The University Against Itself

The University Against Itself

The NYU Strike and the
Future of the Academic Workplace

Edited by
MONIKA KRAUSE, MARY NOLAN,
MICHAEL PALM, AND ANDREW ROSS

TEMPLE UNIVERSITY PRESS
Philadelphia

TEMPLE UNIVERSITY PRESS
1601 North Broad Street
Philadelphia PA 19122
www.temple.edu/tempress

☉ The paper used in this publication meets the requirements of the American National
Standard for Information Sciences—Permanence of Paper for Printed Library Materials,
ANSI Z39.48-1992

Library of Congress Cataloging-in-Publication Data

    The university against itself : the NYU strike and the future of the academic workplace /
edited by Monika Krause . . . [et al.].
      p.   cm.
    Includes bibliographical references and index.
    ISBN-13: 978-1-59213-740-4   ISBN-10: 1-59213-740-7 (cloth : alk. paper)
    ISBN-13: 978-1-59213-741-1   ISBN-10: 1-59213-741-5 (pbk. : alk. paper)
    1. Strikes and lockouts—Graduate teaching assistants—New York (State)—
New York.   2. New York University—Faculty.   I. Krause, Monika, 1978–

LB2335.845.U52N53 2008
378.747'1—dc22   2007024431

Contents

PART II   GSOC Strike

PART III   Lessons for the Future

Introduction

MONIKA KRAUSE, MARY NOLAN, MICHAEL PALM,
AND ANDREW ROSS

Many institutions can trace their founding to the outcome of a conflict, whether over ideas, beliefs, or human relationships. Not a few arose explicitly out of a labor dispute. In the case of New York University, there was a labor conflict over the foundation stones themselves. Convicts from Sing Sing prison were subcontracted from the state to dress stone for NYU's first building on the northeast corner of Washington Square Park in 1834, and local stonecutters rioted in response. The Twenty-Seventh Regiment of the New York National Guard, which used the park as its marching grounds, was called in to restore order. By the turn of the twenty-first century, the university had claimed the whole of Washington Square and was spreading rapidly in all directions, filling out a sizable footprint across the core of downtown Manhattan. After decades of often intense labor friction with its employees, NYU's most recent internal crisis boiled over in 2005, when the Graduate Student Organizing Committee/United Auto Workers (GSOC/UAW) Local 2110, the union for graduate assistants, went on strike to force their employer into negotiations. The square soon hosted picket lines, set up alongside buildings on its east side and in front of the main library, which dominates the south side and houses the offices of the president and senior administrators.

The strike, which straddled two semesters and endured for seven months, drew the attention not only of academics from all over the country and overseas, but also of national labor leaders who hastened to Washington Square to deliver defiant speeches. It was seen by graduate-student organizers across the nation as the front line of their struggle, and many came to join the picket lines. The strike saw a self-proclaimed liberal institution try to break a union in the heart of a union town, and it saw that university administration resort to tactics redolent of a ruthless corporate employer—intimidation, random firings, misinformation, and the promotion of a company union. For many observers, the conflict was seen as a test case of the labor policies that university administrators might pursue in the near future. The strike ended without recognition of a GSOC contract. But it has prompted many analyses of the state of the academic labor movement and widespread reflection on the changing character of the twenty-first–century university, at a time when quickening neoliberal trends are running against the grain of older institutional formations of cultural capital—the university, in effect, against itself.

The strike was noteworthy because of the prominence of the two main actors: the union and the university. GSOC had made history four years earlier as the first graduate-employee union to negotiate a contract at a private university, and that contract remains the only collective-bargaining agreement between graduate employees and a private university in the United States. (Public universities have had recognized graduate unions for almost forty years.) But the employer's profile and conduct had also earned it some distinction. In 2005, just two months before the strike began, the *Economist* presented NYU as the premier example of how an institution of higher education could not only survive through lean times but also thrive and excel by harnessing an entrepreneurial spirit, cultivating ties with the business world, and capitalizing on its location. The key to NYU's turnaround, according to the *Economist*, lay in "the fact that power is concentrated in the hands of the central administration" rather than being distributed among the faculty.[1]

NYU underwent rapid and dramatic change in the decade before the strike. Formerly a commuter school (the percentage of commuting students went down from 60 percent in 1990 to 27 percent in 2006), it was now the nation's most popular choice for college applicants. On a less positive note, these students were graduating with the highest average debt of any university or college students, and they were more likely to be taught by contingent faculty (in 2005, 71.9 percent of NYU faculty were off the tenure track, one of the highest percentages in the country).[2] As part of its image as a global university, NYU enrolled the highest number of international students and sent more of its own students overseas than any other American university. Its much lauded success in faculty recruitment was a testament to the new academic star system that created enormous differentials in pay, workload, and benefits. Its record of physical expansion was a case study in urban real-estate economics. The entrepreneurial profile of the university had been guided by a board of trustees drawn from top executives and investors in the city's FIRE (finance, insurance, and real estate) economy. Its president, John Sexton, provocatively declared that NYU was poised to innovate a new role for urban universities by anchoring a high-growth ICE (intellectual, cultural, and educational) sector as a vital supplement to the FIRE economy.

The University Against Itself

Despite its many successes, NYU remained less well endowed financially and less able to rely on traditional forms of academic prestige than the Ivy League universities with which it was striving to compete. So it was not surprising that a graduate-employee union would succeed at NYU before it did at Ivy League schools such as Yale, Columbia, the University of Pennsylvania, and Brown, which also faced union drives among graduate students. Given NYU's centralized and top-down governance, its fiscal vulnerability, and its entrepreneurial ethos, it was no less surprising that it would be the first university to attempt to bust a graduate assistants' union. The result provided a timely opportunity for this book's contributors to diagnose changes in the landscape of academic labor and university power relations. NYU is not unique in either its embrace of entrepreneurial business practices or its opposition to the unionization of its academic workforce. But the institutional response to the strike, along with the methods adopted by preceding administrations to further NYU's upward mobility and global orientation, illustrate, in stark relief, the impact of marketization on higher education—a topic that many contributors address in these pages.

The March of Privatization

The past two decades in higher education have seen a wave of institutional restructuring in response to demands on administrations to conform with market rationalization. Both private and public institutions rely increasingly on skyrocketing tuition, private sources of funding, and the concentration of power upward, even as critics from government and business have called for greater accountability and efficiency through the more rapid adoption of business practices. The result has drastically eroded the long-cherished buffer zone between academe and corporate America; one symptom is that the salary spread between senior administrators and contingent teachers increasingly resembles its corporate counterpart.[3]

As a consequence of the Bayh–Dole Act (1980), universities have been actively encouraged to generate revenues from the commercialization of research and the licensing of intellectual property. Though research institutions are still regarded as public guardians of the knowledge commons, most have joined the rush to license and generate revenues from the knowledge produced by their employees, sharply limiting public access to that knowledge.[4] Recently, in assessments of academic disciplines and entire universities, competitiveness and profitability are valued as much as, if not more than, impartial inquiry and public knowledge. Teaching resources in subject areas that have no direct commercial potential have been slashed, and students are encouraged to adopt a consumer mentality in shopping for an education that can readily be transformed into market value.[5] A college degree is viewed as a commodity to be bought—increasingly through loans rather than grants—and college administrators treat students as if they were indeed consumers, even as they are also viewed as a "product" of the institution.

Even more troubling, students as a whole, as Marc Bousquet observes, are now often the largest component of any campus workforce, employed more typically in jobs such as food service, day care, janitorial work, building security, interior painting and carpentry, parking enforcement, laundry service, administrative assistance, and warehouse restocking, than in "those that form the dominant image of student work": tutorial, library, and community-service and internship activities. What for most students is the grim reality of "working your way" through college is an economic bonanza for off-campus and on-campus employers in search of low-wage labor.[6] When these jobs are not performed by students, universities and colleges have enthusiastically joined the race to outsource food services, bookstores, and janitorial services to off-campus contractors to lower labor costs and minimize the presence of unions on campus.

A long list of scholarly researchers have concluded that these diverse developments are detrimental to the production and transmission of knowledge and corrosive of the rights, well-being, and interests of students and the academic workforce.[7] Disgruntled employees now routinely lump them under the pejorative rubric of "corporatization." However imprecise—the corporate world comprises a welter of competing strategies for organizing workforces and production techniques—the term functions as a kind of gratifying shorthand for the perceived betrayal of collegiate ideals.

As the culture of privatization spreads throughout higher education, the cruelest toll is taken on public universities. Almost every public college or university has been forced to turn its operations more and more toward private sources of funding, and it is in the public sector that the prodigious rise in tuition fees (and student debt) has been greatest. Like that of so many other private institutions, NYU's ascendancy has been closely linked to the declining fortunes of a public neighbor, CUNY, once the world's greatest working-class university. NYU's very motto—"A private university in the public service"—once was used, proudly, to differentiate its reputation from Columbia, New York City's other major private university, but it has become increasingly incongruous. In the academy, as in neoliberal society at large, the line between public and private is no longer easy to discern.[8]

Despite this blurring, crucial distinctions between public and private higher education remain—not only because private institutions seek to maintain them but also because institutions such as the National Labor Relations Board (NLRB) uphold them. Unlike publicly listed corporations, whose books and financial operations are subject to some degree of transparency, the budgets and finances of private universities are a closely guarded secret, contributing in no small measure to the arcane nature of their prestige. So, too, private universities draw more deeply on the sediment of academic traditions, many of which help obscure the sacrificial labor that keeps the modern university running. Consider the antiquated belief that graduate teaching assistants are not workers but apprentices, or that adjuncts are willing to endure poverty in exchange for practicing a beloved vocation. Each profession has its own way of extracting discounted labor from its youngest and most vulnerable members, but nowhere

A slogan from the global-justice movement adapted by the
PSC, the union for faculty and graduate employees at
CUNY. *(Ashley Dawson)*

else is the gap so great between the self-image of the academic vocation and the
reality of its heavily stratified workforce.[9]

The Right to Organize

As universities increasingly rely on contingent labor for almost every aspect of
their operations, academic organizing is routinely understood, by organizers and
observers alike, as a reaction to commercial pressures and corporate-style university management. Over the past decade, the rise of an academic labor movement has been analyzed in a variety of publications dealing with the struggles of
teaching assistants, the unionization of adjuncts, and the disappearance of the
tenure-track professor.[10] In assessing the GSOC strike, contributors to this volume draw on that literature and on published profiles of corporatization in
higher education. But, as they also make quite clear, the strike was a new chapter
in this history. It involved, from the outset, factors that had not been replicated
elsewhere as well as outcomes that could not be easily predicted.

When GSOC's bargaining committee called for a strike-authorization vote in October 2005, it was not to resist a proposed pay freeze or to take a stand against health-care rollbacks. The union was fighting for the basic right to negotiate with its members' employer over compensation and working conditions. A strike can be a radical tactic, but GSOC's struggle was essentially a conservative effort to retain rights rather than to acquire new ones. Moreover, the students who withdrew their labor in November of that year did so without the protections offered to workers through the National Labor Relations Act (NLRA).

In 2000, the NLRB (the federal agency created in 1935 to enforce the right to organize under the NLRA) ruled that graduate assistants were employees and that NYU was legally obliged to recognize the union.[11] When the administration challenged the ruling, GSOC responded with pressure tactics: publicized visits from elected officials, a mass mobilization of undergraduate support, several petitions for union rights signed by a majority of eligible graduate students, and a call, from a significant portion of full-time faculty, for the administration to recognize the students' democratic choice. The night before a strike vote was to be held, the administration agreed to drop all legal appeals and negotiate.

In 2000, the NLRB decision was a powerful card in the union's deck, but by 2005 it was the employer who held the card. A year earlier, Brown University, facing a graduate-student–unionization drive, had appealed the NYU decision. The NLRB, with new members appointed by President George Bush, overturned the 2000 decision, judging that at private colleges and universities (in contrast with public ones), teaching assistants are "primarily" students and therefore do not qualify for labor rights.[12] The Brown decision clearly emboldened private university employers to crack down on organizing efforts, and the NYU administration (which included several members of the former Clinton administration) came under pressure from its counterparts at Yale, Columbia, Brown, and Penn to withdraw its recognition of GSOC.

Although this ruling was only one of a series of restrictions imposed by the NLRB on the right to organize, its timing, along with the publicity generated by the NYU strike, made the labor movement sit up and take notice. It is fair to say that the AFL-CIO has not been consumed by ruminations about how to organize knowledge workers, though in some unions and among some labor leaders this challenge has been duly acknowledged. Nor had the labor leadership seen graduate-employee organizing, despite its numerical growth, as an especially significant field to which resources and policy ought to be devoted. No decisive shift in mentality on this topic occurred as a result of the NYU strike, though the enduring resolve of GSOC through several months on the picket line helped to convince many trade unionists that the students were "real" union brothers and sisters. If a prolonged strike seemed likely to earn the students laborist credibility, it was not clear that this strategy could really succeed against a large private university, whose financial operations would be much more difficult to compromise than those of a corporate employer.

Nor was it easy to predict how such a strike would play among allies of GSOC. On the inside, they included NYU faculty, whom the administration would seek to divide, and undergraduates whose support would require considerable education on the issues; on the outside, they ranged from community groups and other institutional allies to sympathetic politicians (dozens of city councilors and state senators, U.S. senators Chuck Schumer and Hillary Clinton, and the presidential contender John Edwards). No one could have foreseen that the administration would prove to be quite so intractable, so determined to spread misinformation, and, ultimately, so vindictive in targeting the strikers. To be sure, the administration was expected to abide by the union-busting playbook provided by its legal consultants (the infamous Proskauer Rose, who had advised NYU counsels during the GSOC organizing campaign in the late 1990s and the NLRB hearings in 2000, and who had also been retained by the Yale administration during the Graduate Employees and Students Organization [GESO] grade strike of 1995). But few imagined that it would adhere so closely to the ruthless tactics laid out on page after page.

The course of the strike also saw several unforeseen developments on the side of GSOC support. A sizable number of the NYU faculty came out publicly, either in support of the strike or against the administration's position. Two hundred to three hundred faculty members, a majority of those with whom the teaching assistants worked directly, consistently signed petitions. A new organization called Faculty Democracy initiated its own actions and mounted direct challenges to President Sexton and his senior administrators over their repeated failures to consult faculty on policy positions or observe the kind of transparency required by the culture of shared governance. In contrast to the limited faculty mobilization in support of labor struggles at Yale and Columbia, the NYU faculty efflorescence was highly unusual, if not unprecedented, at a private, research university. But if the NYU administration faced more internal opposition than elsewhere, the very consolidation of power at the top enabled it to push through unpopular policies and actively divide faculty.

The active, day-to-day involvement of organizers from New Haven's UNITE-HERE local, a union that had broken with the AFL-CIO to form the alternative Change to Win coalition in 2005, offered evidence that the recent split within the labor movement might not impede cooperation among unions on different sides. So, too, did rallies attended by other Change to Win and AFL-CIO unions— the Teamsters and the steelworkers, for example. Last but not least, the forward momentum of the union itself proved remarkably resilient. GSOC withstood many severe blows to morale, endured divisive internal struggles, and ended the strike without a contract. Yet the capacity of its members to regroup, re-commit, and embark on new strategies in the years following the strike has confounded those who have experienced the profound demoralization that can follow an unsuccessful strike.

After the strike, GSOC turned inward and focused on rebuilding. The union avoided rallies and other public events, which had been high points of GSOC

Higher education is a knowledge industry. GSOC placards
often reflected the incongruity of knowledge workers' taking strike action. *(Rebecca Howes-Mischel)*

momentum leading up to the strike and during its first weeks, and the growing
infrequency of which signaled to many observers the strike's demise. By the end
of fall 2006, GSOC's first semester back at work, more members were actively
organizing for the union than had been at any point during the strike. During
the spring 2007 semester, for the third year in a row, a majority of eligible graduate students at NYU signed GSOC membership cards, no small feat for any
union, let alone one unrecognized by its employer and still without a contract
after a six-month strike.

The complex social and political life of any strike is not easy to document.[13]
While some contributors to this volume make the effort to do so, that is not the
primary aim of the book. This collection seeks to draw useful lessons from the
strike, as well as from the remaking of NYU as an institution and GSOC as an
organization. Many of the contributors focus on local detail from NYU and New
York City, but most analyze the national significance of economic forces and
patterns of academic life that were highlighted by this local dispute. These tendencies have to be better understood if the freedoms, securities, and vital quali-

ties of the academic workplace are to be preserved and maintained. The alternative is increasing inequality and polarization among the workforce, loss of effective faculty governance and basic rights for non–tenure-track teachers, and falling educational standards and rising costs. Academics never tire of talking and lecturing about justice in society at large, but there is less and less in our own backyard.

In compiling this volume, we want to make a useful, even practical, contribution to the challenges awaiting future academic organizers. We also hope that the lessons found in these pages will help clarify some of the often bewildering changes that are sweeping the university workplace, changes that are occurring at a speed that many find inimical to the measured pace of academic life. Graduate teaching assistants and part-time or non–tenure-stream faculty hardly need a weatherman to know which way the wind is blowing and have organized to protect themselves, but tenured faculty (who have generally acceded to the creation of a two- or three-tier workforce) have not yet recognized, or risen to, the challenges that are transforming academic labor and the university.

The contents of the volume are arranged in three sections: the first devoted to analyses of the restructuring of the university along neoliberal lines; the second focused more directly on the GSOC strike; and the third given over to essays about the future of the academic workplace. The contributors are drawn from several strata of the academic workforce. They include graduate assistants who have been active with GSOC and the UAW; NYU faculty who played a role in Faculty Democracy, the independent organization formed in response to the university administration's unilateral adoption of an anti-union policy and its erosion of the faculty governance system; and non–NYU faculty and trade unionists who are seasoned commentators on the topics of academic labor and university governance.

Notes

1. "Secrets of Success," *Economist,* September 8, 2005. Several articles in the *New York Times* have solidified this narrative of "the NYU miracle." For a good example, see William Honan, "Buying Excellence: How N.Y.U. Rebuilt Itself—A Special Report," *New York Times,* March 20, 1995. See also Joan Marans Dim and Nancy Murphy Cricco, *The Miracle on Washington Square: New York University* (Lanham, Md.: Lexington Books, 2001).

2. See American Association of University Professors, *Contingent Faculty Index* 2006, available online at http://www.aaup.org/AAUP/pubsres/research/conind2006.htm.

3. In 2005–2006, NYU's John Sexton had the second highest salary of any president at a research university, at $915,256, excluding benefits, as well as other income from appointments to corporate boards, also derived in large part from his position. See "Compensation Study of the 25 Universities Involved in Billion-Dollar Campaign Initiatives," *Chronicle of Higher Education,* February 3, 2006.

4. Jennifer Washburn focuses on intellectual-property licensing and technology transfer in *University, Inc.: The Corporate Corruption of American Higher Education* (New York: Basic Books, 2005). See also Corynne McSherry, *Who Owns Academic Work? Battling for Control of Intellectual Property* (Cambridge, Mass.: Harvard University Press, 2001).

5. Frank Donohue, "The Uneasy Relationship between Business and the Humanities," *American Academic,* vol. 1, June 2004, 93–109; Craig Calhoun, "Is the University in Crisis?" *Society,* May–June 2006, 8; Gary Rhoades and Sheila Slaughter, "Academic Capitalism in the New Economy: Challenges and Choices," *American Academic,* vol. 1, June 2004.

6. Marc Bousquet, "The Escape from Contingency, or, Students Are Already Workers," *Works and Days* 23, nos. 45–46 (2005).

7. Sheila Slaughter and Larry Leslie, *Academic Capitalism: Politics, Policies, and the Entrepreneurial University* (Baltimore: Johns Hopkins University Press, 1997); Sheila Slaughter and Gary Rhoades, *Academic Capitalism and the New Economy* (Baltimore: Johns Hopkins University Press, 2004); Stanley Aronowitz, *The Knowledge Factory: Dismantling the Corporate University and Creating True Higher Learning* (Boston: Beacon Press, 2001); Marc Bousquet, *How the University Works: Higher Education and the Low-Wage Nation* (New York: New York University Press, 2007); Cary Nelson and Stephen Watt, *Academic Keywords: A Devil's Dictionary for Higher Education* (New York: Routledge, 1999); David Kirp, *Shakespeare, Einstein, and the Bottom Line: The Marketing of Higher Education* (Cambridge, Mass.: Harvard University Press, 2004); Sheldon Krimsky, *Science in the Private Interest: Has the Lure of Profits Corrupted Biomedical Research?* (Lanham, Md.: Rowman and Littlefield, 2003); Christopher Newfield, *Ivy and Industry: Business and the Making of the American University, 1880–1980* (Durham, N.C.: Duke University Press, 2004); Gigi Roggero, *Intelligenze fuggitive, Movimenti contro l'università azienda* (Rome: Manifestolibri, 2005).

8. For an account of how NYU benefited from the abolition of free tuition at CUNY, see Nathan Glazer, "Facing Three Ways: City and University in New York Since World War Two," in *The University and the City: From Medieval Origins to the Present,* ed. Thomas Bender (New York: Oxford University Press, 1988), 267–288.

9. Andrew Ross, "The Mental Labor Problem," in *Low Pay, High Profile: The Global Push for Fair Labor* (New York: New Press, 2004); Micki McGee, "Hooked on Higher Education and Other Tales from Adjunct Faculty Organizing," *Social Text* 20, no. 1 (Spring 2002): 61–80.

10. Cary Nelson, ed., *Will Teach for Food: Academic Labor in Crisis* (Minneapolis: University of Minnesota Press, 1997); Patrick Kavanagh and Kevin Mattson, eds., *Steal This University: The Rise of the Corporate University and the Academic Labor Movement* (New York: Routledge, 2003); Jim Downs and Jennifer Manion, eds., *Taking Back the Academy! History of Activism, History as Activism* (New York: Routledge, 2004); Randy Martin, ed., *Chalk Lines: The Politics of Work in the Managed University* (Durham, N.C.: Duke University Press, 1999); Marc Bousquet, Tony Scott, and Leo Parascondola, eds., *Tenured Bosses and Disposable Teachers: Writing Instruction in the Managed University* (Carbondale: Southern Illinois University Press, 2004); Gary Rhoades, *Managed Professionals: Unionized Faculty and Restructuring Academic Labor* (Albany: State University of New York Press, 1998); Judith Wagner DeCew, *Unionization in the Academy: Visions and Realities* (Lanham, Md.: Rowman and Littlefield, 2003): Joe Berry, *Reclaiming the Ivory Tower: Organizing Adjuncts to Change Higher Education* (New York: Monthly Review Press, 2005).

Workplace: A Journal of Academic Labor, available online at http://www.cust.educ.ubc.ca/workplace, is an indispensable source of commentary on academic labor (the Fall 2007 issue is a special issue on the NYU strike). *Inside Higher Ed,* available online at http://www.insidehighered.com, has also provided a good deal of coverage and commentary. Print journals that have consistently published articles on academic labor include *Social Text, Radical Teacher, Minnesota Review, Works and Days,* and *Academe,* the monthly publication of the AAUP.

As for organizations, the academic labor movement in toto consists of the Coalition of Contingent Academic Labor, the Coalition of Graduate Employee Unions, the Collective Bargaining Congress of the AAUP, and faculty union groupings in the National Education Association and the American Federation of Teachers.

11. "New York University and International Union, United Automobile, Aerospace, and Agricultural Workers of America, AFL-CIO, Petitioner," case 2-RC-22082, October 31, 2000, 332 NLRB no. 111.

12. "Brown University and International Union, United Automobile, Aerospace and Agricultural Implement Workers of America, ALF-CIO, Petitioner," case 1-RC-21368, July 13, 2004, 342 NLRB no. 42, 7.

13. GSOC members, supporters, and observers documented the strike. Issues of the *GSOC Journal,* a union newsletter circulated to members via e-mail, were produced almost daily during the chaotic early weeks of the strike and posted on many websites and listservs. Several blogs also covered the strike, the most prominent being "Nerds on Strike!" (http://nerdsforgsoc.blogspot.com), a website run by GSOC members in the NYU Sociology Department. There is a strike press archive on the website of UAW Local 2110 at http://2110uaw.org/gsoc/press%20archive.htm. See also the websites at http://www.facultydemocracy.org; http://www.nyuinc.org; and http://www.nyuexposed.org.

Part I

Corporate University?

New York

Academic Labor Town?

Ashley Dawson and Penny Lewis

New York is home to at least one hundred colleges, universities, or professional degree-granting institutions, with hundreds of thousands of residents enrolled in thousands of degree programs taught by close to sixty thousand professors, including part-time and graduate students.[1] In what follows, we analyze the particular trajectories of corporatization that have characterized three of New York City's principal academic institutions: Columbia, NYU, and CUNY. Our primary focus lies with Columbia and CUNY, as much of the rest of the book details NYU. At root, processes at these three schools reflect the global restructuring of the higher-education industry over the past few decades. While local schools such as the newly christened "New School University," Long Island University, Adelphi, and others have similarly transmogrified in this new era of austerity, we have chosen to study Columbia, NYU, and CUNY for their size and renown, as well as their ideal-typical characteristics. Until the 1960s, each had been emblematic of particular statuses within the academic hierarchy and had carved out successful niches educating, respectively, national and international elites, the commuting middle class, and New York City's aspiring and diverse working class. In the decades that followed, this relatively symbiotic balance was thrown over in favor of increasingly intense competition for dwindling city, state, and federal funding. The shifting fortunes, competitive jostling, and cosmetic and structural makeovers of these three universities over the subsequent decades illustrate many of the trends present in the city's academic industry as a whole.

These three institutions share a rhetorical commitment to education as a public good, with the public of New York often enjoying pride of place. CUNY's founding mission was to educate "the children of the whole people," while Albert Gallatin sought "in this immense and fast-growing city . . . a system of rational and practical education fitting for all and graciously open to all" at NYU. Columbia, the least provincial of the three, nevertheless "recognizes the importance of its location in New York City and seeks to link its research and teaching to the vast resources of a great metropolis" and, beyond that, to "convey the products of its efforts to the world."[2] While each of these schools professes to be advancing the public interest in general—and, more specifically, that of the commonwealth of New York City (whose name they have branded and re-branded)—their claims ring hollow when viewed not only through the lens of labor relations, but also in relation to broader questions concerning the long-term sustainability of higher education's mission to advance and disseminate knowledge.

Columbia and the Rise of the Global City

In the closing years of the Fordist era, Columbia held a particularly contradictory relationship to New York City. In conditions that hold true to this day, it operated outside many constraints of place, as the students it served and its institutional peers were national and international in scope. As part of the Ivy League, Columbia has always derived its elite status less from its geographic location than from academic prestige. So when Columbia began to fall in national rankings, first from third place (after 1957), and then from the top ten after student rebellion in 1968, this was cause for deep concern within its leadership.[3] This decline was related in part to Columbia's neighborhood, Morningside Heights, and the city itself. As New York's industrial base went into a steep decline, the deep economic and social problems of surrounding economically marginalized neighborhoods such as Harlem began to have a strong impact on Columbia's self-image. After decades in which Columbia had trumpeted its location in "the country's largest city and [a] world center" as a boon, the university's environs suddenly came to seem an alarming burden.[4] In 1967, Provost Jacques Barzun described Morningside Heights as "uninviting, abnormal, sinister, and dangerous."[5] By the mid-1970s, the city's policy of "planned shrinkage" of ethnic-minority neighborhoods through the slashing of transit, sanitation, and police and fire protection in poor areas to levels that the tax base could support seemed to have damned Morningside Heights, and with it Columbia, to terminal decline.[6]

Decisions taken by Columbia contributed decisively to this sense of decline and crisis. The student takeover of 1968, for example, was precipitated by the university's imperious relations with its predominantly African American, poor, and working-class neighborhood. In particular, Columbia's move to occupy a portion of Morningside Park, a strategic buffer separating the Heights from the Harlem Valley, through the construction of a new gym facility that was to have separate-but-equal facilities for members of each community raised the hackles of members of the neighborhood's predominantly African American and Latino communities.[7] Columbia further alienated members of both working-class and middle-class communities in the area through its use of urban-renewal powers to acquire deteriorating buildings, evict their tenants, and remodel them for faculty and students. Despite snagging a million-dollar grant from the Ford Foundation to ameliorate urban conditions, Columbia seemed to be behaving as arrogantly as the many urban authorities that used the alibi of "renewal" for apparent ethnic cleansing of the city. The decisions made during the city's fiscal crisis in the mid-1970s further impoverished Columbia's immediate locale, and by the early 1980s the school found itself not only facing deficits but caught within many of the same negative "Fort Apache"–type images and conditions faced by the city as a whole. As Morningside Heights struggled with urban blight, student riots, and racial conflict, Columbia, caught in a vicious Catch 22, found that the heavy investment it was required to make in security prevented it from offering the salaries and facilities offered by other elite schools. By 1979, a Presidential Commission on Academic Priorities in the Arts and Sciences report cited Columbia's malaise as a product, first, of the "phenomenal expansion of higher education following World War II," and second, of "circumstances relating to Columbia's location in New York City and its specific location on Morningside Heights."[8]

It should come as no surprise, therefore, that Columbia's revival in the latter part of that decade went hand in hand with the gentrification of the neighborhood, in which it played a prominent role. As middle-class neighborhoods in areas such as the Bronx and Brooklyn decayed—and, in some cases, literally burned to the ground—property values in Manhattan began their steady upward climb. By the mid-1980s, the galloping gentrification of the Upper West Side had reached Morningside Heights, providing a structural form of urban renewal that effectively purged poor communities from the university's environs. By the 1990s, the reversal in the neighborhood's fortunes was virtually complete. The draconian policies of "zero tolerance" that did so much to stimulate gentrification throughout Manhattan during the era of Mayor Rudolph Giuliani sealed this transformation. As Jim Shapiro, an undergraduate student at Columbia during the blighted years of the mid-1970s and a faculty member from 1985 to the present, puts it, "Giuliani did more for Columbia's reputation than anyone else. . . . Columbia has been able to draw on a national and especially an international student population because people aren't afraid to send their sons and daughters to study in the big city anymore."[9] The wheel has come full circle. Indeed, in his five-year report covering the period from 1993 to 1998, President George Rupp cites "extraordinary academic quality," "our New York location," and the university's "history of involvement in the international arena" as Columbia's crucial, defining strengths.[10] Columbia is now firmly anchored in what Saskia Sassen calls the "global city," a core node of the world economy characterized by, on the one hand, an economically and spatially polarized population employed in high-income jobs relating to finance, insurance, and real estate (FIRE) and the culture industry (ICE), and, on the other hand, by low-wage workers in the service sector.[11]

While capital and the middle classes began to flood back into the neighborhood, Columbia took steps to capitalize on government schemes to wean universities off public largesse by turning them into money-making enterprises. On the day that the Bayh–Dole Act went into effect in 1980, Columbia enacted a patent policy that gave the school rights to faculty inventions, allowing for royalties for the faculty members and their laboratories. Since then, Columbia has ranked first among universities receiving licensing revenue.[12] Patenting is overseen by the Office of Science and Technology Ventures, an entity formed in 1982 that quickly made its mark when a team of Columbia researchers led by Dr. Richard Axel was granted a patent for several essential technologies related to co-transformation, a process through which cells can be made to produce particular proteins. The so-called Axel patents, granting ownership over biological processes, proved to be the most lucrative in the history of university patents, placing Columbia at the forefront of the increasing privatization of the scientific-knowledge commons. In 2004, for example, the *Crimson* student newspaper reported that Harvard made $24 million, compared with Columbia's $178 million, from such ventures.[13] Columbia's ambitious plans to expand into West Harlem underline the increasing centrality of biomedical venture capitalism to the university's fortunes. These initiatives in academic capitalism have generated significant friction: In recent years, residents of West Harlem have challenged the university's rezoning plans, and three large pharmaceutical companies have filed a lawsuit against Columbia alleging that the university improperly sought to maintain a monopoly on "biological technologies."[14]

Throughout this period of rejuvenation, Columbia's relations with its workforce remained acrimonious, at best. Fourteen unions currently bargain with Columbia, but the university has done its best to fragment inter-union coordination, demonstrating what workers there call a "plantation mentality, like they need to keep their workers in check or they might do something crazy."[15] The university administration fought bitterly against the campaign for unionization among clerical workers in the mid-1980s, using tactics employed by the most anti-union corporations. Feminism played a prominent role in this campaign, as the predominantly female clerical workers highlighted the gendered pay inequalities facilitated by their lack of access to union representation, a theme that was prominent in similar campaigns among clerical workers at Yale and Boston University. Columbia's paternalism toward its workers, so evident in previous conflicts, such as the clerical workers' unionization drive, played out once again as graduate students sought to acquire union representation over the past half decade. Despite the NLRB's prior recognition of graduate students' right to union representation, like its Ivy League brothers, Columbia consistently drew on the mystique of the feudal university system and its ideological commitment to traditional hierarchical structures to defuse the crisis of consent it faced. The university administration's response to the threat of graduate-student organizing mobilized notions of guild apprenticeships and ancient prestige, articulations of an archaic code that retains its hold over both the public imagination and professional self-image of many academic workers. In addition, the university threatened graduate students with severe punishments, a blatant fear tactic and infringement on academic freedom.[16] While Columbia faculty did not engage in an active anti-union campaign, as professors at Yale had during the 1990s, committed faculty supporters could essentially be counted on one hand, according to union organizers.

Columbia administrators have shown themselves to be every bit as intent on taking advantage of the trend toward contingent labor as have managers of less well-heeled schools, despite the lack of a pressing economic imperative to do so because of Columbia's huge endowment. Columbia's hostile workplace practices, with their echoes from Yale, have served as a model for the NYU administration. Clerical workers at NYU, organized in the American Federation of Teachers, worked in an open shop for years, only winning union security when graduate students organized. Adjuncts, recently organized in the UAW, have gone through multiple arbitrations and fought tooth and nail for their first contract. As private universities, NYU and Columbia can feel somewhat secure from more faculty organizing, as they stand behind the legal cover of the 1980 *Yeshiva* decision, which denied full-time private-school professors the right to organize. But the City University system, with its public base and nearly floor-to-ceiling union organization, also served as a model for NYU. It was at CUNY that the possibility of running a large university system with low-cost labor was realized on a grand scale.

CUNY and Structural Adjustment

While Columbia's fortunes ebbed and then rebounded, CUNY's plummeted. CUNY entered the neoliberal era as one of the great university systems in the country, with its flagship campus at City College internationally recognized as the "proletariat's Harvard." CUNY was home to one of the new higher-education unions, the Professional Staff Congress (PSC), a local of the American Federation of Teachers. Formed in 1969, the PSC brought all CUNY faculty, graduate students, and professional staff together in one bargaining unit.[17] In 1970, as a result of intensive struggle led by African American and Puerto Rican students at City College, CUNY took the historic and radical step of opening its doors to all New York City high school graduates, "arguably the nation's most ambitious attempt to expand college access for minorities." While debates raged over whether this would lower the "standards" of education offered by CUNY, early observations indicated that CUNY could offer universal, free, high-quality education—a contradiction in terms, according to the market logic then ascending.[18] By combining an open admissions policy with free tuition, CUNY broke new ground in democratizing access to higher education in the United States. And in 1973, after voting to strike, CUNY faculty and staff won their first contract.

As a consequence, CUNY quickly drew the attention of those behind the nascent right-wing counterattack against the social movements of the day. The Nixon White House was particularly incensed by the anti-racist and peace activism emanating from U.S. campuses in the early 1970s. Nixon's vice president, Spiro Agnew, attacked open admissions as one of the principal means "by which unqualified students are being swept into college on the wave of the new socialism."[19] In 1970, Roger Freeman, an important adviser to Nixon on educational matters who was working for California Governor Ronald Reagan's reelection campaign, clearly delineated the target of the conservative offensive: "We are in danger of producing an educated proletariat. That's dynamite! We have to be selective on who we allow to go through higher education."[20] While Governor Reagan was able to dismantle the University of California's policy of free tuition after his reelection in 1970, the campaign against CUNY was far more protracted.

It was not until the fiscal crisis of New York City itself in 1975 that conservatives, led by Nixon's successor, Gerald Ford, were able to strike a decisive blow against CUNY. Faced with deepening fiscal difficulties, the Ford administration simply pulled the plug on federal funding of cities. As the famous headline had it: "Ford to New York: Drop Dead." As the gap between revenues and outlays in the city's budget yawned ever greater, a cabal of bankers led by Citibank's Walter Wriston, who equated all forms of government intervention with socialism, refused to roll over the city's debt and thereby pushed New York into bankruptcy.[21] In what was to become the model for the devastating structural-adjustment programs administered around the world by the International Monetary Fund during the 1980s, the debt relief that followed New York's bankruptcy entailed the construction of new institutions of governance that laid first claim to all city tax revenues in order to pay off bondholders. Encouraged by Vice President Nelson Rockefeller, who as governor of New York had long held CUNY's tuition-free status in his crosshairs, President Ford announced he would withhold federal aid from New York City until it eliminated policies of open admissions and free tuition at CUNY.

The threat represented by open admissions was immediately recognized by private schools, which had seen the public universities expand during the postwar era and their own enrollment shrink as inflation and tuition rose. While CUNY students were struggling for public access in 1969, private institutions such as NYU lobbied hard for public resources, persuading the New York State legislature to channel aid to private institutions through the "Bundy" program of Direct Institutional Aid, which guarantees state funds for financial aid at independent colleges on the basis of "graduation productivity."[22] In 1971, NYU's president joined others on behalf of New York State's private colleges in calling for an end to free and low tuition at the public schools.[23] After the federal rejection of publicly supported higher education, their calculations reflected the popular prediction that if CUNY were to introduce tuition, it would lose its middle-class students, who would not qualify for the New York State Tuition Assistance Program or federal Pell grants. Faced with tuition charges, these relatively wealthy CUNY students would begin to migrate to other fee-charging institutions in the metropolitan area. As City College President Robert Marshak put it in his alarmed report on academic restructuring in the early 1970s: "The loss of thousands of these lower-middle and middle-class students from the CUNY system would dilute the social mission of the public sector of higher education in New York City, which is to maintain a balanced academic, ethnic, and class mix in its student body."[24]

Open admissions began as an underfunded mandate, and CUNY entered the 1970s growing rapidly with inadequate resources. In 1974, the PSC successfully fought off an attempt by CUNY's chancellor to limit tenure for new faculty, but CUNY's budget was slashed during the fiscal crisis. Programs were eliminated, hours were shortened, classes were canceled, capital projects were halted, and student services were curtailed. In the midst of these cuts, the city reduced CUNY's budget in 1975 by $32 million, a figure that made transparent its specific goals to starve CUNY: The $32 million was precisely the amount CUNY could expect to yield if it began to charge its students tuition on a par with the State University of New York (SUNY) schools. It was clear to the contemporary observer Michael Harrington that "the tuition demand has nothing to do with raising money and is certainly unrelated to any educational concerns." Instead, "it is a symbolic gesture designed to convince the American money market that New York City has given up its sinful, innovative ways" of educating the public for free.[25]

In 1976, CUNY terminated its 129-year policy of free tuition and fired hundreds of young faculty members who had been recently hired to educate the new students who resulted from open admissions. In total, 3,294 part- and full-time faculty members were laid off. In the eyes of city elites, CUNY had become "an unneeded luxury, a squandering of tax money, a give-away to the poor."[26] Middle-class students who could afford to go elsewhere did, and those who could not afford tuition left school altogether. Sixty-two thousand fewer students attended CUNY after tuition was introduced, and by 1980 the university had 50 percent fewer African American and Latino freshman than it had in 1976.[27] Retrenchment policies have dominated the fiscal management of CUNY for close to three decades. CUNY students have had to endure repeated tuition increases, as state and federal aid dried up during the 1980s and 1990s, as well as the dismantling of the cutting-edge remediation programs set up to integrate nontraditional students into the university setting.[28] The immiseration of students and the elevation of CEO-style university administrators go hand in hand. After receiving a whopping 40 percent pay increase funded through heightened faculty and staff productivity in late 2003, for example, CUNY Chancellor Matthew Goldstein callously proposed two years later to establish annual tuition increases pegged to inflation for the university's working-class student body.[29]

Tuition and fees now cover nearly half of CUNY's operating expenses and have already increased by nearly 200 percent over the past fifteen years, while public funding has decreased by 30 percent over the same period.[30] But rather than identify systemic underfunding as the source of CUNY's hardships or call for meaningful increases in public support, its leaders have promoted "cluster hiring" in "flagship programs," some of which could be used to develop for-profit "incubator companies" like at Columbia. The Master Plan of 2004–2008 continues to promote the "flagship" environment of an increasingly stratified system, in which significant resources are devoted to programs such as the Honors Colleges (schools within a select group of senior colleges) and programs run by the central administration. While the more recent plan calls for more public support, funding is in part sought through "an unprecedented focus on philanthropy as a permanent feature of revenue in support of programmatic initiatives."[31]

Although CUNY's student population began to expand once more as a university degree became increasingly necessary to enter most job markets, a program encouraging full-time faculty to take early retirement further eroded the teaching staff. After a freeze on faculty hiring at CUNY, implemented during the fiscal crisis and lasting for nearly twenty years, a significant generation gap opened among faculty. Although CUNY has added the equivalent of a college and a half since the fiscal crisis, its full-time teaching staff is currently half what it was in 1975.[32] The shortfall in teaching staff was initially made up for through the rehiring of many faculty members laid off during the fiscal crisis as part-time instructors and, subsequently, through employing some of the many talented post–baccalaureate-degree holders who live and work in New York City as adjuncts.[33] Part-time academic workers currently teach between 50 percent and 60 percent of all CUNY courses, down from as much as 70 percent in recent years.[34]

Why this turn to contingent labor? Employment of a contingent labor force obviously saves management money. But it also gives management tremendous power. Part-time teachers do not have the same rights to grievance procedures and due process in general as full-time faculty; they can be hired and fired virtually at will. This insecurity not only eats away at the academic freedom and general well being of part-timers. It also catalyzes a climate of anxiety and fear that helps tame dissent even among those who are tenured and supposedly "secure." As the number of contingent faculty increases, the ability of the faculty as a whole to direct its own affairs diminishes, and the basic character of institutional autonomy and collective self-governance erodes.[35]

CUNY management's recent contract demands (of December 2004 and April 2007) embody precisely this vicious combination of austerity and control. Perhaps the most central component of management's drive to exert greater control over CUNY faculty is its demand that department chairs be removed from the union. If this demand is successfully implemented, the faculty's ability to control its own affairs through democratic election of its own departmental executive officers will be dramatically curtailed: Chairs will essentially become managers. In addition, CUNY management seeks to advance its power over the faculty and staff through the elimination of significant due-process protections, the reduction of annual leave, and the undermining of job security.[36]

NYU, Inc.

In the early 1970s, NYU found itself on the brink of financial ruin, with costs soaring and enrollment declining. In 1973, it sold its prestigious and architecturally distinguished Bronx campus to City University, retreating from what was soon to be the smoldering ruins of the city's northernmost borough, to Greenwich Village as its flagship location. The end of free tuition at CUNY, advocated by NYU's leadership, did not produce the flood of middle-class commuter students who were needed, although NYU was one of the biggest beneficiaries of CUNY's eclipse.[37] By the early 1980s, NYU's future was very much in doubt. A short ten years later, however, the *New York Times* could describe it as "very nearly the Greenwich Village equivalent of Columbia"; today NYU ranks as one of the most popular and expensive undergraduate destinations and is home to many of the nation's leading graduate schools and programs.[38] In the words of the *Economist,* "It is flush with money from fund-raising, 'hot' with would-be undergraduates across the country, and famous for recruiting academic superstars. The Shanghai world ranking puts it at number 32." For the world's premier business magazine the single most important factor determining these results is that "power is concentrated in the hands of the central administration."[39]

With millions in finance capital raised through its magnate-heavy board of directors, NYU became an active player in the growing real-estate sector, helping literally to "rebuild" the city during the booms of the 1980s and 1990s. Like Columbia, NYU was also helped by the gentrification of the city itself, and NYU's efforts in that direction mirrored steps taken in the city as a whole. While capitalizing on and, to a certain extent, facilitating the city's real-estate boom, NYU marketed itself using its distinctive downtown location in a revived New York City. From the 1981 appointment of President John Brademas, one of the creators of the National Endowment for the Arts and National Endowment for the Humanities, the school aggressively branded its location in one of the country's foremost cauldrons of creativity. And while most other institutions were cutting back funding for the humanities and social sciences, NYU expanded support for performing, visual, and communication arts, in particular.[40] The university's financial supporters recognized the appeal of New York's cultural sector, with real-estate moguls such as Laurence Tisch donating $7.5 million for the creation of a school of the arts. NYU thus came to embody the synergy between New York's FIRE economy and the urban-based creative class discussed by critics such as Richard Florida.[41]

As Greenwich Village and the East Village became sites of conflict over this process of radical gentrification, NYU often played the role of the public's enemy number one: driving out local residents and businesses and driving up rents while shadowing one of Manhattan's few "big sky" low-density neighborhoods with towering dorms.[42] The recent struggle over a new dorm on 12th Street typifies NYU's community relations. After years of being identified as the "Villain of the Village," NYU began a kind of listening campaign with its neighbors. After a

community meeting at which new NYU President John Sexton assured concerned residents that "the Village has a fragile ecosystem and we're going to
respect it," local activists were hopeful. But a follow-up meeting never happened,
and ultimately NYU's promise that it would consider the public's input was
"a total snow job," in the words of Andrew Berman, director of the Greenwich
Village Society of Historic Preservation. The dorm is going up as originally
planned. "To be blunt," Berman said, "this exceeded my worst expectations about
N.Y.U."[43]

The bitter conflict over the 12th Street dorm recapitulates battles over urban
development that stretch back to the era of NYU's initial makeover, when President Hester used a massive grant from the Ford Foundation to build Bobst
Library, despite the objections of the surrounding community.[44] This race to
expand NYU's urban footprint typifies its aggressive competition for revenues.
If NYU absorbed many CUNY students whose relatively limited means prevented them from settling in dorms following the city's fiscal crisis, the city's
reviving fortunes have made housing expansion a high priority, and NYU is not
allowing community relations to impede its expansion plans. Other universities
that can afford to are following NYU's aggressive real-estate expansion. CUNY
is building dorms on or near multiple campuses, seeking to better compete for
undergraduate applicants, and Columbia's plans to expand in West Harlem—
potentially through the highly controversial invocation of eminent domain to
evict community residents—are predicated on the need for additional space for
housing as well as research.

Conclusion

Institutions of higher education in the United States occupy a relatively privileged
but also highly contradictory position in the global production of knowledge.
Schools such as CUNY, NYU, and Columbia all benefited from historically unprecedented federal largesse during the era of military-procurement–funded research
and development. While they grew, these paradigmatic embodiments of what
Michael Denning calls the Cold War mass university served to reproduce the
professional and managerial cadres that ran the country, but they also came to
offer a vehicle of mass public education and cognate social transformation.[45] As
the era of the mass university waned, the understanding of education as a public
good was dismantled. Like so many other aspects of social life during the neoliberal era, education and knowledge in general were recast as commodities.

Meanwhile, New York City was transformed by local and national elites from
a bastion of social democracy into a lean and mean global city. In the wake of
the fiscal crisis, the city's tax system was systematically reengineered to eliminate
or minimize New York's pioneering forms of social redistribution and to place
effective control of the public domain in the hands of urban economic elites.
Battles over the fate of CUNY, NYU, and Columbia played an important role in
the city's transformation: As repositories of social capital and pivotal institutions

of socialization, New York's big three were important symbols of the city and the nation's ideological investments. From their vastly different fates during the neoliberal era we may read not simply a tale of changing pedagogical priorities but also the history of a largely successful elite counter-revolution.

The gutting of support for public education and the concomitant shift of funding toward more exclusive private schools has had important implications not just for the city in general, but also for academic workers at each of the big three. With the neoliberal shift has come a fundamental reconfiguration in the terrain of higher education. Polarization takes place on three levels within the increasingly corporate academy: between de-funded public institutions such as CUNY and elite private institutions such as NYU and Columbia; within the faculties of universities, where disciplines that are not oriented toward immediate profit are starved of funds while venture capital floods into areas such as biomedicine and information technology; and between the dwindling core of full-time faculty and the expanding cadre of contingent teachers and service personnel. In other words, New York's academic sector reflects—and, indeed, has helped catalyze—the shift toward an economy in which a small elite controls disproportionate sums of capital, and the ladders of upward mobility are systematically knocked away for everyone else.

In this context, unions threaten each of the three institutions in discrete but related ways. Columbia and its Ivy League brethren must deny that graduate students work in order to uphold the historical fiction of graduate school as a period of apprenticeship. But, more important, the image of elite intellectuals sharing the fruits of their research with an eager audience of students would be undermined if the extent of both graduate and part-time teaching were to be fully understood. CUNY is freed from these particular constraints, but academic unionism remains threatening to its academic management in the most basic senses of money and power. As CUNY pursues an increasingly corporate structure, academic unions are forced to battle not simply for faculty self-governance and autonomy, but also for the very concept of public education itself. Thus, the PSC's campaign on the theme "Another University Is Possible" highlights the issues of endemic race-, gender-, and class-based inequalities of access that underlie struggles over public funding of higher education.[46] In addition, this theme consciously resonates with and draws on the global justice movement's struggle to develop alternatives to the commodification of all forms of public good. As such, the PSC actively seeks to link up with transnational movements within this hemisphere and around the world for the defense of the right to public education.[47]

The obstacles confronted by academic organizers in each of these institutions are, of course, massive. The PSC faces a chilling atmosphere in which the ideology of public austerity has become doctrine, despite budget surpluses from year to year. The PSC's most recent contract won a substantial and historic demand: that one hundred full-time lines be created from CUNY's pool of experienced part-time adjuncts. "For the first time in its history, CUNY has agreed to convert part-time lines to full time positions, instead of the other way around," remarked Bowen.[48] And recent contracts have begun to reverse the wage declines of recent decades, increased sabbatical pay, brought greater parity for part-timers, increased support for professional development for all job titles, and defended staff from management's attempts to erode job security. But the power being exercised by the union has encouraged CUNY management to evade the contract whenever possible. In recent years, the administration has unilaterally implemented policy changes in areas such as computer use, student-complaint procedures, and intellectual property—areas that, the union has argued, fall under bargaining prerogatives. Can the unions representing higher-education workers successfully work together to change the direction of the corporatized university? In recent years, activists and officials in New York City's unions have begun to collectively ask this question in meetings and on picket lines.[49] This recognition of the shared interests among workers in our local "industry" creates, in the words of one PSC leader, "possibilities for a more effective, coordinated approach to organizing and building union power in higher education."[50] University administrations have relinquished the public good; it is up to us to forge it anew.

Notes

1. Exact numbers for these fields are difficult to generate. There are dozens of specialized schools that appear on some official lists and not others. Wikipedia has a fairly good list of ninety-five specific schools, but misses many schools within schools (such as NYU Law School and Columbia Law School), many of the small technical colleges (such as the "Brooklyn Institute of Business Technology"), and most community colleges outside the CUNY system. As many as one million people may be enrolled in some form of postsecondary education; "hundreds of thousands" is a cautious and unfortunately vague estimate. The Bureau of Labor Statistics provides data for "education, training and library occupations," broken down into "postsecondary" positions, within the five boroughs of New York City and including (for some reason) six surrounding counties; its figure of sixty thousand therefore includes Westchester County, New York; Bergen and Passaic counties in New Jersey; and three other counties. The Bureau of Labor Statistics does not provide numbers for non-teaching university employees.

2. See the mission statements on the college websites at http://www.cuny.edu, http://www.nyu.edu, and http://www.columbia.edu.

3. Nathan Glazer, "Facing Three Ways: City and University in New York since World War II," in The University and the City: From Medieval Origins to the Present, ed. Thomas Bender (New York: Oxford University Press, 1988), 267–291.

4. Report of the President's Committee on the Future of the University (1957), as quoted in ibid., 270.

5. Quoted in ibid., 272.

6. For a discussion of policies of "planned shrinkage," see Robert Fitch, The Assassination of New York (New York: Verso, 1993), viii–ix.

7. Glazer, "Facing Three Ways," 274.

8. Columbia University, Commission on Academic Priorities in the Arts and Sciences (1979), as quoted in ibid., 276–277.

9. Professor James Shapiro, personal interview, December 6, 2006.

10. *Columbia University President's Five-Year Report,* available online at http://www.columbia.edu/cu/news/report/98 (accessed January 30, 2007).

11. Saskia Sassen, *The Global City: New York, London, Tokyo* (Princeton, N.J.: Princeton University Press, 1991).

12. Daniel Gilbert, "The Corporate University and the Public Intellectual," draft, Yale Working Group on Globalization and Culture, January 18, 2005, available online at http://research.yale.edu/laborculture/documents/Gilbert_WSF05_draft.pdf (accessed September 8, 2007); Bernard Wysocki Jr., "Columbia's Pursuit of Patent Riches Angers Companies," *Wall Street Journal,* December 21, 2004.

13. Katie Reedy, "Patents Bring in the Cash to Columbia: University Generated More Revenue from Patents than Most of Its Peers in 2006," *Columbia Spectator,* November 28, 2006, available online at http://www.columbiaspectator.com (accessed January 30, 2007).

14. Ibid. The ethical implications of academic capitalism have been aired far more publicly at other institutions, such as the University of California, Berkeley, where a patenting deal essentially gave the multinational pharmaceutical firm Novartis control over government-funded university-research initiatives. For an incisive analysis of this controversy and of the contradictions of academic capitalism in general, see Jennifer Washburn, *University, Inc.: The Corporate Corruption of Higher Education* (New York: Basic Books, 2005).

15. Maida Rosenstein, personal interview, September 25, 2006.

16. Jennifer Washburn, "Columbia Unbecoming," *Nation,* April 25, 2005, available online at http://www.thenation.com (accessed January 30, 2007).

17. "Fighting for the Profession: A History of AFT Higher Education History," pamphlet, March 2003, available online at http://www.aft.org/pubs-reports/higher_ed/history.pdf (accessed September 8, 2007).

18. David Lavin and David Hyllegard, *Changing the Odds: Open Admissions and the Life Chances of the Disadvantaged* (New Haven, Conn.: Yale University Press, 1996); Fred Hechinger, "Open Admissions: Prophets of Doom Seem to Have Been Wrong," *New York Times,* March 28, 1971. See Lavin and Hyllegard, *Changing the Odds,* for the definitive study of open admissions' success—underfunded or not.

19. Spiro Agnew, "Threat to Educational Standards," speech at Republican fundraising dinner, Des Moines, Iowa, April 14, 1970, as quoted in H. Bruce Franklin, *Vietnam and Other American Fantasies* (Amherst: University of Massachusetts Press, 2000), 126.

20. "Professor Sees Peril in Education," *San Francisco Chronicle,* October 30, 1970, quoted in ibid.

21. On the city's fiscal crisis, see Eric Lichten, *The New York City Fiscal Crisis* (South Hadley, Mass.: Bergin and Garvey, 1986); Martin Shefter, *Political Crisis, Fiscal Crisis: The Collapse and Revival of New York City* (New York: Columbia University Press, 1992); William Tabb, *The Long Default: New York City and the Urban Fiscal Crisis* (New York: Monthly Review Press, 1982).

22. For information on Bundy aid, see the Commission on Independent Colleges and Universities website at http://www.cicu.org/learnMore/aidprograms.php?Report_ID=1 (accessed September 8, 2007).

23. Fred Hechinger, "Another Cry for Help: Colleges," *New York Times,* December 19, 1971.

24. Robert Marshak, *Academic Renewal in the 1970s,* quoted in Glazer, "Facing Three Ways," 285.

25. Michael Harrington, "Keep Open Admissions Open," *New York Times,* November 2, 1975.

26. Josh Freeman, *Working Class New York: Life and Labor since WWII* (New York: New Press, 2000), 271.

27. Ibid., 271–272.

28. For a discussion of CUNY's remediation programs, see William Crain, "The Battle for Social Justice at CUNY," *Encounter* 14, no. 4 (2001).

29. On Chancellor Goldstein's nearly half-million–dollar compensation package, see Ellen Balleien, "80th Street, Presidents Get Generous Raises," *Clarion,* December 2003, 3. On tuition hikes, see Hank Williams and Peter Hogness, "CUNY Board Considers Plan for Annual Tuition Hikes," *Clarion,* November 2005, 4, available online at www.psc-cuny.org/ClarionNovember05.pdf (accessed September 8, 2007).

30. Barbara Bowen, PSC testimony before the Higher Education Committees of the New York State Assembly and Senate, October 7, 2005, available online at http://www.psc-cuny.org/fundingtestimonyoct05.htm (accessed September 8, 2007); Steve London, PSC testimony before the Joint Senate Finance Committee and Assembly Ways and Means Committee, public hearings on the 2006–2007 Executive Budget, January 30, 2006, available online at http://www.psc-cuny.org/BudgetTestimonyJan06.htm (accessed September 8, 2007).

31. See CUNY Master Plans for 2000–2004 and 2004–2008, available online at http://www1.cuny.edu/events/press/mplan_tableoc.html and http://www1.cuny.edu/portal_ur/content/2004/chancellor/masterfinal.pdf, respectively (accessed September 8, 2007); "Investing in Futures: Financing the CUNY Master Plan," report by CUNY, November 4, 2005, available online at http://www1.cuny.edu/portal_ur/content/2006/compact_2007.pdf (accessed January 30, 2007).

32. According to PSC President Barbara Bowen, there were 11,600 faculty members at CUNY in 1975; today, there are just under 6,000: Barbara Bowen, personal interview, May 20, 2005.

33. Ibid.

34. Ibid.

35. To its credit, and after many years of pressure from the PSC and other faculty bodies, CUNY is committing to many full-time hires in the coming years and has recently hired hundreds of new full-time professors in the community colleges. While many of these hires are earmarked for programs that stand to increase CUNY's profits or prestige (see "cluster hiring" discussion), the increase in full-time positions is a positive step.

36. Barbara Bowen, "The Union Strikes Back," *Clarion,* January 2005, 11, available online at http://www.psc-cuny.org/PDF/Clarion%20Jan%2005.pdf (accessed September 8, 2007); Meredith Kolodner, "Out to Curtail Tenure, CUNY to PSC: Do More, Get Less," *The Chief,* May 11, 2007.

37. Glazer, "Facing Three Ways," 284.

38. William Honan, "Buying Excellence: How NYU Rebuilt Itself," *New York Times,* March 20, 1995; America's Best Colleges, 2007, *U.S. News and World Report,* special ed.; NYU website, available online at http://www.nyu.edu.

39. "Secrets of Success," *Economist,* September 8, 2005.

40. John Frusciano and Marilyn H. Pettit, *New York University and the City* (New Brunswick, N.J.: Rutgers University Press, 1997), 251.

41. Richard Florida, *The Rise of the Creative Class and How It's Transforming Work, Leisure, Community, and Everyday Life* (New York: Basic, 2002).

42. See Christopher Mele, *Selling the Lower East Side: Culture, Real Estate and Resistance in New York City* (St. Paul: University of Minnesota Press, 2000); Janet Abu-Lughod, *From Urban Village to East Village* (Oxford: Blackwell, 1994).

43. Lincoln Anderson, "Conceding Nothing, NYU Starts Building Megadorm," *Villager,* August 2, 2006; see also Karen Arenson, "The Villain of the Village?" *New York Times,* April 19, 2001.

44. For an account of these earlier conflicts, see Frusciano and Pettit, *New York University and the City,* 248.

45. Michael Denning, "Lineaments and Contradictions of the Neoliberal University System," working paper for "Breaking Down the Ivory Tower: The University in the Creation of Another World," World Social Forum, January 2005, available online at http://www.yale .edu/amstud/denning_lineaments_neoliberal_university.pdf (accessed January 30, 2007).

46. For a discussion of this campaign, see Ashley Dawson, "Another University Is Possible: Academic Labor, the Ideology of Scarcity, and the Fight for Workplace Democracy," *Workplace* 14 (May 2007): 91–105.

47. See PSC International Committee, "Globalization, Privatization, War: In Defense of Public Education in the Americas," booklet, available online at http://www.psc-cuny.org/ international.htm (accessed January 30, 2007).

48. Peter Hogness, "Contract Ratified by Wide Margin," *Clarion,* Summer 2006.

49. Representatives from the New York City academic locals started this discussion a couple of years ago after meeting together under the auspices of the AFL-CIO's Voice at Work campaign. Changes in leadership at the national and local levels interrupted the progress, but interest remains high.

50. John Hyland, PSC treasurer, personal correspondence, 2000–2006.

Academic Freedom in the Age of Casualization

When academic administrators and their faculty allies seek to justify their opposition to the unionization of graduate-student employees, they often cite the damage that such unions would do to academic freedom and the community of scholars. It's an argument based on the notion that the university is, in the words of NYU President John Sexton, a "sacred space" whose denizens cherish their intellectual independence while collaborating in the search for knowledge.[1] But such a harmonious campus bears little relationship to the reality of academe today. Pulled apart by changes within the nation's system of higher education, members of the academic profession no longer share a common identity—if, in fact, they ever did. Since the early 1970s, when professors at top-tier institutions jumped ship rather than associate with colleagues at less prestigious schools who had opted for collective bargaining, membership in the American Association of University Professors (AAUP), the only organization that represents all faculty members as faculty members, has fallen from 120,000 to 44,000.[2] Divided by institution, discipline, and rank, our increasingly stratified profession seems to have lost all sense of solidarity. Can we even conceive of an entrepreneurial biomedical scientist who runs a million-dollar research laboratory sharing the same professional universe as an adjunct English instructor who must cobble together four or five $2,500 composition sections simply to pay the rent?

In the following essay, I will look more closely at the forces that are splintering the academy and destroying whatever sense of community it might once have had. This process has, I believe, deleterious consequences for academic freedom. Not only does that fragmentation diminish the faculty's power and autonomy within the university, but it also weakens its ability to repel external political attacks. There is, I admit, a contradiction at the heart of this proposition. The traditional notion of academic freedom, enshrined in the AAUP's classic 1940 "Statement of Principles on Academic Freedom," was conceptualized during an earlier era, when the common culture of the essentially white, male, and WASP professoriate may well have rested on its narrow exclusivity. Though its clubby attributes may not have actually protected academic freedom (and academe's unfortunate record during the McCarthy years suggests that it did not), the current disunity within the academy not only makes it harder for faculty members to exercise their own political rights, but it also undermines their ability to protect the intellectual integrity of American higher education.

Academic freedom is one of those concepts we automatically embrace and invariably misunderstand. Related, but not identical, to the First Amendment right to freedom of speech, it is both broader and narrower than that constitutional protection. To begin with, because the First Amendment covers only official interference with individual expression, it does not apply to the utterances of faculty members at private institutions. Thus, while people who teach at state or municipal colleges and universities—the vast majority of the academic profession—are shielded by the First Amendment from institutional retaliation for their political speech and activities, people who teach at private schools have no such legal recourse.[3] They must therefore rely on the academic community's own code of conduct—also known as academic freedom—that allows them to address controversial matters without risking their jobs.

The AAUP's 1940 statement maintains that a professor's research and teaching should be free from outside interference as long as he or she abides by the academy's professional standards of integrity, impartiality, and relevance. Its language about extramural speech, however, is more ambiguous.[4] As a result, after dozens of academics were fired during the McCarthy era, the AAUP reinterpreted that language to provide more protection for the off-campus political activities of college teachers. Since the statement's formulation, more than two hundred professional groups and organizations have signed on to it, while many colleges and universities actually include its language in their faculty handbooks or union contracts. Although this traditional definition of academic freedom does not have the full force of law—and some recent judicial rulings imply that the privilege inheres in the institution, not the individual—it does offer considerable protection to all but the squeakiest academic wheels.[5]

But to view academic freedom as the construct that extends the First Amendment to private as well as public institutions is to overlook its primary function of ensuring the quality of American higher education. For above all, academic freedom is a professional attribute.[6] It consists of the practices and procedures, such as tenure and faculty governance, that make it possible for professors to do their job effectively. Academic freedom is central to the university's mission because the nature of teaching and research requires that those activities be free from external constraints. This is not to say that professors can do or say whatever they please. On the contrary: They must conform to the mores of their profession. They must operate within the established boundaries of their disciplines and abide by the same standards of evidence and accountability as their fellow scholars (although they can, and do, push at those boundaries as they search for new insights and information). And, of course, they must not misuse their classrooms by propounding irrelevant material or taking advantage of students.

Over time, the academy has created a variety of institutions to enforce these professional obligations—departmental committees, faculty senates, disciplinary associations, scholarly journals, and the like. By continually assessing the work of individual professors through the process of peer review, these institutions ensure the quality of the academy's scholarship and teaching. Sloppy research will not get published; poorly prepared lecturers will not get tenure. Or so one assumes. Naturally, conflicts arise—academics are, after all, only human—but a general consensus about what constitutes good work within each field ordinarily exists.[7] Academe could not function without it.

Significantly, however, the system requires that the men and women who enforce the norms of the academic world be academics themselves. Who else but another student of Medieval Islam can assess the scholarship and originality of a manuscript about the Hanafi legal doctrines in the Abbasid empire? And who but another molecular biologist has the expertise needed to evaluate a junior colleague's research on CMP-N-acetylneuraminic acid synthetase activity? Though ordinary citizens may well have strong opinions about specific disciplines or lines of research, rarely do they have the background to make thoughtful and informed judgments about someone's scholarship or teaching. In almost every instance in which academic freedom is imperiled, it is because outsiders seek to make academic decisions, a situation that seriously threatens the quality of higher education.

When viewed in this light, as a communal rather than an individual protection, the academic freedom that protects the autonomy of the academic profession also protects the quality of American higher education. It ensures that the faculty controls those aspects of the university that affect its core educational functions and that academically irrelevant considerations do not intrude into such key decisions as the selection and retention of faculty members or the design of curricula. When outside pressures intrude, the integrity of the academy degenerates. German universities under the Third Reich or Eastern European ones under communism offer all-too-dispiriting examples of the intellectual deformations political interference can produce.[8] Even in this country, we know that the chilling climate of McCarthyism induced faculty members to avoid controversial material in their classrooms and shunt their research into safer fields.[9] The current war on terror is taking a similar toll. Excessive post–September 11 security regulations have forced some biomedical researchers to drop work on certain infectious diseases, while outside pressures on people in Middle East

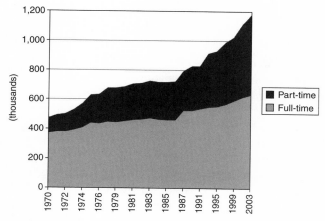

Growth of faculty in U.S. universities. The U.S. Department of Education's National Center for Education Statistics has charted the growth of U.S. universities' growing reliance on temporary faculty since 1970. The proportion of "part-time" faculty has more than doubled from 1970 to 2003, and since 1987 the rate of growth of "part-time" faculty has been more than double that of "full-time" faculty. If this rate of growth remains the same, by 2010 "part-time" faculty will make up well over 60 percent of all faculty hired. *(Graph by Sarah Nash and Maris Zivarts)*

studies make it hard to imagine that junior faculty members in that discipline have not at least *thought* about omitting sensitive topics from their syllabi until they receive tenure.

Today, however, the most serious incursions against faculty autonomy and the academic freedom that it protects come from the structural changes produced by the financial pressures of the past thirty years—changes that have intensified, if they have not actually created, the forces that are pulling the academic community apart. In particular, the increasing stratification caused by those changes has eroded the solidarity of the nation's faculties, thus making it harder for college and university teachers to protect their own and their colleagues' academic freedom. Since the formation of graduate-student unions is itself a response to those changes, let us examine them more closely.

While McCarthyism resulted in the academic community's most extensive purge, most of its victims ultimately returned to the academy. The late 1950s and 1960s were, after all, the golden age of American higher education, when the Cold War competition with the Soviet Union as well as the arrival of baby boomers on campus created an enormous demand for faculty members. As a result, by the mid-1960s even the ex-communists who had lost their jobs during the 1950s could find teaching positions within the nation's rapidly expanding colleges and universities. Research grants were also easy to obtain; the federal government was practically throwing money at scientists.[10] Moreover, because rents in college towns were low, graduate students in every field, assured of decent jobs even before they finished their degrees, could subsist—shabbily, but safely—on but a few thousand dollars a year.

Things changed in the 1970s—for ideological, as well as economic, reasons. Not only did inflation and foreign competition nibble away at previous assumptions about automatic growth, but a more aggressive business community sought to shrink the public sector while promoting a more competitive, individualistic ethos to counter the so-called excesses of the '60s. Government largesse began to dry up, seriously affecting the nation's colleges and universities. The Nixon administration, convinced that "a freer play of market forces [would] best achieve federal objectives in postsecondary education," adopted measures that steered federal aid to individual students instead of to the schools they attended.[11] At the same time, state legislatures, facing taxpayer unrest as well as the same ideological and economic pressures as the federal government, also cut back their aid to higher education.

As their traditional sources of revenue declined, the nation's college and university administrators reconfigured their priorities, adopting strategies that would enhance what NYU's president now calls the "Common Enterprise University." Financial, rather than educational, considerations came to drive their decision making—and not just at public institutions. Operating within a political environment that worshiped the market, many colleges and universities began to adopt a corporate management style. They also looked for new sources of income. They licensed school logos to garment manufacturers, developed office parks on university property, and began to commodify their faculty members' research.

Because tuition dollars became an increasingly important component of their budgets, academic administrators began to devote more of their schools' resources to attracting undergraduates. Both public and private institutions plowed money into big-time sports, invested in state-of-the-art computer facilities, and struggled to raise their rankings in the U.S. News and World Report. NYU, for example, began to hire well-known professors while upgrading its undergraduate housing facilities. Marketing became the order of the day, especially for the institutions that, like NYU, relied on tuition payments to balance their books. One school actually changed its name to attract more applicants, while others began offering ever more vocationally oriented courses. Transforming their admissions officers into "enrollment managers," some institutions even experimented with the corporate world's concept of "branding"—that is, developing a distinctive identity that would somehow attract applicants.[12]

Such measures, in a culture that uncritically celebrated the market, encouraged undergraduates to consider themselves consumers rather than learners, entitled above all to get a good return on their money. Many came to view college primarily as a place to obtain the credentials their future careers required. That it might also offer them an opportunity for intellectual growth seemed almost beside the point. Not surprisingly, academic shortcuts such as cheating and plagiarism flourished, while instructors, themselves enmeshed in the academic market, sought to increase enrollments by giving high grades and little reading. Though such an instrumental view of higher education can only degrade its quality, it is understandable in the light of the financial pressures so many students and their families face. College now costs so much that many otherwise qualified individuals can no longer afford to go, while graduates (and, especially, graduate students) find themselves thousands of dollars in debt.

Ironically, as the sticker price increased—at public universities from an average of $2,712 in 1980–1981 to $12,604 in 2004–2005 and at private universities from $6,569 in 1980–1981 to $34,698 in 2004–2005—and as schools became ever more dependent on tuition dollars, they were also taking measures that increased their students' dissatisfaction.[13] A vicious circle set in: Student complaints undermined public support for the nation's academic institutions, which responded by cutting costs and raising tuition, thus provoking further complaints. With fewer resources devoted to instructional budgets, the educational quality of those institutions began to decline. Classes were larger and harder to get into, making it difficult for students to fulfill the requirements they needed for a timely graduation.[14] And in what has become the most damaging aspect of the current fiscal crunch, fewer and fewer of those classes were being taught by regular tenure-track faculty members.

That problem was aggravated, at least at the major research universities, by the academic community's star system. To attract the widely published authors and cutting-edge scientists who would enhance their institution's reputation, and thus presumably bring in more paying customers and research grants, college and university administrators cut back on teaching loads. Top scholars at many schools no longer taught many undergraduates, if any. Instead, they devoted themselves to their research and Ph.D. students while farming out the less glamorous introductory courses to junior colleagues, part-timers, and off-the-ladder appointees. At NYU, for example, the highly touted analytical philosophers who were hired to raise the department's ranking spend most of their time teaching its thirty graduate students, leaving the undergraduate courses in the hands of adjuncts.[15]

This competition for prestigious faculty has had another deleterious consequence: It has encouraged institutions at every level of the academic world to raise their research requirements.[16] According to a recent study of the criteria for tenure in the fields the Modern Language Association (MLA) represents, not only did more than three-quarters of all the departments surveyed consider scholarship more important than teaching, but a third of them actually expected to see progress on a second book before granting tenure—and this at a time when university presses were publishing fewer monographs in the humanities.[17] We can only speculate about the impact of these requirements (unheard of for earlier generations of college teachers) on junior faculty members at second- and third-tier institutions with heavy teaching loads. But, of course, in the competitive atmosphere of today's academe, productivity is the name of the game.

As is cutting costs. And, like the corporate leaders who dominate their boards of trustees, academic administrators are scrambling to prune their budgets. Thus, besides diverting resources to student-friendly or prestige-enhancing operations, they have been pruning the university's less remunerative activities—such as scholarly publishing, library acquisitions, and building maintenance.[18] Just as in the corporate world, the labor force is taking the main hit. Admittedly, the personnel reductions within the academy seem less brutal than those in the automobile and steel industries. Except when institutions outsource their plant maintenance or bookstores, people do not lose their jobs. The academic workforce is not, in that sense, being downsized, just reconfigured. Despite rising enrollments, American colleges and universities no longer hire full-time tenure-track faculty members, relying instead on graduate students, part-timers, and, most recently, a growing number of post-docs and other full-time off-the-ladder appointees to handle their expanding student bodies and replace retirees.

The figures speak for themselves. A recent AAUP report reveals that between 1975 and 2003, full-time tenured and tenure-track faculty members fell from 57 percent of the nation's teaching staffs to 35 percent, with an actual loss of some two thousand tenured positions. During the same period, however, full-time non–tenure-track appointments grew from 13 percent to 19 percent of the faculties, while part-time positions increased from 30 percent to 46 percent. In other words, fully two-thirds of all the instruction in American colleges and universities is now being handled by contingent faculty members. In some fields, such as foreign languages, these people do most of the teaching.[19] Even at NYU, in the department I know best, out of the seventy-three undergraduate history classes listed for the fall of 2006, only thirty were being taught by full-time tenure-track faculty members. The rest—which, to be sure, included the sections of larger courses—were in the hands of graduate students, adjuncts, and those good old standbys "TBA" and "Staff." In NYU's Italian Department, adjuncts, lecturers, and graduate students handled *all* of the forty-four language classes.

While many of these instructors, at NYU and elsewhere, are as highly qualified as their colleagues on the regular faculty, they remain second-class citizens, without the job security or academic freedom that the tenure track affords. The adjuncts among them experience massive exploitation. Often hired at the last minute with little time to prepare their courses, many can support themselves only by commuting long distances between several of these low-paying positions. The fast-growing cohort of full-time off-the-ladder appointees fare somewhat better than their part-time colleagues; they, at least, have offices and benefits. Even so, because of their heavy teaching loads and lack of institutional support, few full-time instructors (or adjuncts, for that matter) can produce the scholarship that might improve their status and win them a tenure-track job. And (no surprise), most are women—with all the traditional disadvantages that accrue to females within the academy.[20]

Administrators rationalize the creation of this multitiered faculty structure by claiming that it gives them the "flexibility" required to keep up with the

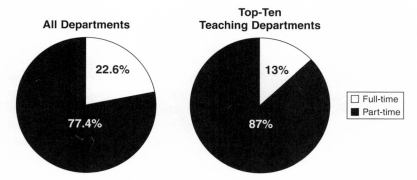

Teaching hours at NYU. Part-time faculty (including graduate employees) teach 77.4 percent of the contact hours in all departments. In the top-ten teaching departments, which account for 60 percent of the total teaching at NYU, part-time faculty and graduate employees teach 87 percent of the contact hours, and tenured or tenure-track faculty teach only 13 percent of the total contact hours. *(Calculations and graphs by Sarah Nash and Maris Zivarts)*

changes in the academic scene while letting students benefit from the special talents of practitioners from outside the academy. But such is not the case. Most contingent instructors are not well-paid professionals teaching for a lark but graduate students and Ph.D.s who could not find regular jobs. Moreover, far from offering unusual or highly specialized courses, they teach the same freshman composition and introductory classes year after year after year. Universities rely on them for one simple reason: They are cheaper than regular faculty members. They are also more easily controlled, since the insecurity of their appointments puts them at the mercy of administrators who can dismiss them at will.

Because of that insecurity, these contingent faculty members do not have academic freedom in any real sense of the term. Many schools—including NYU—claim that they would never interfere with the teaching or political expression of their contingent faculty members. Yet when we examine the (so far, fortunately, small) roster of academic-freedom violations that have occurred in the five years since September 11, 2001, many involve part-timers. While this may be a manifestation of these people's growing presence on campus, it is also the result of the ease with which they can be terminated. Unless they happen to be unionized, they cannot rely on the procedural safeguards that protect their tenured and tenure-track colleagues from being dismissed for political reasons.

There is, however, another and more insidious way in which the growth of the contingent faculty jeopardizes the autonomy and academic freedom of the professoriate: It saps its collegiality. It is demoralizing for faculty members, whose protected status is a partial recompense for earning less money than similarly credentialed professionals, to contemplate the growing presence of an academic underclass that does the same work they do yet has none of their privileges or prestige. Moreover, because outsiders—our students included—do not appreciate the difference between regular and contingent faculty members, the low status and poor working conditions of the latter threaten to undermine the entire academic community. Considerable antagonism builds up—on both sides.[21] While it is easy to understand why adjuncts and off-the-ladder instructors might resent their more fortunate colleagues and even attack the tenure system, senior professors also have legitimate grounds for opposing the employment of contingent faculty members. Though hiring such instructors does lighten some people's teaching loads, it also increases their administrative ones, since the constantly changing cohort of contingent appointees cannot participate in faculty governance. Accordingly, as the tenured faculty dwindles, the remaining senior professors must handle all the departmental and university chores—including the never-ending search for temporary and part-time teachers.

In such a situation, faculty governance becomes more a burden than a privilege, leading many professors to abdicate their control over key academic decisions and thus abandon the autonomy on which academic freedom rests. Administrators, who have long criticized the inefficiency of faculty procedures, are eager to take up the slack. Except in cases where presidents and deans behaved so outrageously that their faculties rebelled, there has been surprisingly little opposition to this assumption by administrators of responsibilities that professors once exercised. Especially when the rewards for community service pale in comparison with those for research, few faculty members are ready to make the sacrifices that maintaining their profession's traditional independence would require. They have other priorities.

On many campuses, those priorities include making money. This is especially the case for people in fields such as molecular biology and computer science that generate commercial applications. Ever since the passage of the so-called Bayh–Dole Amendment in 1980 allowed universities to patent the government-sponsored research on their campuses, institutions have scrambled to cash in on their faculty members' work. As this commodification of intellectual property has proceeded, commercial considerations trump educational ones—with the full cooperation, it must be noted, of the faculty entrepreneurs involved. Though only a few universities actually make money from their faculties' research, the prospect is so glittering that most institutions have embraced the corporate turn.

But academic capitalism has its downside—and not just when a school's investments fail to pay off. In the more remunerative fields, for example, researchers, who are often funded by pharmaceutical companies, must now produce profitable, as well as publishable, results. Moreover, because of their sponsors' desire for exclusivity, these scientists cannot always publish their findings—a serious problem for young researchers when they apply for teaching positions or tenure. An equally serious problem is the way in which these entrepreneurial ventures are reshaping the careers and values of the faculty members involved. Increasingly absorbed into the business world, they scant their educational obligations, often treating their students more as corporate employees than apprentice scientists. As one University of Washington biologist explained, "If you are worried about where you are going to get that next billion dollars, that's not worrying about how your graduate student is doing."[22] While the potential rewards of these ventures induce university administrations to tolerate their faculty members' unprofessional behavior, those administrations can hardly claim it is conducive to the collegiality the academic community allegedly cherishes.

Yet in opposing the unionization of their graduate-student employees, administrators and their faculty allies tout that collegiality, ignoring their own responsibility for its erosion as well as the fact that, even in its palmier days, the academy was never the sanctuary they now revere. Still, until the financial crunch of the past few decades, most college and university teachers did share a common career trajectory as well as a sense of academic professionalism that, if nothing else, treasured its own autonomy. With that autonomy all but defunct, however, references to the damage graduate-student unions inflict on the academic community seem disingenuous. Unionization cannot destroy what does not exist. Certainly, it cannot destroy an academic community that the past three decades of corporatization have already destroyed.

Nor can it destroy academic freedom. University administrators and their allies insist that, besides injecting alien considerations into the "primarily academic" relationship between the university and its students, unionization would violate academic freedom.[23] However, the notion of academic freedom these people espouse emphasizes the autonomy of the university in institutional, rather than individual, terms. In other words, whatever the university does is protected by academic freedom. This was the formulation that an attorney for the University of Pennsylvania propounded in a 2004 Senate hearing on the NLRB's decision to decertify GSOC. "Imposing collective bargaining on Penn's relationship with its graduate students would," he explained, "interfere with each of Penn's 'essential freedoms.'" The "freedoms" that he listed, however—including class size, length, and location—were primarily administrative matters, hardly relevant to the professional rights and responsibilities that academic freedom protects.[24] Moreover, his formulation conveniently overlooked the graduate-student contracts negotiated at many institutions, including NYU, which explicitly excluded key academic decisions from collective bargaining altogether.[25]

What is particularly disturbing about the situation at NYU and elsewhere are the many senior faculty members who share their administrations' hostility to graduate-student unions. Despite the long-term and relatively unexceptional existence of such unions at many of the nation's flagship universities, these academic opponents of unionization claim that it interferes with the educational mission of their schools—in particular, when job actions threaten to disrupt the campus routine. They seem unaware of the inequitable system of academic employment which spawned those unions, ignoring the way in which the growth of the contingent faculty threatens their own power and autonomy—not to mention the overall quality of American higher education.

In many respects, this faculty antipathy to graduate-student unions, especially at major research universities such as NYU, simply reflects the underlying divisions within the academic profession. It also reflects the hostility that senior professors at such universities display toward faculty unions. Claiming that collective bargaining is incompatible with academic autonomy, these well-paid and secure individuals rely on private wheeling and dealing to gain power within their institutions. They also equate their privileged status with academic freedom— and, to a certain extent, they are right. They will not lose their jobs for expressing unpopular opinions. But their academic freedom protects them only as individual political actors; it no longer functions as the collective expression of the professoriate's commitment to maintaining professional standards.

Ironically, as the effort to organize graduate students further divides the university, opponents of unionization insist that it will bring unwanted outsiders onto the campus. Invoking the shade of Jimmy Hoffa and the threat of organizers from Detroit, such allegations merely reveal a lack of knowledge about the growing white-collar presence within today's labor movement. In fact, the outside influences that the unions' opponents claim to fear are already present. Here, I am referring not to the Zionist pressure groups or religious fundamentalists that try to censor outside speakers, art exhibits, and student conferences, but to the business leaders who increasingly determine university policies. The presence of these corporate magnates may in fact account for the tenacity of the major private universities' battle against graduate-student unions. Especially since it costs more in legal fees to fight those unions than to recognize them, it seems likely that ideology, not economics, is driving the campaign. It matters little whether the university's administrators have themselves absorbed the anti-labor views of the businessmen with whom they consort or whether they are mouthing those beliefs to keep the money rolling in. What is tragic, however, is how many other members of the splintered academic community espouse that corporate ideology, as well.

There is some hope. Unions may actually be the most effective vehicles for restoring collegiality to academe. To a certain extent, this transformation has already taken place. GSOC activists at NYU, for example, have found that their organizing campaigns provided them with the sense of community that was otherwise missing from the campus. More important, however, such campaigns may eventually force the rest of the academy to recognize that, besides being a haven for scholarship and serious ideas, the university is also a workplace—and one that is being restructured in ways that are inimical to its essential mission. Thus, while graduate students and other contingent faculty members are struggling for higher pay and better benefits, they are also pushing back against the casualization of academic labor. After all, in a job market where only 35 percent of the Ph.D.s in the fields the MLA represents will get tenure, it is obviously in the long-term interest of graduate students and adjuncts (and the rest of the academic profession, as well) to unionize and to so improve their own salaries and working conditions that their institutions will reopen more tenure lines.[26] Academic freedom would benefit as well—and not just from the greater job security that tenured and tenure-track academics enjoy. Eliminating the glaring inequalities within the nation's faculties might allow for the creation of a real community of scholars that could, at last, protect the intellectual integrity of American higher education.

Notes

1. John Sexton, "The University as Sanctuary," November 2004, available online at http://www.nyu.edu/about/sexton-sanctuary04.html (accessed December 31, 2006).

2. Cary Nelson and Stephen Watt, *Office Hours: Activism and Change in the Academy* (New York: Routledge, 2004), 33.

3. For a discussion of the inability of the First Amendment to protect the free speech of professors at private institutions, see David Rabban, "A Functional Analysis of 'Individual' and 'Institutional' Academic Freedom under the First Amendment," *Law and Contemporary Problems* 53, no. 3 (1990): 227.

4. The relevant section of the 1940 statement reads:

> College and university teachers are citizens, members of a learned profession, and officers of an educational institution. When they speak or write as citizens, they should be free from institutional censorship or discipline, but their special position in the community imposes special obligations. As scholars and educational officers, they should remember that the public may judge their profession and their institution by their utterances. Hence they should at all times be accurate, should exercise appropriate restraint, should show respect for the opinions of others, and should make every effort to indicate that they are not speaking for the institution.

American Association of University Professors, "1940 Statement of Principles on Academic Freedom and Tenure with 1970 Interpretive Comments," in *AAUP Policy Documents and Reports*, 10th ed. (Washington, D.C.: American Association of University Professors, 2006), 3.

5. David Rabban, "Academic Freedom, Individual or Institutional?" *Academe*, November–December 2001.

6. For a recent and compelling discussion of academic freedom as a professional perquisite, see Robert Post, "The Structure of Academic Freedom," in *Academic Freedom after September 11*, ed. Beshara Doumani (New York: Zone Books, 2006).

7. For a thoughtful discussion of the way in which academics maintain the intellectual quality of their own disciplines, see David Hollinger, "What Does It Mean to Be 'Balanced' in Academia?" available online at http://hnn.us/articles/10194.html (accessed April 10, 2005).

8. John Connelly and Michael Gruttner, eds., *Universities under Dictatorship* (University Park: Pennsylvania State University Press, 2005).

9. On the impact of the McCarthy-era purges on the academic community, see Ellen Schrecker, *No Ivory Tower: McCarthyism and the Universities* (New York: Oxford University Press, 1986); Paul Lazarsfeld and Wagner Thielens Jr., *The Academic Mind* (Glencoe, Ill.: Free Press, 1958).

10. Jennifer Washburn, *University, Inc.: The Corporate Corruption of Higher Education* (New York: Basic Books, 2005), 44–45; Mark Ptashne, interview with James Watson, September 1997, Lasker Foundation Award, available online at http://www.laskerfoundation.org/awards/library/1997b_int_pmall.shtml#1 (accessed April 27, 2005).

11. Sheila Slaughter and Larry L. Leslie, *Academic Capitalism: Politics, Policies, and the Entrepreneurial University* (Baltimore: Johns Hopkins University Press, 1998), 72.

12. For an overview of the way in which colleges and universities marketed themselves, see David L. Kirp, *Shakespeare, Einstein, and the Bottom Line: The Marketing of Higher Education* (Cambridge, Mass.: Harvard University Press, 2003).

13. U.S. Department of Education, National Center for Education Statistics, Institute of Education Sciences, "Table 312: Average Undergraduate Tuition and Fees and Room and Board Rates Charged for Full-Time Students in Degree Granting Institutions, by Type and Control of Institution, 1964–5 through 2004–5," *Digest of Education Statistics,* available online at http://nces.ed.gov/programs/digest/d05/tables/dt05_312.asp (accessed January 26, 2007).

14. Slaughter and Leslie, *Academic Capitalism,* 240.

15. Kirp, *Shakespeare,* 73–81, 87; Washburn, *University, Inc.,* 199–200.

16. A former president of Stanford noted that, while half the young scientists there got tenure in 1980, only one-third to one-fourth were getting tenure by the late 1990s—and they had to get 50 percent more grant money, as well: Donald Kennedy, *Academic Duty* (Cambridge, Mass.: Harvard University Press, 1997), 18.

17. Modern Language Association, "Executive Summary," available online at http://www.mla.org/pdf/tenure_summary.pdf (accessed December 23, 2006).

18. Slaughter and Leslie, *Academic Capitalism,* 15.

19. John W. Curtis and Monica F. Jacobe, "Consequences: An Increasingly Contingent Faculty," 2006, available online at http://www.aaup.org/NR/rdonlyres/F05FF88E-B2A8 -4052-8373-AF0FDAE060AC/0/ConsequencesAnIncreasinglyContingentFaculty.pdf (accessed September 17, 2007).

20. A useful introduction to the world of contingent academics is Benjamin Johnson, Patrick Kavanagh, and Kevin Mattson, eds., *Steal This University: The Rise of the Corporate University and the Academic Labor Movement* (New York: Routledge, 2003).

21. Benjamin Johnson, "The Drain-O of Higher Education: Casual Labor and University Teaching," in Johnson et al., *Steal This University,* 61–80, discusses the mutual resentment between regular faculty members and their contingent colleagues.

22. Washburn, *University, Inc.,* 97.

23. Robert Battista, testimony, Hearings, National Labor Relations Board Issues, Subcommittee of the Committee on Appropriations, U.S. Senate, 108th Congress, 2nd session, September 23, 2004, 5 (hereafter, NLRB Hearings).

24. John Langel, testimony, NLRB Hearings, 56, 60.

25. Wilma Liebman, testimony, NLRB Hearings, 43.

26. MLA, "Executive Summary."

A Leadership University for the Twenty-First Century?

Corporate Administration, Contingent Labor, and the Erosion of Faculty Rights

MARY NOLAN

In 2005, the premier international business magazine the *Economist* accorded NYU the dubious distinction of leading American higher education into a brave, new corporate future. American universities are the best in the world, according to the *Economist,* and the secret of their success is attributable neither to American wealth nor per capita spending on higher education. Rather, it is because the best universities are private, faculty are not civil servants, the federal government plays a limited role (except when turbocharging particular research fields), and schools compete for students, faculty, and money. American universities forge links between academe and the corporate world—especially the high-tech knowledge industries.[1]

According to the *Economist,* NYU's rise "from underdog to top dog" came in part from hiring academic superstars. Much more important was NYU's ability to turn its downtown location into an asset and spot and exploit market niches. What made all of these market savvy activities possible was "the fact that power is concentrated in the hands of the central administration." While "most universities in other countries distribute power among the professors," the *Economist* concluded, "American universities have established a counterbalance to the power of the faculty in the person of the president, which allows some of them to act more like entrepreneurial firms than lethargic academic bodies."[2]

The NYU administration, not known for its modesty, shares this positive assessment. Upon becoming president of NYU in 2002, John Sexton proclaimed that the university was "poised to effect a category change" and become "among a handful of 'leadership universities'" in the twenty-first century. Unburdened by "entrenched or anachronistic structures and arche-types," NYU could "capitalize" on its location in the "geographic capital of the world" and "live the interconnection between the world of ideas and the world of action." In language a corporate turnaround expert might employ, Sexton promised that the "university leadership team" would begin "probing our self-definition, concentrating on key issues, and overcoming institutional reticence." NYU would become "the enterprise university," a model of intellectual commu-nity, energetic entrepreneurship, accountability, and governance.[3]

In Sexton's subsequent epistles to the NYU community—there are often sev-eral a year—he elaborated his vision in a much more explicitly market language. The essence of the "common enterprise" (a term adopted when faculty objected to the excessively corporate connotations of the original designation) was "our University's special blend of creativity, entrepreneurship, cooperation, striving and dedication." NYU had "a venture capital attitude."[4] When the Kaufmann Foundation awarded NYU a $1 million grant to "make entrepreneurship educa-tion a common and accessible campus-wide opportunity," NYU agreed to raise $5 million in matching funds. "Entrepreneurship was key to creating the NYU that exists today," Sexton stated. "This grant . . . is a perfect fit for NYU."[5] In 2003, he proudly noted that NYU had developed "a culture of rigorous review and accountability," and talk of "the research enterprise," "the teaching enterprise," and "the intellectual marketplace" is pervasive. Faculty, administrators, students, and staff are described as "stakeholders" and lauded for their willingness "to invest" in realizing NYU's ambition.[6] This is a far cry from the days when NYU could claim to be true to its motto, "A private university in the public service." Even the discussion of NYU as a "global university," the preferred designation in the 1990s, is now couched in terms of global economic competition and entre-preneurial opportunities.

NYU, Sexton insists, must not only pursue fiscal discipline but also "explore new entrepreneurial opportunities" and do more to "develop revenue sources."[7] With government support for higher education declining, "marketplace compe-tition from commercial providers" expanding, and NYU having reached the lim-its of its ability to borrow money and raise funds by expanding the student body, the university needs to reconsider "our techniques for treating our major product [knowledge]."[8] The Development Office, with a full-time staff of ninety-eight and a yearly budget of $26 million, aims to bring in $1 million a day until the goal of $2.5 billion is reached.[9] Like other universities, NYU has aggressively marketed its undergraduate and continuing-education programs and outsourced many activities, such as cleaning and food services. Research universities, Sexton wrote, "will be tempted to act more and more like commercial institutions." Indeed, NYU already has succumbed to that temptation. In 2005, it reported earning more than $133 million from intellectual-property licensing.[10] While acknowledging that intellectual-property licensing is complex and risky, Sexton insists that financially needy universities must pursue revenue this way. The acad-emy should not "devalue research that enters the world." Indeed, "an enlightened approach" might enable social scientists to emulate scientists by linking their research to those outside the academy and thereby produce commercial revenue to support higher education.[11]

To be sure, as befits his doctorate in theology and self-proclaimed identity as a person of faith,[12] Sexton also speaks a religiously inflected language of dialogue and duty, of sacred spaces and spiritual missions. In the enterprise model, he wrote in 2002, "Each person who accepts the title of professor simultaneously accepts a larger duty to the entire community." Students, faculty, administrators, and staff are "privileged" to be at NYU, and "those to whom a good is given must give something back in return."[13] Even as the university pursues commercial revenues, it must "sustain a sacred space for learning and discovery."[14] Sexton has repeatedly called for consultation, dialogue, and cooperation, insisting that he cannot succeed alone: "We will succeed or John will fail.[15]

Faith and the market, communal spirit and entrepreneurship, dialogue and competition coexist in Sexton's vision of the enterprise university. In practice, it has proved easier to corporatize than to create a community. This essay explores how the enterprise university has profoundly restructured the personnel and management practices of the administration, as well as the remuneration and status of academic labor. It suggests how these changes have eroded faculty rights, diminished faculty governance, and destroyed any sense of common interests and goals.

Corporatizing the Administration

Under Sexton, the academic transformation of NYU has been integrally tied to—if not dominated by—the restructuring of its finances. To achieve that, Sexton installed a more corporate administration that introduced new practices of decision making and accountability. Every aspect of academic life was to be profoundly affected.

John Sexton, dean of the NYU Law School from 1988 to 2002, was the insider presidential candidate of the board of trustees, not the choice of a conventional national search, a fact that upset many faculty. Known for his salesmanship more than his scholarship, Sexton had been a superb fundraiser at the Law School and enthusiastically embraced that role, which now dominates the lives of top university administrators. He wooed many legal superstars to NYU, a task made easier because the Law School had financial resources the rest of NYU lacked.[16] His aggressive fundraising undoubtedly enhanced his appeal to the trustees, for NYU as a whole had large ambitions but a small endowment, heavy debt, and a poor record of alumni contributions.

Even before his installation as president, Sexton appointed a new administrative and financial leadership team, whose members came overwhelmingly from the corporate world, government service, and the legal profession. Most top administrators, whose careers had been spent inside the academy, soon stepped down. NYU is hardly alone in this trend. As Craig Calhoun has noted, "Running a university was running a big corporation. As a result, top university managers were more and more often drawn from other fields of managerial work, from professional schools, and/or from long careers in full-time higher education administration."[17] For an increasing number, a stint in a university is simply one stop on a career devoted primarily to business with some government service.

Jack Lew, who headed Sexton's transition team, was appointed executive vice president, a new position, responsible for all budgetary, financial, investment, and operations matters, as well as for administrative services such as real estate and human resources. Before coming to NYU, Lew had served as President Bill Clinton's director of the Office of Management and Budget. Prior to that, he was a partner in a law firm and had been a policy adviser to House Speaker Thomas O'Neill. His only, and brief, academic experience was as a visiting research professor at Georgetown University's Public Policy Institute. When he left NYU in June 2006, Lew became chief operating officer of Citigroup Global Wealth Management.[18]

Lew was replaced by Michael Alfano, dean of the NYU College of Dentistry. Alfano's career has moved among private practice, business, public health, and the academy. Before he became dean, he was senior vice president for research and technology and a member of the board of directors of Block Drug Company, Inc., and was a special consultant to the Board of OraPharma, Inc., on issues "relating to scientific development and the commercialization of the company's interests in oral care medicine."[19] NYU proudly noted that, for several decades, Alfano "has worked to promote improved communications among academic, industrial and governmental scientists; regulatory agencies; and the public. In addition, he has led in the development and clinical evaluation of new products for both the dental and pharmaceutical industries."[20]

Diane Yu, chief of staff and deputy to the president, another new position, "serves as a vehicle by which one can communicate with the President ... and works to ensure the effectiveness of the communication processes of the entire University Leadership Team." Concretely, that means she leads selected policy initiatives, oversees faculty recruitment and retention, and works with deans. Her varied and impressive background was entirely outside the academy and included serving as associate general counsel of Monsanto Company, a life-sciences corporation with $7.5 billion in revenues, and working in private practice, as a government lawyer on trade issues, and for the Bar Association of California.[21] Cheryl Mills was appointed as counselor for operations and soon became senior vice president, general counsel, and secretary of the university, replacing Andrew Schaffer, who had served the university for twenty-seven years. Mills worked first in the nonprofit sector, then gained fame as the deputy counsel who defended President Clinton during the impeachment hearings. She subsequently served as senior vice president for corporate policy and public programming at Oxygen Media.[22] Sexton's senior vice president for development and alumni relations, the new vice president for fiscal affairs, and the counselor to the president all came from the Law School.[23]

Sexton also appointed a new "Academic Leadership Team." David McLaughlin, head of the Courant Institute of Mathematical Sciences, was named provost and given the task of "developing and implementing an academic vision for the University." He committed himself to "making academic priorities a central component of every administrative decision at the University and engaging faculty in these decisions." This rather awkward formulation suggests both the priority given to administrative and financial concerns and a preference for top-down leadership. Richard Foley, dean of the Faculty of Arts and Science, was made head of the Committee on Academic Priorities, and Robert Berne became senior vice president for health, overseeing the academic, financial, and operational aspects of NYU's hospitals and health-education and policy programs.[24] This academic team, however solid the accomplishments and knowledge of its members, lacked the novelty, the national renown, and, seemingly, the close ties to Sexton of its much larger financial and administrative counterpart.

The transformation of the top administration has been quantitative as well as qualitative. In 2006–2007, the thirty-two members of the university administration included the president, his staff, and the upper echelons of the provost's office but only one of the twenty-one deans and directors. The Provost's Office alone now has an impressive array of senior vice provosts, vice provosts, associate provosts, and provost fellows. One cannot begin to count the associate and assistant deans in schools across the university. Within this vastly expanded "University Leadership Team," power is centered, as nearly as one can tell in an utterly nontransparent system, in the president, his chief of staff, the executive vice president, the provost, the senior vice president for health, and the dean of arts and sciences. The Provost's Office is augmented by two advisory committees for academic priorities and undergraduate education, but their members, insofar as they are not ex officio representatives from the Provost's and President's offices, are appointed by and accountable to the provost, not the faculty.[25]

This reconfigured administrative apparatus concentrates enormous power, not to mention budgetary resources. In 2003–2004, for example, Sexton made $862,717, and Lew received $872,994. The provost got $450,000, a substantial gain over his prior salary of $168,967 in 2001–2002. Cheryl Mills was paid $375,000. The salaries for senior vice presidents ranged from $290,000 to $425,000.[26] While salaries for the lower levels of the upper administration and deans are not public, they usually range well above those of faculty.

NYU's revamped administration has introduced a new "culture of accountability." Universities and colleges across the country, under financial pressure from within and criticism from without, have striven to adopt business practices. Line-item budgets and detailed databases on everything from office supplies and classroom use to faculty productivity and class size are assiduously compiled and analyzed by accountants and professional administrators.[27] NYU is hardly distinctive in this regard, although the pace at which these new measures have been implemented has been more rapid and the public information about finances more secret than in public institutions. Managers, such as Dean of Administration

Joe Juliano, take great pride in the "statistical models, financial projections, and operational analyses that have been invaluable in the management of Arts and Science."[28] Certainly, some efforts to track and contain costs, use space more efficiently, and plan better for the future have addressed inefficiencies that benefited no one. But many at the receiving end of these new practices feel mismanaged.

Take the issue of annual salary raises—not individual increases, for salaries are secret at NYU—but what percentage raise will determine the pool from which individual raises will be determined. It is announced from on high and seems to hover at 3 percent, regardless of the university's financial state or fundraising successes. In 2003, however, although NYU had saved $15 million the previous year, Sexton announced a salary freeze for all faculty and administrators in order to "manage austerity." Faculty received a $750 supplement that would not be included in their base pay; Sexton, however, received a 16.5 percent increase, or $122,000. According to the *Chronicle of Higher Education*, this made Sexton the second highest paid president of a research university.[29] In announcing the freeze, Sexton claimed that forgone pay and higher tuition were, in fact, "investments" in NYU.[30]

Every department and program is now required to file an elaborate yearly qualitative and quantitative accounting of its personnel, programs, and budgetary requests. Like any corporation, the university wants information to flow up from the bottom, while decisions come down from the top. Yet it is not clear what mix of financial or academic considerations determine top-down decisions about lines, fellowships, and departmental budgets. Sexton has admonished that "the entire higher education community must find ways to demonstrate its willingness to be accountable, or it will have that accountability imposed upon it by others."[31] That faculty and students are to be accountable and submissive to the administration is clear. But to whom is the administration accountable?

The administration has become much more interventionist on academic as well as financial matters. While previously faculty were given leeway to build new programs, reorient departments, and establish centers, deans now micromanage departments and programs, even as they appear to be micromanaged from above. Increasingly, they block proposed hires or impose unsolicited candidates or override a department's vote for chair and substitute the administration's choice. Faculty hardly feel like they are part of the "common enterprise." They certainly are not management, as the 1980 Supreme Court decision in *National Labor Relations Board v. Yeshiva University* claimed faculty in private universities were, when it denied them the right to bargain collectively.

NYU has developed centralized and secretive information policies typical of the corporate world. It shares little about its endowment, investments, budgets, and compensation packages. It has monopolized communication with the university community via NYU Direct. Sexton's epistles and analyses of GSOC and the strike, as well as the provost's threats to strikers, were e-mailed to all of NYU's employees and students, but no other groups within the university can use NYU Direct. Even the Faculty Senate Council, the highest faculty governance body, must ask the provost for permission. These information policies make a mockery of Sexton's constant calls for "iterative dialogue."

Decisions once within the purview of faculty are increasingly made without consulting elected faculty bodies. The administration has planned for new NYU global branches with belated and minimal formal faculty consultation. The General Studies Program, fully staffed by contract faculty and adjuncts, was moved into the Faculty of Arts and Science with no formal faculty consultation. Sexton decided to close the International Center for Advanced Study, a highly successful faculty research initiative, preferring a pubic-policy think tank instead. This top-down, unilateral decision making has led the Faculty Senate Council, not known for its assertion of faculty rights, to call for a return to the spirit and intent of earlier procedures that encouraged faculty consultation about substantial changes in academic programs.[32]

Marketizing Academic Labor

Faculty have been disempowered and demoralized by the restructuring of the administration. Of equal importance, they have been divided by the restructuring of academic labor that is central to the marketization of higher education and to Sexton's vision of the enterprise university.

In 1969, just over 3 percent of faculty appointments were off the tenure track; in the 1990s, more than half were, and now three-quarters are.[33] In the 1970s, tenured/tenure-track faculty made up 57 percent of academic employees in higher education; today, they represent 35 percent. Full-time non–tenure-track faculty increased from 13 percent in 1975 to 18.7 percent in 2003, while part-time faculty (excluding graduate-student employees) grew from 30.2 percent to 46.3 percent in the same period.[34]

NYU exemplifies these general trends. In 2003, Sexton claimed that, "whereas over the past decade . . . we grew the size of our part-time faculty, our focus on increased attention to our students requires that we shift a greater proportion of our enterprise to full-time faculty."[35] NYU then had 1,899 full-time and 2,403 part-time faculty.[36] In 2006, full-time faculty had increased to 2,043, but the percentage of full-timers remained steady at 44.1 percent. Moreover, 36.4 percent of them were non–tenure-track, well above the 27.9 percent average for that category at private doctoral and research universities, and the 25.2 percent average for public ones. Whereas 55.8 percent of instructional faculty at NYU are part-time, the average for doctoral and research universities is 37 percent. Overall, NYU's percentage of contingent faculty is 71.9 percent, a figure that rises to 77.3 percent when the 1,093 graduate-student teachers are added. The percentages of contingent faculty among the Ivies, the premier public universities, and the "new Ivies"—to which NYU compares itself—are substantially lower. The average for all doctoral and research universities is 48.2 percent.[37]

Contingent faculty are spread across NYU. They are in programs staffed exclusively by full-time contract or part-time faculty: the General Studies Program, the Draper Interdisciplinary Master's Program, and the School of Continuing and Professional Studies. They are in the Gallatin School of Individualized Study as well as in professional schools, which draw from experts whose other commitments preclude full-time employment: the Stern School of Business, the Wagner School of Public Policy, and the Tisch School of the Arts. "Flexibilization" and "adjunctification" have even come to the core of the university: the Faculty of Arts and Science (FAS). Of the fifty-eight new hires in FAS for 2006–2007, forty were non–tenure-track assistant professors or faculty fellows; instructors in expository writing; language lecturers; clinical professors in departments such as journalism; or visiting professors.[38] Men are well represented in the once feminized category of contingent labor. Perhaps 2006–2007 was an anomalous year, for NYU is committed to hiring two hundred fifty tenured/tenure-track faculty over a five-year period. A survey of Sexton's writings, however, suggests his deep commitment to contingent faculty.

In his 2004 paper "The Common Enterprise University and the Teaching Mission," Sexton insisted that knowledge creation was the central function of the modern research university but rejected "the false dichotomy . . . between research and teaching."[39] Nonetheless, he envisioned a highly differentiated faculty for the enterprise university. There would be a core of tenured faculty, who ideally would commit themselves to the common enterprise, feel "genuine faculty ownership of an increasingly complex entity," and "act like members of a symphony orchestra." They would enjoy job security in order to pursue research creatively and without the constraints of intellectual fads or instrumental value and would participate in faculty governance. In turn, the university, by which Sexton seems to mean the administration, "has a significant [but unspecified] interest in circumscribing carefully the membership of this faculty group." While core faculty should recognize the importance of knowledge transmission, he said, they are not suitable for every type of course.

Faculty who are not eligible for tenure and who represent more than half of the full-time appointments in the past decade, were doing much teaching, and "the future will see more of this," he continued. Some would be full-time "university teachers" who were expected to be "an active participant in the institution and a premier participant in the education of students." They do not need tenure to have academic freedom, Sexton asserted, and are assumed to be uninterested in or incapable of research. "Everybody will have a role and respect, but that does not mean that everybody will have the same rights and responsibilities." Moreover, "in a period of hyperchange," in which there are constant demands for new methods and modalities, universities must be free to hire those proficient in the latest pedagogy. The decision to take on this demanding and precarious position is presented as voluntary.

Others would become adjunct professors, Sexton wrote, "selected because he or she, while foreswearing a full-time academic life, comes into the classroom as an exemplar of the application of knowledge creation in the world outside the gates." "Foreswear," according to the *Oxford English Dictionary*, means "to abandon or renounce on oath or in a manner deemed irrevocable." This hardly describes the conditions under which most adjuncts piece together a poverty existence. Nor does it express their aspirations. "It is a part-time commitment in both directions" is Sexton's glib gloss on the grossly unequal power relations. There will also be arts professors, some of whom may be tenured (but most not), as well as a small cadre of elite international visitors appointed as global professors. Finally, cyber-faculty will "integrate research and teaching into the new world of scholarly cyberspace."

"The notion of faculty governance which will characterize this university does not entail the faculty literally running the institution," concluded Sexton. "It entails a commitment by university leadership to conference ideas with faculty in a transparent process that empowers them to participate meaningfully in shaping both aspirations and strategies." Given faculty with unequal rights and status, and given the lack of strong faculty governance institutions, however, it is impossible for the university to become "not only a protected place of open and vigorous exchange but also a sacred space where democratic principles are modeled," as Sexton envisions.

Within the Common Enterprise University, the market is modeled more effectively than democracy. The market accords very different compensation not only among these diverse categories of faculty, but also within the privileged core of tenured faculty. Law and medical schools always offered compensation packages substantially above those in the rest of the university in order to compete in the market. In recent decades, compensation throughout the university has become marketized. NYU, as well as institutions such as the University of Southern California and Vanderbilt University, have bought prestigious senior and mid-career scholars. NYU's purchase of a premier analytical philosophy department is the most discussed such example, but most other departments have participated in star hiring as well.[40] The result has been enormous salary differentials—between divisions, with the sciences on the top and the humanities at the bottom; between departments, depending on whether they are favored by the administration or can readily license their intellectual property or otherwise raise outside funds; and between men and women, with women concentrated in the lower ranks and in departments with overall lower salaries.[41] Within departments, pay differentials can also be substantial, especially among senior professors.

For star hires and those NYU faculty with competitive outside offers, salary, teaching load, research support, housing, child-care funds, and tuition aid are all up for negotiation. Some are promised a center of their own; others are promised the prospect of several lines to fill.[42] While austerity is preached for most, there is money in abundance for some. Just how much is unclear, for salaries are not public, and those who accept an NYU matching offer must sign a confidentiality agreement.

Both individual faculty and department chairs are ambivalent about this pervasive marketization, for it makes negotiations for new hires and retentions difficult and time-consuming. It creates visible inequalities and corrosive suspicions about the magnitude of hidden ones. It requires faculty to pursue outside market recognition. To be sure, Sexton has urged faculty not to consider themselves "independent contractors" and claimed that NYU "need not—indeed it must not—participate in an academic equivalent of baseball's free agency market." Yet he also insists that all faculty have a stake in accepting "the normal, not aberrational market." Despite generating all sorts of differentiations, the market selects "the best colleagues." Furthermore, "allowing the external market to set compensation—to have it value faculty—is less disruptive than a process of ongoing ad hoc internal evaluation." On Sexton's own admission, it is a challenge to create community while using the market as the metric of academic value.[43] It is a challenge NYU has singularly failed to meet.

Eroding Faculty Rights

The GSOC strike did not create division within a once cohesive faculty; rather, it added new disagreements about academic unionization to a host of preexisting differences. The strike both led to substantial faculty protest against administration attacks on faculty prerogatives and showed the power of the administration to impose it own vision.

The faculty experienced three major incursions on its rights and prerogatives in the course of the strike. The first was "Blackboardgate." As the strike began on November 9, several faculty members discovered that deans and directors of undergraduate studies had been inserted onto their Blackboard sites, used to communicate with students and post assignments, thus enabling administrators to monitor all transactions and communicate with students. The second occurred on November 23, 2005, when the provost decreed a radical revision of grading policy that allowed students who felt their learning had been disrupted to take courses pass/fail *after* they had received a grade from the instructor. Pass/fail grades could now be used to fulfill general education and major requirements, and students could drop courses long past the usual deadline, with no notation on their transcripts. Students could retake a course for free in a later semester or at another university and NYU would pay. An Academic Resources Center (ARC), staffed by administrators, was opened to offer assistance to undergrads once they reported whether the teaching assistant was on strike and the professor had moved classes off campus.[44] The third unilateral administration action occurred on November 27, 2005, when punitive sanctions against strikers, which would not only dock pay for the period struck but also prohibit strikers from teaching the following semester, were announced.

Faculty were deeply upset by these actions, all of which were undertaken without faculty consultation. In a Faculty Democracy petition signed by two hundred faculty members, as well as in letters and departmental resolutions, faculty protested "invasive intimidation," "deepest violation of academic freedom," and the compromising of "the principles of free conversation and exchange" that are integral to the classroom.[45] They insisted that only faculty could determine grading policy and departmental regulations and evaluate students' work. In February 2006, two hundred seventy faculty members signed a letter to the president and provost arguing that the penalties were excessive and antithetical to values integral to academic and civil society. They were imposed in a unilateral manner that ignored standing disciplinary procedures at the school and departmental levels and interfered with departmental prerogatives to determine who should teach.[46]

The protest was encouraging, coming as it did from both strike supporters and many who were ambivalent about the union, but it came disproportionately from the humanities. Of greater importance, the administration saw no cause for indignation or need for apology. Intruding onto Blackboard sites was not "surreptitious or malicious," claimed Sexton; rather, it was "a responsible approach to ensuring educational continuity."[47] The provost used an identical justification for his radical revision of grading policy.[48] The administration did not deign to reply to protests about threatened punishments against strikers. In each case, the administration refused to engage with the underlying issues of such concern to faculty. As Professor of Politics Christine Harrington noted, questions of morality, ethics, and academic freedom were reduced to issues of procedure.[49]

The administration was able to impose its policies during the strike at the expense of faculty because the prior corporate restructuring of the administration had centralized decision making, weakened the institutions of faculty governance, and encouraged those on top to ignore the concerns of chairs or ad hoc faculty groups. Sexton had a clear vision of the enterprise university, which had as little room for strong faculty governance as it did for unionized teaching assistants. He presented the rest of the university with the choice of buying in or being marginalized.

The restructuring of the faculty contributed significantly to its inability to defend its rights. Those protesting were drawn primarily from the minority of faculty who were tenured and on the tenure track, and many of their colleagues were ambivalent or hostile toward GSOC/UAW, in particular, and toward unions in general. Faculty were ambivalent about collective action in an institution that marketized every aspect of academic labor and about faculty governance institutions, which had a history of timidity and deference toward the administration but were nonetheless ignored by it. NYU had created a culture in which "voice"— a favorite administration term—was to be individual and ad hoc, not collective and institutionalized. Both those who opposed the union and those who sought—sometimes publicly, often privately—a third way between the UAW and union busting engaged in secret meetings and backstairs bargaining, floated proposals to a select few faculty and administrators, and thrust them on graduate students. Such actions undermined the potential effectiveness of public, collective protest letters and meetings. They reflected and reinforced a culture in which privileged faculty presumed that a better market position translated into more influence on key decisions. The administration might meet with them, whereas it would not even accept petitions delivered by members of Faculty Democracy, but it listened only to those who shared its determination to destroy the union.

On the day before the strike began, more than fifty members of Faculty Democracy asked Sexton to negotiate with GSOC, warning that a prolonged strike would create ongoing contention and lasting bitterness, as it had at Yale. Sexton did break the strike, but GSOC continues to organize. NYU faculty members, much more divided about GSOC than their very anti-union counterpart at Yale, are angrier and more suspicious of one another and the administration than before. But for the leaders of the enterprise university, faculty demoralization, cynicism, and division are a small price to pay for union busting, the erosion of faculty governance, and rave reviews from the *Economist*.

Notes

1. "The Best Is Yet to Come," *Economist*, September 8, 2005, available online at http://www.economist.com/surveys/displaystory.cfm?story_id=E1_QPQDDRP (accessed March 8, 2006).

2. "Secrets of Success," *Economist*, September 8, 2005, available online at http://www.economist.com/surveys/displaystory.cfm?story_id=E1_QPPJJQQ (accessed March 8, 2006).

3. John Sexton, "The Enterprise University," September 17, 2002, available online at http://www.nyu.edu/provost/communications/communications-091702.html (accessed December 14, 2006).

4. David L. Kirp, *Shakespeare, Einstein, and the Bottom Line: The Marketing of Higher Education* (Cambridge, Mass.: Harvard, 2003), 277, fn. 4.

5. NYU Office of Public Affairs, press release, "New York University Awarded $1 Million by the Kaufman Foundation to Unleash Entrepreneurial Spirit," December 14, 2006, available online at http://www.nyu.edu/public.affairs/releases/detail/1359 (accessed January 2, 2007).

6. John Sexton, "Beginning a New Year," Fall 2003, available online at http://www.nyu.edu/about/sexton-newyear03.html (accessed October 2, 2006).

7. Idem, "Managing Austerity while Seizing Opportunities," March 30, 2003, available online at http://www.nyu.edu/about/sexton-entrepriseupdate.html (accessed October 2, 2006).

8. Idem, "The Research University in a Global Context," available online at http://www.nyu.edu/about/sexton-globalization.html (accessed October 2, 2006).

9. Jonathan D. Glater, "Seeking $1 Million a Day, NYU Mines Personal Data for a Fund-Raising Edge," *New York Times*, December 25, 2006.

10. This made NYU the second-highest earner among those universities that agreed to publish their intellectual-property revenues: *Chronicle of Higher Education*, March 2, 2007, A29.

11. Sexton, "The Research University in a Global Context."

12. Idem, "Dogmatism and Complexity: Civil Discourse and the Research University," August 2, 2005, available online at http://www.nyu.edu/about/sexton-dogmatism.html (accessed October 2, 2006).

13. Idem, "The Enterprise University."

14. Idem, "The Research University in a Global Context."

15. Kirp, *Shakespeare*, 89.

16. James Traub, "John Sexton Pleads (and Pleads and Pleads) His Case," *New York Times Magazine*, May 25, 1997, 28.

17. Craig Calhoun, "Is the University in Crisis?" *Society* (May–June 2006): 9.

18. "NYU Appoints Jack Lew as Transition Director, Executive Vice President," *NYU Today,* October 9, 2001; NYU Office of Public Affairs, "Administrative and Financial Leadership Team Named," May 1, 2002, available online at http://www.nyu.edu/public.affairs/releases/detail/401 (accessed December 18, 2006).

19. Dentsply, Management, Dr. Michael C. Alfano, available online at https://www.dentsply.com/defaut.aspx?pageid=32 (accessed December 18, 2006); "Michael Alfano, D.M.D., Ph.D., Appointed as Special Consultant to OraPharma, Inc.," available online at http://www.smilefinder.com/index.php?name=News&file=article&sid=1570&theme=Pri (accessed December 18, 2006).

20. NYU Office of Public Affairs, "Michael C. Alfano, D.M.D., Ph.D., Dean, College of Dentistry," available online at http://www.nyu.edu/public.affairs/leadership/alfano.html (accessed December 18, 2006).

21. Idem, "Diane C. Yu, B.A., J.D., Chief of Staff and Deputy to the President" available online at http://www.nyu.edu/public.affairs/leadership/yu.html; Lloyd Johnson, "From the White House to Monsanto, Yu Is Dedicated to Diversity," Minority Corporate Counsel Association website, available online at http://www.mcca.com/site/data/magazine/movers andshakers/Johnson/0299.htm (accessed December 18, 2006).

22. Idem, "Cheryl Mills, B.A., J.D., Senior Vice President, General Counsel, and Secretary of the University, Acting Senior Vice President for Operations and Administration," available online at http://www.nyu.edu/public.affairs/leadership/mills.html (accessed December 18, 2006).

23. Idem, "Administrative and Financial Leadership Team Named," May 1, 2002, available online at http://www.nyu.edu/public.affairs/releases/detail/401 (accessed December 18, 2006).

24. Idem, "Academic Leadership Team Named," April 25, 2002, available online at http://www.nyu.edu/public.affairs/releases/detail/402 (accessed August 16, 2006)

25. New York University, "University Administration," available online at http://www.nyu.edu/about/administration.html (accessed August 16, 2006); NYU Office of the Provost, "About the Office," available online at http://www.nyu.edu/provost/about.office (accessed November 9, 2006). Whereas only three of the eighteen members of the Academic Priorities Committee were initially ex officio representatives from the provost's and president's offices, now eleven of twenty-eight are.

26. NYU Exposed, "How NYU Works; NYU Administration," available online at http://www.nyuexposed.org/works_administration.htm (accessed January 6, 2007).

27. Richard Daniels, with Lisa Blasch and Peter Caster, "Resisting Corporatization of the University," in *Campus, Inc.: Corporate Power in the Ivory Tower,* ed. Geoffry D. White and Flannery C. Hauck (Amherst, N.Y.: Prometheus Books, 2000), 64; Christopher Newfield, "Recapturing Academic Business," in *Chalk Lines: The Politics of Work in the Managed University,* ed. Randy Martin (Durham, N.C.: Duke University Press, 1998), 80.

28. Joe Juliano, memorandum to Arts and Science Community, December 21, 2006, in the author's possession.

29. NYU Exposed, "How NYU Works: John Sexton's Salary," available online at http://nyuexposed.org/works_sexton.htm (accessed January 6, 2007).

30. Sexton, "Managing Austerity."

31. Ibid.

32. *Faculty Senators Council Newsletter,* September–October 2006, 3.

33. Joseph Entin, "Contingent Teaching Corporate Universities and the Academic Labor Movement," *Radical Teacher* 73 (2006): 27.

34. John Gravois, "Tracing the Invisible Faculty," *Chronicle of Higher Education,* December 15, 2006. See Jack H. Schuster and Martin J. Finkelstein, *The American Faculty: The Restructuring of Academic Work and Careers* (Baltimore: Johns Hopkins University Press, 2006), for the most exhaustive compilation of these trends.

35. Sexton, "Managing Austerity."

36. Preclinical and clinical medical faculty as well as graduate students are omitted from these figures.

37. AAUP Contingent Faculty Index 2006, 18–35.

38. New York University, "New Faculty 2006–2007," September 2006, available online at http://www.nyu.edu/provost/pdf/new.faculty.06-07 (accessed January 6, 2007). More recent listings of new faculty on the provost's website give only tenured and tenure-track faculty and omit contingent faculty.

39. John Sexton, "The Common Enterprise University and Teaching Mission," November 2004, available online at http://www.nyu.edu/about/sexton-teachingmission04.html (accessed October 2, 2006). All quotes in the next five paragraphs come from this document.

40. Kirp, *Shakespeare.*

41. Report of the FAS Faculty Equity Committee, March 10, 2006, available online at http://www.nyu.edu/fas/wfc/3-10-06.doc (accessed January 6, 2007).

42. David L. Kirp, "How Much for That Professor?" *New York Times,* October 27, 2003, 27.

43. Sexton, "Common Enterprise University," 8.

44. Provost David McLaughlin to deans, directors, and department chairs, November 23, 2005, in the author's possession. Bryan Pirolli, "Some Fear ARC May Be against Striking Grads," *Washington Square News,* December 9, 2005; Andrew Nusca, "Center Helps Students Cope with Strike," *Washington Square News,* January 17, 2006.

45. History Department resolution passed at November 11, 2005, meeting, in the author's possession. Barbara Leonard, "Administrators Access Class Blackboard Sites," *Washington Square News,* November 10, 2005, and "Blackboard Access Infuriates Profs," *Washington Square News,* November 14, 2005; "Letter to President Sexton: Regarding Electronic Surveillance," November 10, 2005, available online at http://facultydemocracy.org/surveillance.html (accessed December 14, 2006).

46. Phillip Harper, draft of letter from department officers to the provost, December 1, 2005, in the author's possession; faculty to Sexton and McLaughlin, "Protest against Punitive Sanction," letter, February 5, 2006, available online at http://www.facultydemocracy.org/punitivesanctions.html (accessed January 9, 2007).

47. Richard Foley and Matthew Santirocco to chairs and deans, letter, November 10, 2005; John Sexton, "Letter to the NYU Community," n.d., and David McLaughlin to Sexton (circulated to NYU Community), "Implementation of Blackboard," memorandum, n.d., available online at http://www.nyu.edu/provost/communications/ga/communications-111405.html (accessed December 14, 2006).

48. McLaughlin to deans, directors, and department chairs, November 23, 2005; Pirolli, "Some Fear ARC"; Nusca, "Center Helps Students."

49. Scott Carlson, "NYU Professors Blast Inclusion of Administrators on Course-Management Site," *Chronicle of Higher Education,* November 25, 2005, A44.

Building a Statue of Smoke

Finance Culture and the NYU Trustees

CHRISTOPHER NEWFIELD AND GREG GRANDIN

When it comes to the role of trustees in graduate labor issues—indeed, in all of university life—much is assumed, but little is researched. One historian noted that "the most evasive group within American higher education has been one of its most powerful groups—namely, trustees."[1] Boards of Trustees, sometimes called Regents, Overseers, or, in the case of Yale University, a "Corporation," have in almost all cases legal possession and ultimate fiduciary authority over their institutions. Boards take full formal charge of the business side of their universities, often have high-level business connections and sophistication, and are in many cases dominated by lawyers and corporate elites. They rarely have formal training or demonstrated achievement in the world of higher education; rather, they are associated with the fund-raising side of the enterprise, where their social and business connections are expected to increase philanthropy and related opportunities for the university. Trustees can and do sometimes pull administrative strings and sometimes ignore or set policy for faculty; before the parameters of tenure were well established, trustees used to fire suspect or dissident faculty.[2]

In recent times, trustees have occasionally intruded into educational policy against the wishes of the majority of both faculty and administrators. In 1995, University of California (UC) Regent Ward Connerly, a small-business man acting with the full backing of the state's governor, Pete Wilson, persuaded the Board of Regents to eliminate affirmative action in UC hiring and admissions. But this kind of spectacular strong-arming is the exception rather than the rule, and Connerly had so clearly dragged the University into Governor Pete Wilson's campaign for the Republican presidential nomination that he became a poster child for unregental behavior. His claims that the regents "share too damn much" with the faculty, that he was "sick and tired of the faculty thinking we're supposed to roll over and play dead," are still cited as blatant trustee overreaching.[3] There is no evidence that Connerly's *public* brand of activist trusteeship has caught on.

Organizational frameworks do not clarify much, either. "Trustees" appear in the title of the American Council of Trustees and Alumni (ACTA), a conservative advocacy organization co-founded by Lynne Cheney and operating in close alignment with David Horowitz's crusade to purge liberals and leftists from campuses. Although ACTA hopes to influence trustees to reshape their faculties toward the right, it cannot be said to be a trustee organization. The more mainstream Association of Governing Boards of Universities and Colleges (AGB) has recently issued a sober report defining such concepts as "board accountability" and "board performance."[4] This is a worthy group committed to good trustee governance, but its practical influence over sitting trustees is unknown and probably limited.

Lacking better information, we often fall back on the model of trustees as a "board of directors." Its most famous expression emerged from the 1964–1965 Free Speech Movement at UC Berkeley, when the student negotiator Mario Savio expressed his frustration with UC President Clark Kerr and the "autocracy which runs this university":

> If President Kerr actually tried to get something more liberal out of the Regents in his telephone conversation, why didn't he make some public statement to that effect? And the answer we received—from a well-meaning liberal—was the following: He said, "Would you ever imagine the manager of a firm making a statement publicly in opposition to his board of directors?" That's the answer! Now, I ask you to consider: if this is a firm, and if the Board of Regents are the board of directors, and if President Kerr in fact is the manager, then I'll tell you something: the faculty are a bunch of employees, and we're the raw material! But we're a bunch of raw material[s] that don't mean to have any process upon us, don't mean to be made into any product, don't mean to end up being bought by some clients of the University, be they the government, be they industry, be they organized labor, be they anyone! We're human beings![5]

In the 1960s, trustees often seemed to be the power behind throne of figurehead university presidents, routinely maneuvering on behalf of established powers, particularly those invested in heavy industry and national defense. So we might start thinking about the NYU Trustees in the 2000s by comparing them to their predecessors.

A Genuine Power Elite

In 1971, the New University Conference Publications Collective produced a well-researched and analytically sophisticated overview of the trustees of their day.[6] Most strikingly that board could be described, at least superficially, as representing a political and business aristocracy with international reach. The report, "NYU Inc.," posited a theory of the trustee as industry representative, meaning that trustees brought their industrial group's financial interests to the NYU table and carved up the university's resources in friendly competition with other trustees. The board consisted of seven Financial Groups, each an empire or, at least, a major fiefdom unto itself: the "Lehman Group," the "Morgan Group," the "Manufacturers Hanover Group," the "Rockefeller Group," and so on. Trustees own the NYU Corporation, the report noted, meaning that they "see it as an important instrument for amassing wealth, avoiding taxes, generating research and development, processing the technical and managerial labor power they need for their enterprises, and forging international, national, and local policy studies. Their overlapping positions, which include more than one hundred corporations and forty foundations, help them to link business, education and government into a single powerful tool for their own aggrandizement, with a cultural cover and nicety which befits the liberal world view."

The conclusion was largely deductive, with little direct supporting evidence. But given several factors, it was certainly a plausible interpretation of what seemed to be happening. One was a set of known financial transactions in which board members appeared to be on both sides of the deal. In at least one case, a trustee appeared to unload an unprofitable real-estate asset onto the university (ironically, this was Washington Square Village, today home to many NYU faculty and a prized bargaining chip used by the university to attract professors). A second was the plausible assumption that the combination of intimacy and secrecy made it easy enough to hide special deals and mutual enrichment, so that the ones that had become public could be read by skeptical onlookers as the tip of the iceberg.

The third was the overall corporate feeling of NYU at the end of the 1960s. It was a fragmented urban university with two main campuses, in the Bronx and Greenwich Village, intermingled with hundreds of Manhattan businesses. It was a major property owner with serious budgetary problems. It was manager of dozens of auxiliary enterprises whose core operations were directed by administrators drawn from the finance, insurance, and real-estate (FIRE) sector that dominated lower Manhattan. NYU already had six thousand faculty, one-third of whom were part time. It enrolled forty thousand students, yet half of these students were part time, and there was little feeling of an academic community. NYU also employed a large number of low-wage workers and had already become known as an anti-union employer, one that tried to break strikes and paid poverty-level pensions. NYU was in essence a "corporate university" long before the term entered the national vocabulary.

Finally, NYU's public presence was dominated by figures drawn from the financial, military, and foreign-policy establishments. Senior managers came from Alcoa Aluminum, IBM, the Federal Reserve Bank, military contractors large and small, the Office of Naval Research, and the U.S. Department of Defense. NYU's staff in the 1950s had many former military commanders, including its vice president, the hard-line anticommunist Brigadier-General Frank L. Howley. This grouping did not add up to a bloc, and was well within normal parameters for a large research university, but its ties to the military and political establishments were significant.

The central figure in all this was the president of the university, James McNaughton Hester, who, according to the report, "manages NYU, Inc. for the Trustees."[7] Hester served with the U.S. Military Occupation Government in Japan, where he oversaw the restructuring of three thousand Japanese schools and had become close to General Lucius DuB. Clay, commander-in-chief in Europe and Governor of the U.S. War Zone in occupied Germany after the end of World War II. Clay later became head of the Continental Can Company when it was owned by Lehman. He then became a senior partner at Lehman when Hester was NYU's president. Hester sat on the boards of Prudential Life, Union Carbide, Lehman, and the Irvine Trust company, as well as on the Board of Governors of the Federal Reserve Bank of New York. "NYU Inc." noted that Hester could be found at the top of New York's financial and insurance industries at the same time that he served as university president and that his boards were at the center of major political and economic policies of the era, ranging from manufacturing nuclear weapons to mining in apartheid South Africa.

Hester could not accurately be described as the puppet master pulling entangled strings. But the report correctly noted a conflict between his official academic self-presentation and his institutional affiliations. Most important, the report was correct to depict the NYU Board of Trustees as composed of people with influence over public policy as well as financial matters. The board did "represent," though it did not control, dominant and generally conservative powers in Cold War America. It was an establishment board and was one element in the wielding of *visible*—and not merely backroom—political, military, and financial power.

A Post-Industrial Board of Trustees

Can the same be said of the NYU Board of Trustees that sat during the graduate-student strike? Several features of the trustees of the mid-2000s stand out. The first is the board's almost complete professional detachment from higher education itself. With the exception of the position held by an NYU president emeritus, not a single trustee held a major post in higher education, though several are involved in arts and educational charities. These activities have a somewhat narrow institutional range. Nearly all the museum work of the NYU Board of Trustees, for example, involves the Whitney Museum.

The second feature is the almost complete silence of the board members on matters of public life. Representatives of the higher levels of the government, the military, electoral offices, or even public administration do not appear on the board. It is very difficult to find an NYU trustee who has gone on the public record advocating a strong position on civic issues—from anywhere on the political spectrum. The leading organization among board members is the Citizens Budget Commission (CBC) of New York; Trustees Marc H. Bell, H. Dale Hemmerdinger (as chair), Lester Pollack, Joseph S. Steinberg, and Michael H. Steinhardt have served in various capacities. The CBC has had various preoccupations over the course of its history, but in recent years it has focused almost entirely on the cost of government in New York City and New York State. It has published a repetitive series of reports recommending various methods of reducing public-sector costs, with a special interest in cutting pension and benefit costs for public employees.[8] It has argued that public-sector wages are no longer sufficiently below private-sector equivalents to justify generous defined-benefit pensions and each year urges the governor to veto the legislature's pension-allocation bill.[9]

The CBC's peculiar focus on wage and pension costs as the main problem facing New York public life is consistent with finance culture's attempts to weaken the political power of unions and of the non-elite college-educated middle class that provides society's teachers, social workers, nurses, and other "safety-net" caregivers. This worldview requires shrinking their economic portion, as well. The middle-class has been split in recent decades between the high-end professionals such as lawyers, bankers, and engineers whose salaries have risen consistently and rapidly since the early 1980s, and the "in-person servers" among the white-collar ranks who get 5 percent raises, at most, in excellent years, and who are cut at the slightest downswing in a business cycle. This latter group includes the municipal, state, and federal government employment that has been the foundation of the African American and, to a lesser extent, the Latino job market in the same urban areas that have experienced acute, long-term deindustrialization. A blunt way of putting the point is that the FIRE sector that numerically dominates the NYU Board of Trustees (see Table 4.1), having eliminated many or most well-paying, high-benefits manufacturing jobs in the old industrial belt, is coming back to public- and private-sector employment to finish the job.

The NYU Board is overwhelmingly skewed toward finance, a sector that encompasses many trustees who at first glance seem independent of it. For example, although Trustee Courtney Ross-Holst technically appears under media, her wealth derived originally from her status as Time-Warner CEO Steven R. Ross's third wife at the time of his death in December 1992. Ross's personal fortune was created through a series of cleverly engineered corporate mergers into which he wrote enormous payouts for himself and his inner circle. His final major merger brought Time Inc. together with his company, Warner Communications International, and the last year of his life was overshadowed by the protests of shareholders and fired workers over various problems in the merged firm, including

TABLE 4.1 NYU TRUSTEES IN 2006–2007 BY GENERAL INDUSTRY SECTOR

INDUSTRY	APPROX. NUMBER	TRUSTEE AND PRIMARY ORGANIZATION
Finance	17	1. Martin Lipton, Wachtell, Lipton, Rosen and Katz
		2. Lawrence D. Fink, BlackRock
		3. Ronald E. Blaylock, Blaylock and Company
		4. Kevin R. Brine, Brine Management
		5. Paul E. Francis, Cedar Street Group
		6. Jay M. Furman, RD Management Corporation
		7. Richard A. Grasso, NYSE
		8. Richard D. Katcher, Wachtell, Lipton, Rosen and Katz
		9. Richard Jay Krogan, Bank of New York
		10. Jerry Labowitz, Merrill Lynch
		11. Donald Baird Marron, Lightyear Capital
		12. Lester Pollack, Centre Partners Management
		13. E. John Rosenwald, Jr., VC Bear Stearns
		14. Daniel R. Tisch, Mentor Partners
		15. William D. Zabel, Schulte, Roth and Zabel
		16. Evan Chesler, Cravath, Swaine and Moore
		17. David C. Oxman, Trusts and estates law
Insurance	2	1. Joseph S. Steinberg, White Mountains Insurance Group
		2. Anthony Welters
Real Estate	7	1. Larry A. Silverstein, Silverstein Properties
		2. Leonard A. Wilf, Garden Commercial Properties
		3. H. Dale Hemmerdinger, Hemmerdinger Corporation
		4. Constance J. Milstein, Ogden CAP Properties
		5. William C. Rudin, Rudin Management Company
		6. Henry R. Silverman, Cendant Corporation
		7. Lisa Silverstein, Larry Silverstein's daughter
Media & Art	9	1. Thomas S. Murphy, Capital Cities/ABC
		2. Marc H. Bell, Penthouse International
		3. Arthur L. Carter, *New York Observer*
		4. Joel S. Ehrenkranz, Whitney Museum
		5. Barry Diller, InterActive Corporation
		6. Brooke Garber Neidich, Whitney Musuem
		7. Michael H. Steinhardt, *New Republic*
		8. Casey Wasserman, Wasserman Media Group
		9. Shelby White, art collector
Manufacturing	1	1. John L. Vogelstein, Mattel
Retail	2	1. Kenneth G. Langone, Home Depot
		2. Jay Stein, Stein Mart
Education	2	1. L. Jay Oliva, NYU President Emeritus
		2. John Sexton, NYU President

a declining stock price and Ross's own $78 million take from the merger.[10] The current chair of NYU's Board of Trustees, the prominent mergers and acquisitions attorney Martin Lipton, was Steve Ross's attorney during some of Ross's most important, latter-day internecine conflicts.

To take another example, the member of NYU's board most likely to be seen as an active mogul—Barry Diller—has had a media career that has involved studio filmmaking, the Home Shopping Network, cable network ownership and other interactive services that have found him at the forefront of the convergence of media and retailing. But each step in the construction of his companies has required full exploitation of the world of financial services represented more directly by trustees such as Lipton, Richard Grasso, former president of the New York Stock Exchange (NYSE) and many others. The board boasts one other significant figure from the retailing world, mostly known from his earlier role as one of the founders of Home Depot, Kenneth Lagone. Yet as we will see, Langone's fortune and influence flows from financial engineering.

Most NYU trustees, in short, come either from finance or from a sector where their elevated status has been determined by their expertise or connections to finance. The NYU Board of Trustees seems to be something very close to a monoculture of high finance—to the point that, while many of its members exert financial control over America's ultra-competitive industries such as computers, telecommunications, and biotechnology, they by and large are not invested in the research, development, or manufacturing of these sectors. Notwithstanding its attempt to brand itself as a global university, NYU—at least, as it is represented by its trustees—has become increasingly provincial, tied nearly exclusively to the narrow vision and interests of New York finance, real estate, and insurance.

The Culture of Finance

America's financial culture is complex and very much in motion, but a few major features are especially relevant to the question of student labor. First, the watershed of contemporary finance was the transformation of the firm into a commodity to be bought and sold. Henceforth, firms would not simply develop and produce commodities but would themselves be commodities that could be exchanged and whose value would rise or fall as a result of sales, mergers, and takeovers—not only as a result of the goods they produced. Though financial control is both an ancient idea in economics and predated the 1980s advent of major financial deal making, finance became central to American corporate life *and* profitability only during the Reagan administration. The most notorious figure in this world was Michael Milken, but "corporate raiders" became widely known in American culture at that time, and the wealth and prominence of figures such as Steve Ross in media and Martin Lipton in financial law signaled the dominion of finance in American economics and politics alike.

Second, mergers and acquisitions had eliminated hundreds or thousands of jobs by the late 1980s.[11] Financial control became the arch-rival, even enemy, of "steady work."

Third, financial culture has largely caused, endorsed, and presided over the greatest boom in economic inequality in modern history. This inequality shows up in the business world itself. Large companies have benefited at the expense of many mid-sized companies, and financial firms have succeeded in two decades

TABLE 4.2 COMPARISON OF SELECTED REVENUES IN FINANCE AND RESEARCH AND DEVELOPMENT, 2006

AGENCY	REVENUES
University of California ten-campus federal research funds, without Department of Energy labs	$2.2 billion
National Nanotechnology Initiative (NNI) budget, all agencies	$1.06 billion
NNI budget, risk analysis (Wilson Center estimate)	$0.011 billion
Goldman Sachs, funds to distribute as bonuses	$16.5 billion[a]

[a]See Christopher Newfield, "Useful Dubious Analogies: Nanotech and Nanosociety," available online at http://centernanosociety.blogspot.com/2006_12_01_archive.html (accessed March 13, 2007).

in doubling their share of the after-tax profits of non-financial firms.[12] The more dramatic form of inequality is wealth and income inequality among individuals in the United States, both of which have reached their highest level since the 1920s.

This recent shift toward the top of the wealth and income ladder and away from the bottom and middle has been accelerated by the financial sector, which has delivered materially in the form of tens and occasionally hundreds of millions of dollars for executives and deal-making insiders, and ideologically in the form of natural-law theories of markets in which principals always "earn" their pay and deals always increase efficiency. One example that received enormous attention at the end of 2006 was the investment bank Goldman Sachs's bonus pool for that year, which we express in the form of a research-funding comparison (Table 4.2). Just one good year's bonus pool at the leading Wall Street investment bank could pay for seven years of research in the nation's largest public research university, for sixteen years of the National Nanotechnology Initiative, and for sixteen *centuries* of nano-related risk analysis. Finance culture has helped make us impervious to the ascendancy of finance over the research and development on which the economy supposedly depends.

Finally, throughout the 1990s, finance culture increasingly came to treat white-collar, middle-management, and intellectual labor in the same way it treated blue-collar labor in the 1980s: as an entirely fungible element in financial equations. Much skilled labor can be outsourced and off-shored as readily as can semiskilled or unskilled labor. Years ago, major companies began to contract customer service to companies in India and elsewhere, where salaries were a fraction of those in the United States. Recently, the same has been happening to computer programming, digital design, architectural rendering, pharmaceutical research, and radiology. Education, too, is being outsourced, starting with the lower-division introductory teaching done by adjuncts and graduate students. The e-outsourcing of higher education has not advanced as quickly as its promoters had hoped, yet "enterprise" universities such as the University of Phoenix are quite successful. One predictable and, indeed, silently desired result is that wage increases for college graduates are beginning to fade, as did those for factory workers thirty years ago. The decent wage advances now belong largely to those with professional or advanced degrees.

Under the previous New Deal order, finance tended not openly to oppose strong labor protection because it was not a labor-intensive industry. Now, though, with its increased investment in restructuring labor-intensive industries, it has been on the vanguard of the campaign to weaken labor rights in the United States and elsewhere.

Finance on the NYU Board

We now have a sense of how prominent financial culture is on NYU's board. We also have an idea about the general features of financial culture: Organizations are commodities, and there is no obvious reason universities would be excluded; mergers and acquisitions generally increase layoffs and come close to fulfilling traditional views about the binary opposition of capital to labor; financial law is often private law—within minimal regulatory standards, it is a realm of non-public rules made by financial insiders; wealth and income inequality will naturally and steadily increase, with no logical endpoint in sight; and with the exception of some financially and technologically oriented elites, white-collar employees—the old managerial cadres, both public and private—will be made cheaper and less secure.

This suggests that a trustee board overwhelmingly composed of financial-sector players will generally be at odds with its own university community, which (by ideals, if not always by policy) values humanist notions of culture, tradition, and self-governed social relationships over economic and market calculations; where job security remains a standard (even if a shrinking one); and where the quality of professional labor is seen as both the fountainhead of intellectual innovation and an end in itself. In this context, can we say some more specific things about whether current NYU trustees are in conflict with these university ideals?

The evidence is thin for reasons we have already mentioned. The NYU trustees make few public statements about education—or about any civic issue, for that matter. But what evidence does exist is uniform, in terms of both business activity and policy statements. In the interests of space, we focus on the officers of NYU's Board of Trustees and organize their positions around major topics. We should be clear that our emphasis is not on the personal competence, politics, or even ethics of the individual trustees, but on the larger culture of finance that they exemplify and, in many cases, have helped to construct.

Nearly the entire NYU Board of Trustees is composed of "high net worth" individuals. This is especially true of the board's officers, and the process of becoming individually wealthy has led several of them into public controversies about enormous executive pay. The best known is Richard Grasso, who was the outgoing chair of the NYSE when he arranged $139.5 million in farewell compensation for himself. Grasso unabashedly defended his gigantic parachute, arguing that under his watch, the stock market grew rapidly in worth, and the "value of a membership seat nearly tripled."[13] "The men and women who set my compensation," he said, "knew exactly what they were doing." These men and women were chaired by NYU Trustee Kenneth Langone, who approved the amount.[14]

Around the time the Grasso scandal broke in the press, the independent Council of Institutional Investors said that a serious conflict of interest was created by the fact that many members of the stock-exchange board, including Laurence Fink, Kenneth Langone, and Martin Lipton, were also NYU trustees, which gave them special access to John Sexton, who at the time served on the committee that nominates new exchange members. NYU spokesman John Beckman dismissed the report, saying that any "attempt to make some sort of singular or special connection between NYU and the NYSE is like trying to make a statue out of smoke," but Sexton did resign from his position on the NYSE shortly thereafter.

Similar attention was brought to bear on the chair of NYU's Board of Trustees, Martin J. Lipton. Lipton is a founding member of Wachtell, Lipton, Rosen and Katz, chairman of the NYSE's legal advisory committee and chief counsel to its corporate governance committee, and one of the highest-paid lawyers in New York City. The Council of Institutional Investors criticized Lipton for conflicts of interest, in particular for his role as an adviser to fellow NYU Trustee Grasso. As the *Times* put it, "Mr. Lipton's offering advice to Mr. Grasso at the same time that he was serving in crucial advisory roles at the exchange underscores in critics' eyes how the stock exchange remains a warren of insider relationships and cozy, if not conflicted, ties." Added to Lipton's and Langone's role in the Grasso scandal is Laurence D. Fink, another NYU board member and chief executive of BlackRock, a New York investment-management company, who chaired the search committee that chose Grasso's successor. "It's almost as if they got the NYSE and the NYU initials mixed up," Sarah Teslik, executive director of the Council of Institutional Investors, mordantly observed.[15]

Even after Grasso's pay became a public scandal, Langone was unapologetic. A billionaire entrepreneur and a leading figure on Wall Street, he had launched his own career by helping to construct the initial public offering of Ross Perot's company Electronic Data Systems in the 1970s. He was one of the founders of Home Depot, which transformed local hardware stores into a dominant national chain with more than $80 billion in sales in fiscal year 2005. When asked how he felt about stratospheric CEO pay, he replied:

> I was recently asked whether I was ever bothered by the fact that CEOs pay now is 567 times the average worker. I said, do me a favor. Tell me how much Sam Walton would have been worth to Kmart stockholders if he was running Kmart instead of Wal-Mart. There's one Sam Walton.

There's one Jack Welch. Tell me how much better off GM would have been today if Jack Welch had become CEO of GM in 1980 instead of GE.[16]

This is as clear a statement as any of the belief that value is created not by what a company produces through the labor of its employees, be they GE's 300,000 or Wall-Mart's 1.2 million, but through the acuity of a single CEO. In this world, value is created not by labor but by the price level of investors' bids. Similarly, Langone's ownership of 16.5 million shares of Home Depot stock is the market's accurate judgment of the value he personally created as a company founder, and not merely the return to his ownership position. The same would apparently be true of Grasso's $140 million at the end of his presidency of the NYSE—it is supposedly about value creation and not about placement and power. The same is true, Langone argues, for the CEO of Home Depot:

> If I gave you $80 billion and you were Vanguard, you'd charge me 10 basis points, which is $80 million. Very modest management fee. I trusted [Home Depot CEO Robert] Nardelli with $80 billion worth of market value, and we paid him five basis points to protect it. The first rule of investing is don't lose any money. So you're telling me he's got $80 billion in value under his charge and I paid him $40 million? That's a lot of money? I don't think so.[17]

Forty million dollars is not a lot of money only in the two-tier system that finance has established even in a complex business, where a CEO such as Nardelli is transformed from the lead operating executive to the chief investment manager. All regular employees are paid a flat salary that reflects the presumably modest value they individually create, measured usually in the five figures and almost never more than the middle six figures. Above them lies a small elite that is paid as a percentage of assets under management, or assets in play. At all points, these pay packages are said to reflect the market's impartial judgment about the individual's true worth to the company: CEOs are thus allegedly worth five hundred or one thousand times more than other employees, including all "brain-worker" university graduates such as heart surgeons and computer-hardware designers with Ph.D.s. What could trustees from the top of the FIRE sector possibly think of a graduate-student strike, having helped devise, and then directly benefited from, a system in which all labor outside the large financial transaction lives under regular salary rules and is distinctly second class?

The health sector sometimes succumbs to a similar logic, and here NYU Trustees are again not lagging behind. NYU Trustee Anthony Welters has been involved with the founding and development of several HMOs with large Medicare and Medicaid components, and these HMOs, as we will see, have been under investigation from time to time, first for extravagant management fees and later for allegedly excessive rationing of medical care. In the mid-1990s, auditors from the State of Pennsylvania and the federal government charged that "the Welters group had paid itself millions of dollars in management fees—paid to other companies they controlled—and millions more in bonuses."[18] Welters had learned the lesson of carving points off the top of any transaction, apparently some of the time by multiplying the number of brokers involved and controlling more than one of them. Welters's response: "What [should] a person who takes a $200,000 investment and turns it into a billion-dollar company . . . receive? I don't know. But I know this: I'm not going to apologize for it."

The mostly men who sit on NYU's Board of Trustees have, at critical moments, endorsed the replacement of the labor-theory *and* even the combined labor–capital partnership theory of value with a theory that traces value to financial managers. Absent a vision of the common good—even the very mixed version that motivated Cold War elites—financial wealth appears to be the main object of admiring attention for the board's leading figures. The board is virtually silent on any public purpose beyond cutting the overhead on public services. Its members are involved in sectors that have successfully built enormous transaction costs into the consumption of their products, be they legal and financial services, health care, or insurance. Where they have successfully lowered costs, as in large-scale retail, they have done this by separating much or most of their workforces from job security and group-based economic advancement. Even the rebuilding of Ground Zero has been financialized into delays and extra costs by site controller and NYU Trustee Larry Silverstein.

It is difficult to square the trajectory of the board's primary activities with the university's traditional missions of knowledge creation, public service, and, ironically, low-cost social development. As finance culture intensifies the inequality that has spread through the United States in the past two decades, it will subject research universities to the same conditions, in which all the cost-cutting and insecurity occurs at the bottom—among adjuncts and teaching assistants, among others—while revenues boom at the top.

That the university is not a profitmaking institution, and that less money is saved by breaking a teaching-assistant union than, say, by stopping a unionization drive at Home Depot—these things matter less than the fact that both Sexton's NYU and Langone's Home Depot share similar negative opinions when it comes to workplace democracy. Indeed, were "NYU" substituted for "Home Depot," an excerpt regarding unions from Home Depot's 1996 Orientation Handbook could easily be confused with administration statements during the strike: "We believe that Home Depot associates are much better off remaining union-free rather than dealing with third-party outsiders. We believe outsiders would destroy the open and direct communication we have with our associates. Home Depot is strongly opposed to union organizing and will resist organizing attempts by unwanted outsiders." Not for nothing does Sexton insist on calling NYU an "enterprise university." And at an enterprise university, given its culture of finance, there will be no negotiating with labor.

Notes

1. John R. Thelin, *A History of American Higher Education* (Baltimore: Johns Hopkins University Press, 2004), 405.

2. Tenure policy remained variable into the Cold War period, although job security had improved markedly in most major research universities. Clark Kerr, however, noted that the University of California did not have "continuous tenure" with removal only for "good cause" until the end of 1958: Clark Kerr, *The Gold and the Blue: A Personal Memoir of the University of California, 1949–1967,* vol. 1 (Berkeley: University of California Press, 2001), 140.

3. See Joan Wallach Scott," The Critical State of Shared Governance," *Academe* (2002): 2, available online at http//www.aaup.org/publications/Academe/2002/02ja/02jasco.htm (accessed January 23, 2007).

4. Association of Governing Boards of Universities and Colleges, "AGB Statement on Board Accountability," Washington, D.C., 2007.

5. Mario Savio, speech, University of California at Berkeley, December 3, 1964, available online at http://www.fsm-a.org/stacks/mario/mario_speech.html (accessed June 7, 2005).

6. New University Conference, Publications Collective, "NYU, Inc.," typescript report, 1971. All pagination refers to this two-column typescript at the NYU library collections.

7. Ibid., 23.

8. These reports are available on the organization's website at http://www.cbcny.org.

9. See, e.g., "CBC Urges Governor to Veto Bills That Would Increase the Cost of Fringe and Pension Benefits for Public Employees," available online at http://www.cbcny.org/07-27-05_CBC_Pensions_Letter_Release.pdf (accessed March 11, 2007).

10. The best overview of Steve Ross's life and times is Connie Bruck, *Master of the Game: Steve Ross and the Creation of Time Warner* (New York: Penguin, 1994). Bruck's unflattering portrait of Courtney Ross appears on 323 *et passim.* On Ross-Holst's current projects, see http://www.ksg.harvard.edu/leadership/about/people/board/index.php?id=551 (accessed February 16, 2007).

11. The indispensable history of the rise of the normal layoff is Louis Uchitelle, *The Disposable American: Layoffs and Their Consequences* (New York: Alfred A. Knopf, 2006).

12. For example, between 1990 and 1995 "nonfinancial corporations paid 78% of their after-tax profits out as dividends." This is a huge increase in the "rentier share of the corporate surplus," which had been between 20 percent and 30 percent of pretax profits in the golden age of the 1950s and 1960s. "Far from turning to Wall Street for outside finance," the economic journalist Doug Henwood concluded, "nonfinancial firms have been stuffing Wall Street's pockets with money": Doug Henwood, *Wall Street* (New York: Verso, 1997), 73.

13. Richard Grasso, "My Vindication Will Come," *Wall Street Journal,* May 25, 2004, A16

14. Finance insert, *Economist,* February 2007.

15. "Consultant to Grasso on Pay Is Also Adviser to Exchange," *New York Times,* September 24, 2003, 1

16. "Make My Day," an interview with Kenneth Langone, on "Directorship: The Business Resource for Directors," available online at http://www.directorship.com/publications/makemyday.aspx (accessed March 11, 2007). Langone continues:

> My point of view is based on being an owner. I own 16.5 million shares of stock, period. Nothing more. I don't have any business or side deals with Home Depot.

I'm a founder but that doesn't make me any less independent. Compare this with those people who go on corporate boards where they collect $300,000 a year and vote with their wallets. Do you think at the end of the day they're going to go against the CEO? I'm sorry, but I can't work with such people on a board. When they come on I depart. I have great concerns about the independence of people whose directors fees comprise a significant portion of their income.

17. Ibid.

18. Bill Brubaker, "Confronting Health Care 'Demons' Anthony Welters Took an Unlikely Route to Head AmeriChoice, an HMO for the Poor," *Washington Post*, May 27, 2002, available online at http://www.pnhp.org/news/2002/may/confronting_health_c.php (accessed March 11, 2007).

ICE from the Ashes of FIRE

NYU and the Economy of Culture in New York City

STEPHEN DUNCOMBE AND SARAH NASH

In the early winter of 2004, New York University President John Sexton and Abraham Lackman, president of the Commission on Independent Colleges and Universities, published an op-ed article in the salmon-colored pages of the *New York Observer*. The occasion was the unveiling of a new model for thinking about the economic future of New York City. The city, they argued, has prospered by adapting to an ever changing marketplace. First, it was the port that generated the wealth of the city, followed by manufacturing. In recent decades, the engine of economic wealth has been composed of the finance, insurance, and real-estate industries, or FIRE, as they are commonly known. But to thrive in the new millennium when "today's chief executives can conduct business from Aspen or make deals from the Caribbean" and thus do not have to locate their businesses within its borders, they argued, the city must adapt yet again to retain its attraction for commercial ventures. New York City must become a destination not of necessity but of choice, "creating a different value premium." That value premium, Sexton and Lackman declared, is culture. Drawing a conscious comparison to the older economic engine of FIRE, they labeled their model "ICE." And ICE, they predicted, would eventually extinguish FIRE: "Our intellectual, cultural and educational (ICE) assets—already among the world's greatest—will become the essence of New York's being."[1]

Given the occupations of both John Sexton and Abraham Lackman, it was not too surprising to read a few paragraphs later that they envision a primary component of the new ICE economy as "independent" (read, private) higher education. There is a certain level of irony in Sexton's promotion of this model when one remembers that many members of NYU's powerful Board of Trustees made their money from that same threatened FIRE economy whose demise Sexton and Lackman happily charted in the op-ed.[2] Further, it is the funds and powerful connections granted by those trustees that continue to infuse NYU with the grandeur necessary to make it a viable institution to put at the center of the new ICE engine.

Sexton and Lackman present the ICE economy as a "*different* value premium" (emphasis added). What is different is that they are suggesting that culture can take on the role of more traditional business—for example, insurance. What is not different is that the value premium is the same, only shifted from products generated by big business onto the "products" produced by big university business. The ICE model allows institutions such as NYU both to tout themselves as cultural beacons and, at the same time, to sell themselves as sound financial investments.

Although the *Daily News* reported in late 2004 that Sexton and Lackman "hatched" the idea of ICE, and within a few days the *Gotham Gazette* deemed it a "big story" to watch out for in the future (one detects the hand of NYU's public-relations office here), both the concept and the term significantly predate the *Observer* op-ed.[3] Back in 1969, the French sociologist Alaine Touraine observed the growth of a new type of economy, one that was based in culture and creativity. "All the domains of social life," he wrote, "education, consumption, information, etc.—are being more and more integrated into what used to be called production factors."[4] In the early 1990s, Robert Reich, President Clinton's first secretary of labor, made the case for a national economy for the twenty-first century based on the creative work of "symbolic analysts."[5] And in the new millennium, the "creative class" found a cheerleader in Richard Florida, the indefatigable public-policy professor who advises regions to woo artists, intellectuals, and educators or face economic ruin.[6] Nor is the acronym ICE entirely original. As early as 2000, "ICE" was a term widely used among economists and planners in India; by 2001, the term had become familiar enough for a journalist in the *Hindustan Times* to raise the question of whether India's ICE economy was in decline.[7] In Indian usage, ICE stands for information, communication, and entertainment, but the industry and employment categories largely line up with those accounted for under Sexton and Lackman's definition.

The initial temptation is to dismiss Sexton and Lackman's neologism as an old term encapsulating an even older idea—a concept recycled by an ambitious university president eager to make a name for himself (Sexton's doctoral thesis was on Harvard's famous president Charles Eliot), and a private-sector colleague eager to convince government and private interests of the importance of "independent" higher education. So really, who cares? Those of us interested in intellect, culture, and education should care. For ICE is more than a catchy acronym for an economic sector. It encapsulates a way of understanding culture and creativity that has a real impact on the university, its faculty and students, and the surrounding community. Because of efforts like Sexton's and Lackman's to package, brand, and value cultural activities, thinking within and about universities has changed, and will continue to do so, in some of the most prestigious arenas and think tanks that influence university education across the nation.

The slipperiness and lightning dissemination of measuring intellectual, cultural, and educational pursuits as viable economic models capable of producing all the profits and products of previous economic engines is exemplified most profoundly in the report "The Responsive Ph.D.," created by the Woodrow Wilson Foundation in September 2005, a mere nine months after Sexton and Lackman's op-ed piece.[8] The report accounted for an initiative undertaken by twenty deans and provosts from twenty prestigious doctoral-degree–granting institutions who were willing to design programs at their universities to improve the doctoral-educational experience.[9] One of the efforts governing the initiative was to encourage doctoral students to seek jobs in the business world instead of in academe, where the number of positions for tenure-track faculty is falling every year. Considering that the people involved in these "innovations" are a collection of administrators who make and create hiring opportunities for tenured positions, it seems odd at first that they did not come together to decide collectively to push back on the reliance their own universities have on temporary staff to teach their courses, which, they readily admit, is one of the main reasons that so many Ph.D. students cannot find tenure-track jobs when they graduate.[10] But it was easier for these deans to think of pushing graduates to look for work outside of academe because it also provides a convenient "assessment" of their education. The "assessment," or value, of doctoral education is much easier to assign when universities can use the language of commerce—for example, by framing Ph.D. graduates' worth in terms of income earned, which is readily intelligible to the business world, instead of producing their own measurement system to determine the value of independent thinkers in their fields.

Aside from the convenience factor, the overriding goal is to represent the doctoral degree in quantifiable terms that can be understood outside academe in order to show that academe is no longer governed by "self-determination" but can, instead, foster "a continuing dialogue between the producers and the consumers of doctoral education."[11] Arizona State University, for example, has implemented a "Career Goal Setting Workshop." One can attend a "Career Conversations" workshop at Princeton or the "Ph.D. Career Seminar Series" at the University of California, Irvine. The University of Texas, Austin, even goes so far as to offer its graduates the "Entrepreneurship Course."[12]

Thinking of culture and education in terms of economic value has not been relegated only inside the walls of academe. In the summer of 2006, a year and a half after Sexton and Lackman's original op-ed, the idea of culture as a "different value premium" returned. The Center for Governmental Research (CGR) issued a report provocatively entitled "Solutions for New York."[13] The title of the brief intentionally begs the question: What's the problem? The problem, the report quickly tells its readers, is that the economy of the state and its biggest city are in grave danger of economic failure. Paralleling Sexton and Lackman's argument, and in places quoting at length from the *Observer* op-ed, the report argues that the FIRE economy is growing cold. Jobs in the finance and insurance sectors have shrunk 14 percent over the past fifteen years. If this does not seem all that worrying (particularly as real-estate jobs have grown and the overall wages of FIRE employees have heated up considerably), the author warns of a cold, dark future: "It is only a matter of time before this relative stability ends. Facilitated by the precipitous declines in the cost of telecommunications and the increasing sophistication of offshore providers, global competition for a wide array of services will only accelerate."[14] The once booming but now desolate industrial cities of Schenectady, Buffalo, and Rochester, New York, are offered as cautionary tales of what happens when a city links its fortune to a declining industry. One can almost picture the writers of the report fantasizing a *Daily News* headline of the future: "President to City: Drop Dead . . . Again."

Fortunately, there is a remedy: It turns out that Sexton and Lackman's ICE economy of New York is healthy and steadily expanding. The report tells us that, between 1990 and 2005, the number of jobs in the ICE sector expanded 16 percent, and the total amount paid to people working in these fields increased 36 percent. The growth rates for the educational sector as a whole seem particularly impressive: jobs growing by 47 percent and payroll jumping by 64 percent over the past decade and a half.[15] This is good news for the group who bankrolled the report, Lackman's own Commission on Independent Colleges and Universities, and especially good news for the president of the largest private university in New York State, NYU's John Sexton.

Opinion pieces and reports such as these are written to convince public and private actors that private higher education offers a sound return on investment. State money and private donations are fed into this cultural institution, and out comes profit in the form of taxable and free-spending citizens, new ideas for new products and services, and the creation of a cultural milieu attractive to other free spenders and product and service producers. We oppose the idea of defining intellect, culture, and education as an investment in future financial value, but even if one accepts the tenet propelling the CGR report, another, different question lurks at its margins: Does ICE really deliver on its promise as the economic dynamo of the future?

There is little doubt that ICE is growing as a sector, but it is instructive to put the numbers into perspective. For simplicity's sake, we will look just at private-sector employment in "Educational Services," the category most germane to Lackman's and Sexton's argument and the one that shows the most impressive growth in the CGR report. According to this report, the number of people employed in private-sector education in New York State grew 47 percent between 1990 and 2005, from 185,337 to 272,169 employees. Over the same fifteen years, total payroll increased 64 percent, from $6,378,000 to $10,473,000. At first blush, this seems impressive. However, the 272,169 people employed in private education in 2005 make up only a little more than 3 percent of the 8,528,300 people working in New York State that year. According to U.S. Bureau of Labor Statistics data, far more people—69 percent more—were employed in the less glamorous field of "Food Services and Drinking Places" (459,600 in 2005). This, too, was a "growth economy" in New York, with the number of waiters, fry cooks, and bartenders steadily increasing between 1990 to 2005, albeit at a slower rate (16 percent) than educational workers.[16] While the wages of food-service workers—and, thus, their payroll contribution to the consumer (and tax) economy—tend to be lower than those of educators (with the notable exception of most teaching assistants and adjunct instructors), there are many other economic sectors whose employees "contribute" a great deal more. According to the *New York Times*, the *average* pay in the now ostensibly archaic financial sector topped out in 2006 at a whopping $8,323 *per week*—up nearly $3,000 a week in just three years. The starving artist or intellectual has always been a bit of a romantic myth, but very few jobs in the ICE economy come close to paying as well as this.[17]

But counting the number of employees and the discretionary income they have to spend on products and services, or pay in taxes, is only part of the ICE equation. Universities, for example, are brick-and-mortar properties, and the building of laboratories, classrooms, and, especially, dormitories pumps additional value into the economy through capital construction. Further, proponents of the cultural economy frequently talk about indirect and "multiplier" effects: economic value generated not by the direct payment of wages or construction of buildings, but through more intangible forces. In the case of universities, this might be money spent by students on food, entertainment, or off-campus housing, or the splurging on hotels and Broadway shows by their parents when they come to visit. One is also encouraged to factor in "spin-offs"—money generated and jobs created by the licenses, patents, and royalties that come with university research. Add it all up and, according to the CGR, educational institutions such as NYU create more than 3,285,000 jobs, $15 billion in wages, $41.4 billion in spending, and almost $1 billion in tax revenues for New York.[18]

Recently, however, this sort of math has come under suspicion. Researchers at the Rand Corporation issued a report in 2004 that questioned the economic value of the creative economy and raised doubts about the ways in which cultural institutions have grown to define their "success" in economic terms. The conclusion of Rand's report, "Gifts of the Muse," is that many of these claims are overblown and unfounded.[19] A recent, and local, example of this culturo-economic wishful thinking are the extravagant assertions made for the economic value of Christo and Jeanne-Claude's "The Gates"—the undulating, saffron-draped frames that arched the pathways of New York City's Central Park in the winter of 2005. Before the installation was erected, the city's Economic Development Corporation (EDC) predicted that "The Gates" would generate "over $80 million of economic impact" through increased tourism, museum receipts, hotel stays, restaurant bills, tips received by waiters, and so on—creating at least $2 million in city taxes. But Randall Weiss, the chief economist of the EDC, was quoted by the *Wall Street Journal* as admitting that his estimate was "as much art as science" and, as the *Journal* went on to report, the number was based on the "dubious data" of an earlier, self-serving study produced by the Metropolitan Museum of Art to justify the budget of its 2003 blockbuster "Leonardo" show.[20]

This is not to argue that the figures trotted out in defense of ICE are mere fiction. In fact, we found the economic arguments in the CGR's "Solutions for New York" to be a model of empirical restraint. But no matter how carefully one calculates the impact of ICE on the local economy, such calculations invariably do not address what the Rand researchers (and the *Wall Street Journal*) argue is the most important question to be asked when making the case for the economic value of any endeavor: Could some other activity or investment or outside factor have the same—or better—economic impact? To quote the Rand report:

> The multiplier effect driving the direct economic benefit of the arts to local communities is essentially the same whether what is producing the effect is the arts or some other type of economic activity (high-technology industry, for instance). Similarly, the comparative advantage that an arts-rich environment provides for stimulating local economic development could also be provided by other types of local amenities (say, a pleasant climate or a location along a seashore).[21]

NYU certainly generates money for the local economy. But might not the expansion of light industry paying substantial union wages deliver a more stable tax base? Couldn't casinos attract even more free-spending tourists? There are plenty of reasons to support some economic initiatives and reject others, but it needs to be acknowledged that indirect economic benefits (and detriments) flow from all sorts of economies.

The more direct benefits claimed by ICE proponents need to be interrogated, as well. The CGR's report boasts that private educational institutions such as NYU spend more than $1,944,000 a year constructing buildings in New York to house classes, laboratories, faculty, and students, and $1,050,000 in wages for construction workers and others.[22] But the same materials would be bought and the same construction workers employed no matter whether the structure was the latest NYU dorm or a high-end residential building. In terms of money pumped into the economy, FIRE is just as good as ICE and, in one critical way, better.

In a revealing aside in "Solutions for New York," the study's author points out—as further evidence of the importance of private education—that while employee payroll has risen 57 percent in private education over the past fifteen years, it actually fell 9 percent in the public sector. In addition, over the same period, student enrollment grew nearly twice as fast in private colleges as in public colleges.[23] The reasons for this decline in the fortunes of public higher education are not hard to trace. For the past thirty years, public financial support for the City University of New York (CUNY) has shrunk dramatically, recently hitting its lowest per-student rate in history. Between 1991 and 2005—when New York City's economy was booming—state *and* city support for CUNY dropped by more than one-third each. Meanwhile, the revenue generated by tuition increased by nearly 90 percent.[24] In other words, today CUNY is receiving fewer tax dollars, and the university's already poor students are shelling out more money.

What does this sad story have to do with the success of institutions such as NYU? Property taxes are New York City's single largest source of revenue, making up 37 percent of all the tax monies collected. When a FIRE developer builds residential properties, the owners—ideally—pay property taxes; when a nonprofit ICE institution such as NYU builds a new school building, student dorm, or residential high-rise for its faculty, it pays . . . *nothing*.

The promise of ICE is that institutions such as NYU pump money into the economy, and with the rising tide all boats are lifted: A booming economy means swelling tax revenues, which means more money for parks, services, and education—a virtuous cycle. But there is one, big problem. Private educational institutions are distinguished from many other private industries that contribute to the growth of New York's economy in that, unlike most other businesses, they, as "nonprofit" institutions, are exempt from property taxes. So rather than being part of the solution to the declining fortunes of public education, it turns out that institutions like NYU and other nonprofit ICE organizations are actually part of the problem.

This is what Bonnie Brower and Rachel Hays argue in their 2006 City Project policy paper "Fatal $ubtraction." The case they make is simple but compelling: Property-tax exemptions cost New York City more than $7 billion in lost revenues in 2005; the share *not* paid by private educational facilities was $385,826,261.[25] This number has also increased over the past thirteen years as the value of tax-exempt college and university properties has almost tripled.[26] New York University is a major culprit in this legal tax evasion. Other universities own more tax-exempt property than NYU (Columbia's real-estate portfolio is two and a half times larger), and other institutions are more egregious abusers (the Chrysler building, owned by Cooper Union, has not paid a single cent in property taxes since 1930), yet NYU still did *not* pay $42,133,034 in taxes on its 105 properties in 2005.[27]

Where might these tax dollars have otherwise gone? Well, between 1991 and 2005 city support for CUNY dropped 33.5 percent, from $266.1 million to $176.9 million. NYU's missing $42.1 million in tax revenues would go a long way in helping to make up that $89.2 million cut; add in Columbia's absent tax money, and the gap would be closed.[28] Other universities around the country offer at least a token to their host communities. Harvard and the Massachusetts Institute of Technology make "payments in lieu of taxes" (PILOTS) to Cambridge and Boston; Yale does it for New Haven; and Stanford does it for Palo Alto, but no private nonprofit educational institutions make such payments to New York City.[29] The expansion of private education at New York University may be driving the success of ICE, but the university achieves this expansion at the cost of government revenues that could go to public education.

As this example suggests, what is at stake here is considerably more than whether the ICE industries provide an economic stimulus and whether that contribution is unique. One primary effect of valuing intellectual, cultural, and educational endeavors as a means to economic ends is a radical change in the definition of culture. Certain types of culture, those that are "assets"—to use Lackman and Sexton's term—are valorized while other expressions are marginalized.

Moreover, while ICE boosters are eager to promote the indirect economic benefits of the creative industry, there are other ways to view the "multiplier effects" of ICE industries that raise serious questions about their impact on culture and creativity. As mentioned previously, the CGR's "Solutions for New York" report brags about that discretionary spending of private college students and the value of those expenditures—$1.6 billion—to the local economy.[30] Where do students spend their money? Bars, cafes, restaurants, clubs, and movie theaters— all arguably cultural assets but also commercial businesses that garner significant profits and pay high commercial rents. Since there is no commercial rent control in New York City, this results in the eviction of less profitable businesses and services. Students who choose to live off-campus also spend money on rent. Because students are willing to put up with smaller spaces and more roommates than older or more settled residents, and because they are frequently subsidized by their parents, they tend to be willing to pay more for smaller spaces. In addition, because students usually stay for a couple of years and then move on, landlords can legally and regularly increase rent levels at each vacancy. Both of these factors contribute to a steady increase in residential rent. The result, if not quite gentrification, is a "studentification" of a neighborhood.

Located in the heart of Greenwich Village, New York University makes the most of its setting in a neighborhood internationally known for providing a haven in a heartless world for artists and intellectuals. In his 2006 commencement address, President Sexton paid homage to this rich cultural heritage recalling when, nearly a century ago, a group of artists spent the night atop the arch in Washington Square. "And, as dawn broke," Sexton evoked, "those artists and poets issued from the top of the arch a boisterous declaration of independence by which Greenwich Village seceded from the physical union of the United States to form its own state of mind."[31] Sexton neglected to mention to the assembled students and their parents that Marcel Duchamp, John Sloan, and the others who had camped out overnight in the arch unveiled their utopia in the name of, among other things, "sex [and] socialism." What was also left unsaid was the reason that artists and poets made Greenwich Village (and later SoHo and the East Village) their home in the first place: the availability of cheap apartments, cafes, and gallery spaces—that is, the conditions for creativity currently being undermined by NYU's physical expansion.

While NYU is certainly not solely responsible for the skyrocketing rents in the neighborhood—Malcolm Cowley was complaining about businessmen moving into "studios" in the Village and displacing artists in the 1920s—it certainly has continued and accelerated creative flight as artists and poets have had to move elsewhere in search of cheaper rents and affordable performance or exhibition spaces.[32] Sitting on a panel with John Sexton at the 2006 Creative New York conference, the choreographer Bill T. Jones lyrically summed up the impact of ICE on the future of artists. Jones listened patiently to Sexton's presentation of his case for the ICE economy. When Sexton was done, the famous choreographer began singing: "Start spreading the news, I'm leaving today. . . ."[33]

Jones went on to explain that, when he began as an artist a quarter-century ago, rehearsal spaces were cheap, it was easy to stage a performance, and there was more public (tax-generated) funding for the arts. All this had changed in recent years and was making creativity, and creative experimentation, more difficult. But what really got the choreographer's ire was how the president of NYU was talking about culture, how culture was being *valued*:

> I'm asked to sit on this panel and talk about being part of the new economic engine of New York City: are we serious? Are we serious? . . . Let's use dance—not for me to say mea culpa, mea culpa—but dance is the idea of what do we mean by a spiritual activity? This one's not going to make anybody any money. The culture, the culture talking all this highfalutin' talk today about creativity, [can it] truly value something that does not have a product?[34]

Oddly enough, the researchers at the Rand Corporation—a think tank better known for its hard-headed analysis of body counts during the Vietnam War than for mushy pronouncements about culture—came to a similar conclusion in their study of the benefits of the arts. "People are drawn to the arts not for their instrumental effects, but because the arts can provide them with meaning and a distinctive type of pleasure and emotional stimulation," they said. "We contend not only that these intrinsic effects are satisfying in themselves, but that many of them can lead to the development of individual capacities and community cohesiveness that are of benefit to the public sphere."[35] The Rand response is a bit drier than Jones's, but the point is largely the same. The "value" of culture is lost when you define it solely in terms of its economic contribution.

Perhaps the most telling example of the tensions hosted by this effort to assign a value premium to culture occurred in 2000, the year NYU announced plans to build a new building for its law school. The proposed site included a small brick house on West 3rd Street in Greenwich Village, where Edgar Allan Poe lived in 1844–1845 and published his poem *The Raven*. The destruction of yet another historical building, this one a former home to one of America's first great writers, did not sit well with the Greenwich Village community. Residents and preservation activists staged rallies and demonstrations. Burton Pollin, a CUNY professor emeritus and the author of twelve books on Poe, provided lengthy arguments about the cultural importance of the site. The Municipal Arts Society, the Landmarks Conservancy, and the Mystery Writers of America, along with artist celebrities such as the musician Lou Reed and the writer (and NYU faculty member) E. L. Doctorow, registered complaints. Reverend Billy, a local activist and performance artist, garnered media—and police—attention with a staged reading of *The Raven* atop the construction scaffolding erected in front of the site. Like the raven, bad press began to haunt NYU: "The Villain of the Village?" ran one *New York Times* headline, as media outlets portrayed the situation as yet another instance of the university's insensitivity to the local community and its culture.[36] Faced with a public-relations disaster, NYU brokered a compromise: It would respect the artistic heritage of Greenwich Village and integrate the Poe House into the building of its new law school.

What was unveiled after two years of construction was especially revealing. NYU had built a facsimile of the front of the Poe House half a block away from its original site and stuck it on the surface of its new law building. Nonetheless, a brass plaque on the building front informs the passerby that this is the Poe House—or, more precisely, "an interpretive reconstruction" thereof. The front door is locked. To enter (it is open from 9 to 11 A.M. on weekdays only), visitors have to proceed through the law school's lobby, check in with a security guard, and make their way down the hall to a little side room, next to the student cafeteria. There, a portrait of Poe hangs on a wall, along with a manuscript page from *The Raven*. Comfortable chairs are scattered across the carpeted floor. A glass case near the far wall displays a few broken pots and trinkets unearthed in the excavation; in the center of the case, prominently displayed with its own identifying tag, is one of the original bricks that was supposed to be used in the reconstruction. To the right is an odd staircase: the remains of the house's original banister and six steps built into the wall, leading to nowhere. To the left is a door to the cafeteria. Leaving the stark room, one might look back and notice the sign that marks the interior entrance. Here, inside NYU, there is no mention of the Poe House or even a Poe room. Instead, there is a plaque that states that the room just visited is the "Honorable Frank J. Guarini and Caroline L. Guarini Study Lounge." The Poe House serves double duty, and the timid and half-hearted perpetuation of Poe's memory is reframed—or encased, if you like—as a wealthy benefactor's vanity gift to the university.

Andrew Berman, executive director of the Greenwich Village Society for Historic Preservation, described the new Poe House as "tacked on . . . a façade, literally and figuratively."[37] It is an apt description of the possible future of culture in a world of ICE: Sexton and Lackman's "value premium," tacked on and hollowed out.

Notes

1. Abraham Lackman and John Sexton, "City's Economic Future Linked to Brain Power," *New York Observer*, February 21, 2005, 5. Lackman and Sexton's op-ed does differ from the CGR report in one important respect. Perhaps in deference to the financial-minded readership of the *Observer*, Lackman and Sexton take pains to reassure that ICE is a supplement and stabilizing force for FIRE rather than its replacement.

2. NYU's Board of Trustees is one of the largest, with fifty members. Those who claim the title "Officers of the Board" alone read like a FIRE list in miniature. Among those on the list are Martin Lipton, the lawyer who invented the "poison pill defense"; Lawrence Silverstein, of Twin Towers fame; Kenneth Langone, co-founder of Home Depot and former chair of the New York Stock Exchange Compensation Committee that granted Richard Grasso his compensation package; Anthony Welters, CEO of AmeriChoice Medicaid Insurance Company; and Leonard Wilf, CEO of Garden Homes, the mega-company that deals in shopping malls and apartments in New York, New Jersey, Florida, Arizona, California, and Israel. For more on NYU and the historical role of university trustees, see Christopher Newfield and Greg Grandin, "Building a Statue of Smoke," in this volume.

3. Richard Schwartz, "City's Economy Is Getting Artsy," *New York Daily News,* December 16, 2004, 43; "What Will Be the Biggest Stories of 2005 in New York City?" *Gotham Gazette,* December 17, 2004, available online at http://www.gothamgazette.com/article/feature-commentary/20041220/202/1222 (accessed August 31, 2007).

4. Alain Touraine, *The Post-Industrial Society: Tomorrow's Social History: Classes, Conflicts and Culture in the Programmed Society,* trans. Leonard F. X. Mayhew (New York: Random House, 1971), 5.

5. Robert Reich, *The Work of Nations: Preparing Ourselves for 21st Century Capitalism* (New York: Alfred A. Knopf, 1991).

6. Richard Florida, *The Rise of the Creative Class* (New York: Basic Books, 2002).

7. Alok Agarwal, "Zee Targets to Become the Largest Integrated Convergence Company," September 26, 2000, available online at http://www.domain-b.com/companies/companies_z/Zee/20000926zee_targets.html (accessed August 31, 2007); "India Needs Many More Computers," interview with F. C. Kohli, *Hindustan Times,* December 10, 2001, available online http://www.tata.com/tcs/media/20011211.htm (accessed August 31, 2007); N. K. Singh, "India's Economy: The Next Five Years," working paper no. 186, October 2003, Stanford Center for International Development, Stanford University, Palo Alto, Calif. Singh is a member of the Indian government's Planning Commission.

8. Woodrow Wilson National Fellowship Foundation, "The Responsive Ph.D.: Innovations in U.S. Doctoral Education," policy report, September 2005.

9. The complete list of participants can be found on page 11 of the report or on the Woodrow Wilson National Fellowship Foundation's website at http://www.woodrow.org/responsivephd/RPHDmember.php.

10. Woodrow Wilson National Fellowship Foundation, "The Responsive Ph.D.," 6.

11. Ibid.

12. Ibid., 29.

13. The CGR was founded in 1913 by George Eastman of Eastman Kodak as part of the wave of "good government" efforts by industrialists to "study and promote efficient and effective city government"—in other words, to take back cities from the, albeit corrupt, immigrant-run political machines and run them like rational corporations. See the CGR website at http://www.cgr.org (accessed November 26, 2006).

14. Kent Gardner, "Solutions for New York: The Economic Significance of Independent Colleges and Universities in the New York State Economy," report, July 2006, Center for Governmental Research, July 2006, p. 2.

15. Ibid., ii.

16. U.S. Department of Labor, Bureau of Labor Statistics, "State and Area Employment, Hours and Earnings: New York," "Total Non-Farm," and NAICS 22: "Food Services and Drinking Places," data available online at http://www.bls.gov (accessed November 27, 2006).

17. "Bonanza on Wall Street," *New York Times,* November 26, 2006, 2.

18. Gardner, "Solutions for New York," 10–11.

19. Kenneth F. McCarthy, Elizabeth H. Ondaatje, Laura Zakaras, Arthur Brooks, "Gifts of the Muse: Reframing the Debate about the Benefits of the Arts," Rand Corporation, Santa Monica, Calif., 2004, 67–68.

20. Lee Rosenbaum, "The Gates Receipts? Not Even Ballpark Figures," *Wall Street Journal,* March 1, 2005, D9.

21. McCarthy et al., "Gifts of the Muse," 32.

22. Figures for 2005 in Gardner, "Solutions for New York," 10–11.

23. Enrollments rose 12 percent between 1995 and 2004 for private universities and rose only 7 percent for comparable (four-year and graduate) public institutions: ibid., 14–15.

24. Bonnie Browert and Rachel Hays, "Fatal $ubtraction: How State-Mandated Property Tax Exemptions Subsidize New York City Private Education at the Expense of Public Schools and CUNY," City Project policy paper, April 2006, 38.

25. Ibid., 5, 18, 22.

26. Ibid., 21.

27. Ibid., 53, table 8.

28. Ibid., 39, table 6.

29. Ibid., 90.

30. Gardner, "Solutions for New York," 7.

31. John Sexton, "Commencement Address," 2006, http://www.nyu.edu/about/sexton.commencement.2006.html (accessed August 31, 2007).

32. Malcolm Cowley, *Exile's Return: A Literary Odyssey of the 1920s* (London: Penguin, 1976).

33. Bill T. Jones, transcribed remarks, Creative New York conference, New York, April 4, 2006, 29.

34. Ibid., 30.

35. McCarthy et al., "Gifts of the Muse," xv.

36. Nina Siegal, "Rapping on Poe's Door: A Hint of Nevermore," *New York Times,* July 19, 2000, B1; Karen Arenson, "The Villain of the Village?" *New York Times,* April 19, 2001, B1.

37. Denny Lee, "The Poe House and Its Mask of Red Bricks," *New York Times,* October 19, 2003, sec. 14, 7.

The High Cost of Learning

Tuition, Educational Aid, and the New Economics of Prestige in Higher Education

ADAM GREEN

I n 2005–2006, while the war on GSOC raged on New York University's campus, a different struggle pitting administration against student on Washington Square was declared. Frustrated for years by tuition increases well outpacing inflation, undergraduates at NYU the previous summer had organized as the Tuition Reform Action Coalition (TRAC), a group dedicated to informing the campus and public about the affordability crisis at NYU and compelling the institution to enact meaningful reforms. Calls for moderated increases, full disclosure of the university budget, and meetings between students and President John Sexton fell at first on deaf ears. By January 2006, after outreach by TRAC to other organizations and a savvy media campaign, President Sexton was finally compelled to respond in writing. Claiming that concerns about tuition were "never far from our thoughts," Sexton cited faculty salaries and staff benefits as a justification for high tuition rates, even as he avoided citing more specific details of the budget. Sexton's pleas that NYU was fiscally dependent on tuition as its primary source of revenue were met, predictably, with ire from the students. In an open letter later that winter, TRAC's president, Asaf Shtull-Trauring, denounced further increases in NYU tuition, renewed calls for fiscal transparency, and promised more organizing and demonstrations, warning President Sexton that "this year will be the last in which student voices are ignored."[1]

The furor over tuition and accountability at NYU is but a local phase of a national problem. Increases at NYU of more than 20 percent in the five years since 2002 have been mirrored by figures nationally. Public college

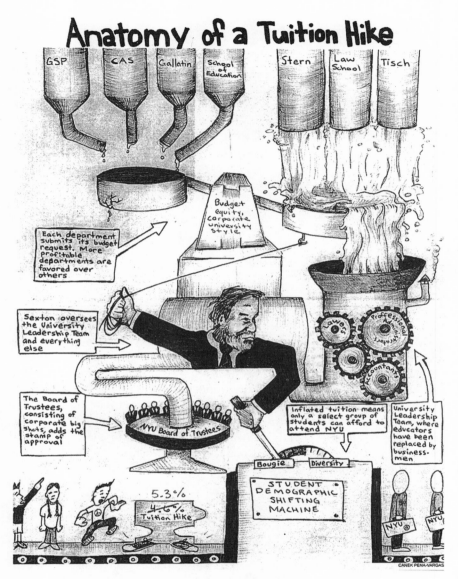

Anatomy of a tuition hike. *(Canek Pena-Vargas,* NYU Inc., *vol. 3. no. 1, March 2004.)*

tuition in the United States increased 14 percent and 10 percent in 2003 and 2004, respectively. While four-year private-school tuition rose at a more moderate rate of 6 percent in 2004 and 2005, that figure was still nearly double the inflation rate for that year.[2] Estimates by the College Board were that, over the decade from 1995 to 2005, inflation-adjusted tuition costs increased 36 percent at private colleges and 51 percent at public schools.[3] The year 2004 saw higher education affordability emerge as a national political issue, with the Democratic presidential nominee John Kerry suggesting federal incentives to help colleges and universities hold down their costs for students.[4] On the other side of the aisle, House Republicans led by Howard (Buck) McKeon called for cutting off federal student-aid funds to colleges and universities that raised tuition too dramatically.[5] While this proposal was ultimately tabled, campus cost control remains a potent Republican talking point, as the Spellings Report on Higher Education, released in the fall of 2006, makes clear. Stressing concerns that U.S. higher education was largely unaccountable to monitoring, hard to access for underserved communities, and losing its competitive advantage globally, the Spellings report has been justly seen as a warning of greater federal micromanaging to come on matters ranging from academic-standards compliance and skills training for the new economy to a stronger push for universities to restructure themselves along privatized and corporate lines.[6]

The high cost of learning—at NYU and at institutions across the country—makes manifest the institutional contradictions of the higher-education industry, and of educational policy generally, at the start of the twenty-first century. State and citizen concerns about affordability reflect broader anxieties concerning the ability of colleges and universities to meet the needs of society, as indicated by widespread criticism concerning executive compensation, legacy admissions, and accessibility.[7] Challenges to colleges and universities to deliver "equity" as well as "excellence" have historically served as spurs to the flanks of the modern American university, as campaigns to remove quotas against Jewish students, women, and racial minorities transformed flagship private and land-grant campuses alike.[8] Prohibitive tuition fees and crushing debt loads remind us that this struggle continues today, with the emergence of even stronger barriers to poor, first-generation, and immigrant students who look to higher education as a road to social mobility.

The muted and contradictory responses of colleges and universities to the outcry over tuition indicates that this mission of mobility is becoming a thing of the past, if it could ever have been spoken of as reality. Beyond the splashy stories of well-endowed campuses footing the bill for needy students, higher education as a whole is regressively reworking aid formulas, pursuing ambitious and expensive growth plans, and privileging merit over diversity in admissions to best appeal to the legion of national ranking institutions, from the National Research Council to *U.S. News and World Report* and *Princeton Review*.[9] The rise of the new economics of prestige has affected how colleges and universities relate to undergraduates and, in a broader sense, to the public at large—generally for the worse. It seems inevitable, then, that the tuition wars will grow more dramatic in coming years. How those battles progress—and who is left standing as they run their course—will determine whether the American university can realize the progressive social mission many have charged it with over the past half-century.

College affordability has been a nagging question among policymakers, public advocates, and even forward-thinking university leaders in recent decades. In

1988, the Congressional Budget Office found average tuition and fees for full-time–equivalent undergraduate students had more than tripled in nominal terms, and increased nearly 30 percent in real terms, between 1970 and 1986.[10] According to their findings, increases were steeper during the years 1980 and 1985 than in previous years, and private institutions far outpaced public in rates of increase: On average, overall increases in private tuition rates rose from $1,680 to $6,320, a 43 percent increase in terms of real dollars.[11] If anything, the figures worsened during the 1990s. According to the College Board's 2002 report on higher-education pricing, average tuition at four-year private colleges stood at $18,273. The comparable figure for four-year public institutions was $4,081. In each case, the rate of increase, adjusted in value for 2002 dollars, stood at well over 100 percent for the three decades between 1971–1972 and 2001–2002.[12]

Despite this rising cost, talk of a clear and present crisis in college afford-ability was not as widespread as it has become recently. Much emphasis was placed, by university spokesmen, lobbyists, and even reviewing agencies them-selves, on rich streams of resources—primarily state grants for public schools and endowments as well as revenues for private institutions—that subsidized the actual cost of education for enrolled students. In policy circles (if not yet in the public mind), the unit of measure for tuition costs was redefined from the "pub-lished price" of listed tuition to a "net price" that reflected an array of real costs, including faculty salaries, maintenance of the campus physical plant, health care for students and staff, and overall services and amenities, which were represented as in fact far greater than the sticker cost of a college education.[13] One can see hints of this conception even now. NYU President John Sexton, for instance, challenged the indexing of college costs relative to inflation rather than the more generous Higher Education Price Index (HEPI),[14] and emphasized institutional austerity measures that, by his thinking, constituted effective subsidies to the cost of an NYU undergraduate education.[15]

Also serving to allay affordability concerns prior to the mid-1990s was the presumption, especially in Washington, that federal aid programs were an effec-tive supplement for college students and their families. The Congressional Bud-get Office's 1991 report on student aid and postsecondary education, for example, concluded that federal aid effectively facilitated attendance of needy students at public institutions and that aid at private schools, while not functioning as well, could be made to do so through moderate and feasible corrections.[16] Estimates in the early years of this decade were that 90 percent of dependent students receiving federal financial aid for higher education were from families with annual incomes below $40,000.[17] The acknowledged merits of the Perkins and Stafford loan programs, as well as the Pell grants, rested largely on this correlation of aid with need.

Of course, there were those voicing concerns before 2000 as to whether these programs truly bridged the gap between college pricing and many families' incomes. According to the National Center for Public Policy and Higher Educa-tion, the percentage of four-year public-tuition costs covered by the average Pell grant fell precipitously from 98 percent in 1986 to 57 percent in 1999, with still worse figures for private institutions.[18] These figures led researchers such as Thomas Keane to question whether Pell grants in fact served to ease access for lower-income students.[19] By 2000, the extent to which federal aid was effective in mitigating the impact of increasing tuition on low-income students, as well as in expanding educational access—particularly at more desirable schools—was increasingly understood to rest on three factors:

1. Whether colleges and universities approached their pricing policies in a way that placed a priority on encouraging access for a variety of students, in terms of class as well as other categories of social identity;
2. Whether real incomes of poor and lower-middle-class families maintained value relative to incomes generally in American society, enabling them to even consider enrollment on the part of college-age members at a variety of schools, particularly four-year private schools; and
3. Whether the federal government remained committed in its traditional vision of student-aid programs as fundamentally *need*-based rather than *merit*-based.

As it has turned out, each of these conditions has tracked precipitously against the interests of poorer students and families from 2000 to today in ways that make broad higher-education options less feasible for these students than at any time over the past generation.

Recent years have seen a strong turn toward reformulating federal student-aid programs around principles of merit rather than those of need. To be sure, signs of this turn were evident as early in the 1990s, in accord with general hostility toward any organization of the American state around the principle of public welfare that is by now well acknowledged.[20] Initially, states took the lead, establishing new aid initiatives such as Georgia's HOPE scholarships and Texas's State Scholars program that relied on strict standards concerning class credits and grades to move state aid for higher education toward a merit principle. This, of course, correlated with larger ambitions to institute standards and workforce re-skilling that have animated much of conservative educational reform in the past decade. State Scholars, for example, relied on partnerships between statewide business organizations and secondary schools to establish eligibility criteria for applicants.[21] And with state appropriations for higher education generally, and aid programs in particular, seeing significant decreases during this time,[22] the turn toward merit criteria for aid at the state level represented a particular crisis for needy students seeking to meet tuition bills.

Federal interest in moving toward a merit basis for higher-education aid was evident during the 1990s, with the Clinton administration's implementation of its own Hope Scholarship program, as well as a Lifetime Learning Credit tax reform program, both of which moved federal educational aid in more regressive directions.[23] But it has been the administration of George W. Bush that has pushed for this shift most aggressively. In 2004, Bush sought to restructure the entire Pell grant program—a $12.7 billion program at the time—along the lines of the States Scholars program from his home state of Texas. To close a $3.7 billion deficit in the Pell grants budget, the Bush administration, with the blessing of Congress, restructured the program's eligibility formula in such a way as to deauthorize nearly ninety thousand students assisted by the program and restructured the Perkins loan program to make another sixty-nine thousands students ineligible.[24] The following February, the Bush administration targeted the Perkins loan program, LEAP, Upward Bound, and other federal programs directed toward increasing first-generation and underrepresented student populations on college campuses for elimination. It also required colleges and universities nationally to return some $6 billion in Perkins funds that would otherwise have gone to fund loans for low- and middle-income students. To date, these changes have not yet been approved in Congress, despite the lobbying efforts of the administration.[25] Bush and Education Secretary Margaret Spellings, however, have been successful in winning congressional approval of a proposal to eliminate borrower ability to lock in fixed rates on federal student loans, a change projected to save the government $14.3 billion, cost student borrowers and their families nearly $7.8 billion, and open a bonanza for lenders seeking to exploit more market-variable conditions.[26]

It is worth turning back to the case of NYU, specifically in relation to the changing rules of federal aid under Bush. In his January 2006 response to TRAC, President John Sexton took pains to emphasize that NYU had among its undergraduate students a higher percentage of Pell grant recipients (17 percent) than any institution ranked ahead of it. In Sexton's mind, this was clear proof that "NYU has a more economically diverse student body than any of those institutions."[27] Yet given the restructuring being pursued for the Pell program, and the total elimination of Perkins money, it is unclear how long such a claim can be made by NYU. Given the profound instabilities of nationally funded aid programs generally, it is hard to imagine any student programs, other than direct institutional grants, offering the requisite security to low- and middle-income users who are already stretched to the limit in terms of their capacity to pay tuition fees on the order of NYU's—$33,370 in 2006–2007.[28] Of course, it is impossible to know with any certainty just how many students at NYU are in fact low or middle income without disclosure of the relevant budgetary figures. In the absence of such transparency, though, relying, as Sexton does here, on Pell grants as indicative not only of who among NYU's students are in need, but also to what degree that collective need is being reliably met by the institution, inspires less than full confidence.

But what is clear is that low- and middle-income students have uniquely pressing needs for assistance at present, given the effects of the wealth gap. According to the Economic Policy Institute's report "The State of Working America, 2006/2007," the top-earning 1 percent of households controlled 34.4 percent of total assets in the United States in 2004, while the bottom 90 percent held only

28.7 percent of total assets. This same top 1 percent controlled an average of $15 million in assets, as compared with $81,000 in average assets held by those at the median income level. The lowest 17 percent of incomes, by contrast, had zero or negative net worth in assets, while the 30 percent above that controlled, on average, less than $10,000. The stark distinction in life chances derived from these figures is evident in the Economic Policy Institute's projection that, given current material conditions, it would take the average family of four at the poverty line ($19,307) nine or ten generations to reach middle-income status, and still longer to reach the median level of assets. Though there have always been significant discrepancies in wealth in the United States, the gap has become especially pronounced in the past twenty years—mirroring the acceleration in tuition rates and the corresponding restructuring of financial aid within higher education. While the wealthiest 1 percent in the nation held 125 times the median wealth in 1962, and 131 times that figure in 1983, by 2004 the wealthiest 1 percent controlled 190 times the median figure—in other words, an increase in wealth disparity of 45 percent in the past generation, as opposed to 5 percent for the generation preceding this one.[29]

As is now well documented, the increase in the wealth gap is the single most significant factor decreasing prospects for social mobility at present. It is symptomatic, of course, of the steeply regressive flow of assets upward throughout the world in the wake of economic restructuring associated with changes in world financial administration and globalized processes of production, labor flow, and investment. According to the United Nations World Institute for Development Economic Research, the richest 10 percent of the world's inhabitants currently own more than 85 percent of global household wealth. North America's and Europe's control, each, of a 33 percent share of the world's assets compares with 1 percent for the entire African continent.[30] Yet even in the United States—the country that enjoys the greatest per capita share of global wealth, along with England, prospects for social mobility are becoming increasingly remote for the majority of citizens. Such statistics, national and international, make a particularly dire appeal to U.S. colleges and universities to redouble efforts to enable prospective students who are otherwise unable to afford higher education to enroll, matriculate, and, ultimately, graduate. Yet the signs are not encouraging: According to the Economic Policy Institute, a high-achieving student from a low-income family has a lower probability of successfully completing college than a low-achieving student from a high-income family. Changing patterns of recruitment and aid support have made the well-off the preferred pool for incoming undergraduate students.[31]

One sobering indicator of the growing disparity in educational opportunity is the intensifying condition of student labor on campuses in recent years. Citing U.S. Department of Education figures, Laura Bartlett points out that 80 percent of undergraduates nationally were working while in school in 1999–2000. Of that number, 56 percent were working twenty-four hours per week or more, with 39 percent working more than thirty-five hours—the normal work week for several

European countries. These figures—which have surely gone up in subsequent years, given the widening gap between college costs and student resources—signal labor conditions mirroring the casualization and flexing of the university teaching pool, composed overwhelmingly of adjuncts and graduate students, as well as the overall move toward disposable labor within the new service and information economy here in the United States.[32] The ways in which these conditions sort students into distinct categories in terms of academic performance and quality of undergraduate experience are clear. Working nearly full-time hours, often in temporary or outsourced work that has little correspondence to an academic major or aspired-to middle-class career, working students find themselves making up a captive and thoroughly exploitable pool of labor to be delivered by colleges and universities to various corporate partners.[33] The sweat equity of the efforts of this undergraduate majority, moreover, is becoming increasingly difficult to locate. According to Tom Mortenson, from 1964 to 1982, it was possible to pay the average cost of four years of public college by working nineteen to twenty-one hours a week at minimum wage for fifty-two weeks. As of 2002–2003, the figure stood at fifty hours at minimum wage. Average private-college tuition required 136 hours of minimum-wage work over fifty-two weeks for a working student to meet costs.[34]

This makes the question of rising tuition at colleges and universities across the country all the more urgent. By now, the high cost of education is acknowledged as a concern across the spectrum of groups that make up the community of higher education—everywhere, it seems, except for among those in fact setting tuition charges for this country's colleges and universities. It is certainly not for lack of ready evidence that the problem of cost has not emerged at the forefront of policy discussions internal to colleges and universities. One need only look at a major newspaper for a week to come across a prominently placed story related to college costs and access. Nor are those in positions of national authority, or those aspiring to occupy those positions, uninterested in this question. As mentioned earlier, the problem of the affordability of higher education was prominent in the 2004 presidential campaign. It has been a central preoccupation on the part of the Bush administration at the start of each annual budget process. It has constituted a standard for activist legislators on both the left and the right. And it is already being invoked prominently by several candidates in the 2008 presidential election. Thus, it seems appropriate to briefly outline the scope of the problem concerning high college charges and then explore the factors driving the desire to set them, in spite of the perils involved.

National figures on tuition paint a picture that, while sobering and even dire in places, should not be seen as historically unique. The rise in public-institution charges are, without question, nothing short of lamentable, given the role of storied state systems in California, Wisconsin, Massachusetts, and elsewhere not only in making a world-class education accessible to a majority of state residents, but also constituting the cutting edge in intellectual innovation in a variety of fields. Increases higher than 50 percent in fees for public higher education nationally over the past decade have all but ended the first part of that legacy, while the effects of state budget cuts raise questions regarding the viability of the second. Among private institutions, however, the increases have been less dramatic—still severe, as anyone required to meet the $40,000 in fees charged at ranked private institutions can attest, but in line with the 100 percent rate of increase in private-school tuition between 1971 and 2001 cited earlier. Without question, the decline in relative value of the income and savings of poor and middle-income Americans is hugely important here. It matters little to speak of "net pricing" or abundant options of subsidy to individuals and families when discretionary spending powers, for all intents and purposes, are effectively held at levels approaching that of poverty.

Nonetheless, overall figures tell us that the current tuition crisis is equal parts perception, projection, and reality. Yet that is not the same thing as saying that public anxiety over the high cost of education is the result of exaggeration or hysteria. Coupled with the adverse developments concerning state- and federal-aid programs, affordability is an irrefutable concern, especially as one looks into the future. And given that many colleges and universities, especially those that count themselves at the top of the pile in reputation, notoriety, and prestige, seem indifferent, if not arrogantly dismissive, in their responses to these concerns, it may be that a change in institutional attitude must precede effective changes in policy.

Here again, the case of NYU proves revealing. Despite the unwillingness of the NYU administration to open its fiscal books, members of the group TRAC, through extensive research, have established several insights into how that administration sees the problem of access and affordability. Given that NYU's limited endowment (approximately $1.6 billion as of January 2007) and a student body exceeding fifty thousand (within which undergraduates total 19,401),[35] it has relatively few discretionary resources to devote to each student—about $30,000–$40,000, depending on whether non-degree students are factored in. Schools such as Princeton, Harvard, and Stanford—all of which have announced comprehensive internal grant programs in recent years—have comparable per-student endowment figures ranging from $1.1 million to $1.9 million.[36] President Sexton took pains to emphasize this disparity in his January 2006 letter to TRAC while emphasizing his "pride" that NYU was nonetheless able to offer a "high quality educational experience" seen as comparable to those found at "schools with which we compete."[37] Yet pride by itself cannot pay the bills, as members of TRAC pointed out in their response. Of the top fifty private universities in the country, NYU has among the highest rates of aid offered in the form of loans or work study (41 percent), the lowest rates of meeting demonstrated student need (68 percent), and, not surprisingly, the highest average debt carried by undergraduates following graduation ($29,480).[38] Little wonder, then, that NYU, which has famously topped out many survey measures of popularity among prospective applicants nationally, ranks dead last in the category "satisfaction with financial aid resources," according to the *Princeton Review.*[39]

Yet NYU, like many colleges and universities across the country, is far more focused on the rising market value of its product than actual customer satisfaction. Aggressive price pointing has become the trend in how tuition rates are set, as schools ranging from George Washington University and the University of Richmond to Bryn Mawr or Bates College in Maine seek to generate recognition for their education "brand" by pricing themselves alongside the Ivies.[40] A recent report in the *New York Times* on how Ursinus College, a Pennsylvania liberal-arts school, increased applications and acceptance yields dramatically through steep tuition increases at once exemplifies the current boom cycle in educational costs and reminds us that this model for growth has been seen before.[41] Recent arrivals at the head table of academe, such as Duke and NYU, have used aggressive tuition pricing as a component of their campaigns to challenge traditional flagship universities' monopoly as "first choice" schools in the 1980s and 1990s, and by many analysts' lights, this strategy has proved successful. What is different today is how widespread the ambition to be compared to the elite standard has become in American higher education, setting off an escalating race for reputation that deeply distorts all sense of institutional mission and threatens to make university access still narrower than it historically has been.

Throughout higher education today, prestige constitutes the governing measure of value. It provides the basis on which faculty are recruited, hired, and compensated. It has become ever more integrated into merit review, with services ranging from the Philosophical Gourmet Report to the Faculty Scholarly Productivity Index offering new metrics to fuel departments' and institutions' dreams of rapid rise in national reputation.[42] It has shaken up the traditional institutional hierarchy that ordered academe for decades, setting off the equivalent of an arms race in attracting the attention of college applicants and recruiting students whose test scores, grade-point averages, and resumes in turn can be converted into still more lustrous placement in the *U.S. News and World Report* and *Princeton Review* annual surveys. And it has increasingly compelled campus presidents, administrators, and trustees to extol the virtue of growth—growth in infrastructure, splashy amenities, star faculty, name recognition, and tuition pricing—over values of social service on the part of academe.

The emphasis placed on prestige has operated in particular to drive colleges and universities to charge the maximum cost that the market will bear while seeking to increase the number of students positioned to pay full or nearly full cost. With elaborate integration of development and admissions functions at most leading institutions, there is already a discernable turn toward concentrating on the well-heeled and well-off in fashioning incoming undergraduate classes.[43] Given the shift in federal policies regarding educational aid from need to merit, colleges and universities have that much more cover to seek to approach admissions, aid, and matriculation questions with an eye to toward profit and revenue rather than the ethic of access advocated by progressive educational policymakers such as William Bowen, student advocates such as the members of TRAC at NYU, and national campaigns such as the "free higher education" initiative coordinated by the Debs-Jones-Douglass Institute.[44] The value of these interventions loom that much larger when one contemplates how much more regressive this country's colleges and universities may become—regarding tuition and aid, specifically—and the larger question of social access to higher education in general.

The battle over tuition charges, then, is a key entry point into the battle over the soul of contemporary higher education, as well as the broader struggle to prevent social mobility from being closed off in American society. All of us associated with the work of higher education would do well to learn the terms of this coming struggle and make clear where we stand in relation to it.

Notes

1. NYU President John Sexton to TRAC, letter, January 31, 2006; Asaf Shtull-Trauring, TRAC, to President John Sexton, open letter, February 15, 2006; both available online at http://www.makeNYUaffordable.com (accessed January 25, 2007).

2. "Public Colleges See a 10% Rise in Tuition for 2004–5," *Chronicle of Higher Education,* October 29, 2004, A1.

3. College Board, *Trends in College Pricing, 2005* (Washington, D.C.: College Board, 2005), 7.

4. "Kerry Offers Proposals to Hold down Tuition Costs," *Chronicle of Higher Education,* July 9, 2004, A1.

5. "A House Divided over Tuition-Control Bill," *Chronicle of Higher Education,* January 23, 2004, A27.

6. "Plan to Punish Big Increases in Tuition Is Dropped," *Chronicle of Higher Education,* March 12, 2004, A1; U.S. Secretary of Education, Commission on the Future of Higher Education, "A Test of Leadership: Charting the Future of American Higher Education," Washington, D.C., 2006, esp. 2–3, 9–11, 18–20.

7. Daniel L. Golden, *The Price of Admission: How America's Ruling Class Buys Its Way into Elite Colleges and Who Gets Left outside the Gates* (New York: Crown, 2006); William G. Bowen, Martin A. Kurzweil, and Eugene M. Tobin, *Equity and Excellence in Higher Education* (Charlottesville: University of Virginia Press, 2005).

8. Golden, *Price of Admission;* Bowen et al., *Equity and Excellence.*

9. "Upping the Ante for Student Aid," *Chronicle of Higher Education,* February 16, 2001; "Harvard Gives a Break to Students Who Are Earning Less than $40,000 a Year," *Chronicle of Higher Education,* March 12, 2004, A35; "Stanford Eliminates Tuition for Neediest Students," *Chronicle of Higher Education,* March 16, 2006.

10. Congressional Budget Office, "Staff Working Papers: Trends in College Tuition and Student Aid since 1970," report, Washington D.C., 1988, 17.

11. Ibid., 23. A subsequent follow-up report by the Congressional Budget Office on the matter set the full average cost of private higher education, including room and board and other miscellaneous charges, at $10,351 in 1986, with average tuition set at $6,525 at that time. See idem, "Student Aid and the Cost of Postsecondary Education," report, Washington, D.C., 1991, 46.

12. College Board, *Trends in College Pricing, 2002* (Washington, D.C.: College Board, 2002), 8.

13. Congressional Budget Office, "Student Aid," 85–86; Bowen et al., *Equity and Excellence,* 88–89; College Board, *Trends in College Pricing, 2005,* 28.

14. HEPI was first developed as a statistical index in 1961 and, according to the Commonfund Institute, "measures the average relative level in the prices of a fixed market basket of goods and services purchased by colleges and universities . . . excluding expenditures for research." In this sense, it is meant to offer an alternative to the Consumer Price Index for measuring the cost of higher education. It is published monthly by Research Associates of Washington, D.C. For information, as well as an archive of HEPI figures, see http://www.commonfund.org/Commonfund/Investor+Services/HEPI.htm.

15. Sexton to TRAC, January 31, 2006.

16. Congressional Budget Office, "Student Aid," xiii–xxv.

17. Susan Dynarski, "The New Merit Aid," in *College Choices: The Economics of Where to Go, When to Go, and How to Pay for It*, ed. Catherine Hoxby (Chicago: University of Chicago Press, 2004), 63–100, as cited in Bowen et al., *Equity and Excellence*, 196.

18. National Center for Public Policy and Higher Education, *Losing Ground: A National Status Report on the Affordability of American Higher Education* (San Jose, Calif.: Center, 2002), 6; as cited in Bowen et al., *Equity and Excellence*, 200.

19. Thomas J. Kane, *The Price of Admission: Rethinking How Americans Pay for College* (Washington, D.C.: Brookings Institution, 1999), 118; as cited in Bowen et al., *Equity ad Excellence*, 200.

20. Thomas Byrne Edsall and Mary D. Edsall, *Chain Reaction: The Impact of Race, Rights and Taxes on American Politics* (New York: W. W. Norton, 1991); Kevin Phillips, *Wealth and Democracy: A Political History of the American Rich* (New York: Broadway Books, 2002); Lisa Duggan, *The Twilight of Equality? Neoliberalism, Cultural Politics and the Attack on Democracy* (Boston: Beacon Press, 2003); Thomas Frank, *What's the Matter with Kansas? How Conservatives Won the Heart of America* (New York: Henry Holt, 2004).

21. Bowen et al., *Equity and Excellence*, 196; "Bush Proposes Larger Pell Grant, but with a Catch," *Chronicle of Higher Education*, March 26, 2004, A24.

22. "State Spending on Colleges Drops for the First Time in 11 Years," *Chronicle of Higher Education*, January 16, 2004, A24–27. Fiscal year 2003–2004 represented the first year since 1992–1993 in which total state expenditures on higher education declined, and the 2.1 percent loss was cited by analysts as perhaps the largest rate of decline ever. In states experiencing especially severe cuts—notably California, which slashed 5.9 percent from its $9 billion higher-education budget, and Wisconsin, which saw cuts of 7.8 percent to its $1.2 billion higher-education budget—the adverse effects are still being felt. In other states, targeted cuts in state student aid—7 percent in Connecticut, 16.3 percent in Colorado, 35.6 percent in Florida—had a predictably chilling effect on figures for enrollment and matriculation.

23. Bowen et al., *Equity and Excellence*, 196.

24. "Congress Gives Lean Increases for Student Aid and Research" and "Spending Bill Allows Government to Cut Back on Pell Grants," *Chronicle of Higher Education*, December 3, 2004,) A1, 22–24; "Change in Federal Formula Means Thousands May Lose Student Aid," *Chronicle of Higher Education*, January 7, 2005, A1, 34–35.

25. "Bush Budget Takes Aim at Student Aid and Research," *Chronicle of Higher Education*, February 18, 2005, A1, 21–24. Though these cuts have not yet been approved by Congress, Bush and Secretary of Education Margaret Spellings have been consistent in their advocacy to eliminate Perkins and other programs and shift Pell toward more of a merit criteria. See "Not Much Help for Needy Students in 2007 Budget" *Chronicle of Higher Education*, February 17, 2006, A23, 26.

26. "House Narrowly Passes Bill That Cuts into Student Loans," *Chronicle of Higher Education*, December 2, 2005, A24.

27. Sexton to TRAC, January 31, 2006.

28. The tuition figure for an incoming freshman in the College of Arts and Science is taken from the university's financial-aid website at http://www.nyu.edu/financial.aid/tuitiongeneral.html (accessed January 25, 2007).

29. Economic Policy Institute, "The State of Working America, 2006/2007" (Washington, D.C.: Economic Policy Institute, 2006). The poverty figure for a family of four in 2004 can be found in the U.S. Census Bureau Report for that year, available online at http://www.census.gov/hhes/www/poverty/threshld/thresh04.html (accessed January 27, 2007).

30. United Nations University, World Institute for Development Economic Research, "The World Distribution of Household Wealth," report, New York, 2006.

31. Economic Policy Institute, "State of Working America."

32. Laura Bartlett, "Introduction: The Information University," *Workplace* 5, no. 1 (October 2002).

33. The work of Marc Bousquet is especially instructive on this point. See Bousquet, "The Informal Economy of the Information University," *Workplace* 5, no. 1 (October 2002); idem, "The Escape from Contingency, or Students Are Already Workers," unpublished paper, in the author's possession.

34. Tom Mortenson, "I Worked My Way through College; You Should, Too, 1964–5 to 2002–03," spreadsheet, available online at http://www.postsecondary.org/archives/Reports/Spreadsheets/1251102WorkedShould.pdf, as cited in Bousquet, "Escape from Contingency."

35. Total institutional enrollment is 50,917, of which 19,401 are undergraduates, 18,990 are graduate and professional students, and 12,526 are enrolled in non-credit programs. Figures are posted at the university's official web-based almanac "About NYU," at http://www.nyu.edu/about/facts.html. For figures on endowment, see the *Chronicle of Higher Education*'s report on college and university endowments in the January 2, 2007, issue.

36. Student enrollment at Stanford is 17,747 (6,422 undergraduates, 11,325 graduate and professional students), while its endowment now stands at more than $14 billion. Harvard's enrollment is at 19,650 (6,650 undergraduates, 13,000 graduate and professional students), with an endowment of $28.9 billion. Princeton University has 7,085 students (4,790 undergraduates, 2,295 graduate and professional students), with an endowment of more than $14.8 billion. See www.stanford.edu/home/statistics, www.stanford.edu/home/stanford/facts/finances, www.harvard.edu/budget/factbook/current_facts/2007Online Factbook.pdf, www.princeton.edu/pr/facts/profile/07/about, www.princeton.edu/pr/facts/profile/07/finances (accessed September 19, 2007). For endowment figures at comparable universities, see the *Chronicle of Higher Education*'s annual report on college and university endowments in the January 2, 2007, issue.

37. Sexton to TRAC, January 31, 2006.

38. "50 Top Private Universities: A Comparison," available online at http://www.makeNYUaffordable.org (accessed January 25, 2007).

39. For results of the *Princeton Review* survey, see "Students Dissatisfied with Financial Aid," available online at http://www.princetonreview.com/college/research/rankings (accessed January 27, 2007).

40. "How Much Is Too Much?" *Chronicle of Higher Education*, October 21, 2005, A30; "In Tuition Game, Popularity Rises with Price," *New York Times*, December 12, 2006.

41. "Tuition Game."

42. "Deep Thought, Quantified," *Chronicle of Higher Education*, May 20, 2005, A8; "A New Standard for Measuring Doctoral Programs," *Chronicle of Higher Education*, January 12, 2007.

43. Golden, *Price of Admission.*

44. The Free Higher Education Campaign, ongoing since 2001, seeks to establish a universal full-funding policy for public higher education funded through progressive restoration of tax revenues and redirection of budget priorities. It is modeled on the historical example of the Servicemen's Readjustment Act of 1944 (GI Bill). For further information on the campaign, see Adolph Reed Jr., "A G.I. Bill for Everyone," *Dissent* 48, no. 4 (Fall 2001), as well as the campaign's website at http://www.freehighered.com.

Blue Team, Gray Team

Some Varieties of the Contingent Faculty Experience

MICKI MCGEE

According to a recently released report prepared by the American Association of University Professors (AAUP), the composition of the American professoriate has been undergoing a steady and significant shift: The proportion of tenure-track and tenured appointments to contingent faculty appointments at degree-granting colleges and universities in the United States has declined by 21.8 percent, shrinking from 56.8 percent in 1975 to 35.1 percent in 2003.[1] Tenure, one of academe's most important traditions, has been disappearing more rapidly than the polar ice caps, and yet there was no substantial response on the part of the professoriate until the emergence of the contingent-faculty labor movement in the late 1990s.[2] Much as formerly middle-class Americans have watched passively as real wages have declined since 1972 and the single–wage-earner family has all but disappeared, the full-time professoriate has been largely complacent as tenure (and the associated principles of academic freedom and faculty governance) have been under gradual but continuous assault.

During this shift in the working conditions of academic labor, university administrations have managed to walk a fine line—embracing the ideal of a traditional tenured faculty that has long been associated with excellence in higher education while relying on part-time and temporarily contracted faculty to perform the bulk of the teaching work that is central to the university's mission. Although ostensibly committed to the academic traditions of faculty governance, academic freedom, and rigorous peer review, college and university administrations nationwide have cultivated faculties composed predominantly of part-timers and non–tenure-track full-timers who have little or no role in the governance of their schools, who are hired and fired at will, and who are seldom subject to formal peer-review processes within their departments or programs. Attempts to reconcile such contradictions require that university leaders mobilize all the rhetorical, administrative, legal, and political devices at their disposal.

New York University has played a leadership role in this arena. Not only have its administrations developed innovative new rhetorical and practical strategies to manage the contradictions that emerged as they cultivated the use of contingent labor over the past three decades, but in recent years NYU's part-time faculty and graduate-student employees have waged groundbreaking union-organizing campaigns. NYU's GSOC achieved a historic victory in 2000 when it won the right to organize as employees, and NYU's part-time faculty made history when they came together in late 1999 to launch an organizing campaign that resulted in the 2002 certification of ACT-UAW Local 7902 as the union representing NYU's part-time faculty. Since September 2004, the union has also represented the part-time faculty of the New School University, with a total membership that numbers more than four thousand, making it the largest part-time–faculty union in the nation.

As both the NYU administration and its activist faculty and graduate students have been on the forefront of the important skirmishes around the future of academic labor, this chapter will take the case of NYU as exemplary as it analyzes a series of policy statements crafted in part as a response to the widely publicized 2002 unionization campaign of the university's adjunct faculty. At that time, NYU faced an emerging public-relations problem as the fact that nearly three-quarters of all courses were taught by low-wage adjunct faculty (most of whom had no job security, benefits, or even office space in which to meet and advise students) came to light.[3] Specifically, this chapter will look at the disjunction between the university's rhetorical claims and the empirical realities of faculty composition while considering the newly expanded role of full-time non–tenure-track faculty—the fastest-growing category of faculty labor at the university.

Reconciling Opposites: The Phantasm of the Common Enterprise University

Along with the unionization of part-time faculty, 2002 marked another important change at NYU: the Board of Trustees appointed a new president, former NYU Law School Dean John E. Sexton, whose administration would be faced with the challenge of negotiating with the newly certified adjunct faculty union. President Sexton approached the situation by announcing early in his appointment that reducing the ranks of part-time faculty would be part of his agenda and by issuing a series of policy statements in which he articulated his vision for the "Common Enterprise University."[4] As early as spring 2002, NYU's student newspaper, the *Washington Square News*, reported that Sexton planned to reduce the use of adjunct faculty: "The first step in making it the kind of institution he envisions will be in building a top-notch faculty, one that is stable beyond what students are accustomed to, with fewer adjunct professors."[5] In a March 2003 missive to the NYU faculty, Sexton also noted, in somewhat oblique language, that the university's use of part-time teaching faculty had peaked and that full-time tenured faculty would need to return to the classroom. Paying "increased attention to our students," he said, "requires that we shift a greater proportion of our enterprise [teaching] to full-time faculty."[6] As most labor activists know, reducing the size of the bargaining unit is a common strategy for weakening the effectiveness of a unionized group, particularly when other parts of the labor force are not unionized or are subject to restrictions on their efforts to unionize (as are full-time faculty under the provisions of the yet-to-be overturned *Yeshiva* decision).[7]

By June 2003, Sexton had drafted a policy document, "The Role of Faculty in the Common Enterprise University," that was presented to a subcommittee of the NYU Board of Trustees.[8] The fifty-eight–page statement sketches a vision of the university as a multi-tiered, highly stratified organization in which non–tenure-track full-time faculty ("university teachers") would shoulder the bulk of teaching responsibilities without the benefits of tenure or any other form of job security, while part-time faculty would once again be adjunct to (rather than outnumbering) full-time faculty. The policy statement, and a subsequent 2004 version of it ("The Common Enterprise University and the Teaching Mission") are notable in several ways, but particularly so in their masterful attempts to reconcile the traditional values associated with the ethos of a community or cultural commons with the enterprising values of the marketplace, where "free agent" academics may auction themselves to the highest bidders. The statements envision an enterprising university community composed of a majority who are largely willing to sacrifice individual gain for the success of the group and who are willing to forgo even a commitment from the university that their continued membership in the community is assured (in the form of tenure or some other mechanism for job security). This is not an egalitarian community; it is, rather, a super-stratified organization in which under-compensated teaching faculty are expected to eagerly greet the arrival of superstar faculty poached from other universities with six-figure salaries and penthouse suites.[9] (Sexton writes: "I would submit that every member of the common enterprise faculty has a stake in accepting this normal market because everybody at the university benefits from having the best of colleagues.")[10] The competitive values of enterprise and entrepreneurship are to be articulated on behalf of the university as a whole, and among a limited few, but most individuals are urged to eschew their own self-interest, as the policy document decries the idea of entrepreneurial professors acting entirely in their own individual self-interest.

As part of its rationale, "The Common Enterprise University" suggests that tenure is no longer relevant because it has been in decline for more than two decades:

Just thirty years ago the National Center for Education Statistics reported that just over twenty percent of university professors in America were part-time; by 1999, that proportion had nearly doubled. According to the American Council on Education's Center for Policy Analysis, the number of part-time faculty grew nearly eighty percent in the last two decades of the twentieth century—to more than 400,000. Two thirds of the faculty appointed in the last five years of that century were part-time.

But the increased use of part-time faculty merely illustrates the emergence of a set of new—and sometimes creative—relationships between the university and some of its faculty. Over half of all new full-time faculty appointments in the past decade have been to positions that are not tenure eligible; or, to put it differently (and to incorporate the increased use of the part-time faculty) in the year 2001, only one in four new faculty appointments were to tenure track positions. The future will see more of this, and the common enterprise university will embrace the development of these new relationships and will integrate them consciously into the academic team.[11]

The erosion of tenure is offered as evidence of its increasing irrelevance and of the need for "creative relationships." Part of the proposed plan is an expanded teaching role for the tenured professoriate and the development of a hyper-stratified array of faculty, including untenured "university teachers" who are charged with focusing on teaching rather than research. In the midst of his essay, Sexton reminds us that teaching should be understood as a "sacred duty and privilege" that demands some sacrifice.

For tenured research faculty, the sacrifice is straightforward: They would be called on to renew their commitment to undergraduate teaching, to come down from the lofty realm of knowledge creation and engage in the previously low-status activity of undergraduate teaching. Since this activity was now to be considered sacred, it would no longer sully their time and reputations:

> Every faculty member—from the most senior world-renowned scholar to the most junior adjunct—must embrace the importance of integrating knowledge creation with knowledge transmission and understand their place in the process. Without this, the justification for undergraduate education, and even for the new Master's Colleges at research institutions, disappears.[12]

For others—among them the "university teachers"—the sacrifice would lie in giving up all hope of tenure-track appointments, thereby allowing the university to remain flexible, fleet and nimble in its ability to hire and fire at will and thus remaining economically positioned to "seize opportunities."

This "common enterprise university" policy statement envisaged the creation of a new hierarchy of mostly untenured teaching faculty comprising five types: the "university teacher," imagined as a full-time faculty member whose focus would be primarily on teaching; the "arts professor," a master practitioner of a particular art called on to share his or her craft and who would sometimes be tenured and other times be an untenured "university teacher"; the "global professor," who would include world business and political leaders from outside the borders of the United States; and the "cyber professor," who would disseminate his or her knowledge via the Internet. But if tenured faculty are supposed to be once again devoting more time to teaching, why would an untenured teaching faculty be necessary? Equally contradictory is the imperative that "university teachers"—who are defined as faculty not engaged in seriously focused research—would "embrace the importance of integrating knowledge creation with knowledge transmission." So, too, if faculty are selected specifically for their focus on teaching rather than research, one wonders how their unsupported research would be expected to inform or infuse their teaching.

Sandwiched neatly in the middle of these four new categories of the professoriate was an already existing type, the adjunct faculty, the group that had by the sheer force of numbers and organizing efforts generated the need to formulate this panoply of new classifications. However, in Sexton's lexicon, adjunct faculty are redefined as a rare phenomenon—limited to cases where world-class experts will share their expertise on a very limited, part-time basis. (The filmmaker Spike Lee and the corporate attorney, financier, and chair of NYU's Board of Trustees Marty Lipton are his examples of adjunct faculty.) Thus, in the blueprint for the common enterprise university, teaching by adjuncts will be rare, their ranks will dwindle, and, accordingly, their union might dissolve, resolving the tribulations of contract negotiation, employment security, collective bargaining, and other forms of due process that accompany a union contract.

By circulating these reflections on new models for the academy, NYU's astute leadership managed to make a virtue of the potential publicity liability that the part-time faculty represented. With 70 percent of courses taught by part-time faculty in 2002, and with 72 percent of its faculty off the tenure track by 2005, NYU had to get out "way ahead of the story"—as any good public-relations professional would advise.[13] The administration tacitly acknowledged that the university had begun to rely too heavily on part-time faculty as it crafted a detailed proposal that attempted to reconcile its perceived need for a flexible, expendable teaching labor force while preserving academic traditions (tenure, academic freedom, and faculty governance) for a tiny minority. These attempts to bring the contradictory values of the collective or the commons into harmony with the enterprising ethos of the corporate university marks one of the most ambitious efforts to make a philosophical argument for the reconciliation of these counter-posing tendencies and the diminution of tenure. But in the effort to shape this emerging vision of the university, the newly announced president indulged in an unfortunate, but revealing, analogy that warrants our consideration.

The Blue and Gray Teams

Prior to releasing his June 2003 policy statement, President Sexton endorsed a bifurcation of the faculty into what he called the "blue team" and the "gray team." The concept emerged in January 2002 when a group of faculty activists from NYU's AAUP chapter met with the newly designated, but not yet installed, university president at his old office in the NYU Law School, where he had served as dean for twelve years. Surrounded by the baseball memorabilia that reminds visitors of Sexton's passion for the sport, Sexton is reported to have commented that "the blue team was made up of professors who could get jobs at the drop of a hat at any of the top five universities in the country; the gray team represented the rest of the faculty." The sports analogy was widely circulated when the idea was discussed in David Kirp's *Shakespeare, Einstein, and the Bottom Line: The Marketing of Higher Education* and in a related October 23, 2003, op-ed piece Kirp published in the *New York Times*.[14] Sexton told the group of faculty activists that his goal was to increase the "blue team" from 10 percent to 30 percent of the faculty. It was clear to those present that "blue team" members would be afforded every traditional academic privilege, as well as celebrity compensation and perquisites, while many of the gray team's members would be denied even the traditional employment protections of tenure, an academic tradition available even to New York City public-school teachers.

The blue- and gray-team language proved, not surprisingly, to be enormously divisive and demoralizing among NYU's faculty, the vast majority of whom do not make celebrity salaries. At that time—prior to the ratification of a union contract—more than half were adjuncts making less than $3,000 per course. Even those in the ranks of the full-timers, who were relatively better off, had been asked to acquiesce to a wage freeze when the administration claimed it faced a financial crisis as it fretted publicly over the implications of its pending negotiations with the adjunct faculty union.[15] And it is perhaps worth noting that the gray team—at least the the part-time members of the team—has grown increasingly gray. According to the national center for Education Statistics and the U.S. Department of Education, the age of part-time faculty has grown steadily since 1992, when 50.8 percent of part-time faculty were forty-five or older, through 2003, when 63.5 percent of all part-time faculty in the United States were over forty-five.[16]

It seems plausible to suggest that "blue team–gray team" metaphor stands in for another color dyad that reverberates throughout American culture: the blue and pink color coding that inscribes a gendered division of labor (and rewards) that has only been marginally revised, despite the accomplishments of second-wave feminism. Of course, the university president would not have spoken of blue and pink teams—after all, what Major League Baseball team competes in pink jerseys? However, the classic division of lofty–lowly, extraordinary–ordinary is enunciated in his off-the-cuff rhetoric. I am not suggesting that the gray team comprises only female players, or even a majority of female players, though there is evidence that women have been as over-represented in the ranks of the non–tenure-track full-timers as they are unrepresented in the ranks of the tenured professoriate.[17] Rather, I am suggesting that the color-coded division recapitulates a well-worn line of thinking that creates a gendered set of ideas about work that is masculine, and labor that is feminine,[18] about the creation of knowledge (masculine) and the transmission of knowledge (feminine), about research faculty and teaching faculty.

The idea of separate gendered spheres of production and reproduction has its roots in the nineteenth century: As agrarian forms of living gave way to industrialization, the home and family ceased to be a site of farming and craft production and, instead, became a site of biological and cultural reproduction. The spheres, at least for the middle classes, were largely gendered, with women presiding over the management of the household and the moral development of children while their menfolk went forth into the commercial arena and labor market.[19] At home, traditional virtues and self-sacrifice were to be rewarded; in the marketplace, enterprising individualism was valorized. Out of this division of labor and values, the cult of true womanhood, that phantasmatic assemblage of purity, self-sacrifice, and generativity was born. The values of this cult were transferred to teachers, traditionally unmarried women who were to sacrifice themselves in the classroom, that other site of social reproduction.[20] It is this ideal of the self-sacrificing teacher for whom teaching is a sacred vocation that is at the heart of the ideology that ensnares teachers in self-defeating relationships with their institutions.[21] However sacred teaching may be, the use of this rhetoric has had eminently profane results for education.

Rhetoric versus Realities, or Less Reconcilable Differences

According to the AAUP's *Contingent Faculty Index, 2006*, the largest group of NYU faculty by far is the part-time or adjunct faculty, who accounted for 55.8 percent of all faculty in the 2005–2006 academic year. The next largest group are those who are tenured or on the tenure track), who account for 28 percent of all faculty. Finally, there are the non–tenure-track full-timers, who constitute 16.1 percent of all faculty but who will be the largest group of faculty if "the common enterprise university" vision were to be realized. These figures do not include graduate-student employees, who at this point outnumber the non–tenure-track full-timers. Graduate-student labor, if included, would account for 18.75 percent of all teaching staff, while the part-time faculty would account for 45.25 percent and tenure-track (tenured and tenurable) appointments for 22.75 percent. According to this AAUP accounting, graduate employees outnumber non–tenure-track-full timers, who would account for only 13.03 percent of all faculty.

The AAUP's figures, drawn from the U.S. Department of Education's Integrated Postsecondary Education Statistics, closely matched demographic figures available from NYU's Office of Institutional Research and Program Evaluation

How to identify an adjunct at NYU.

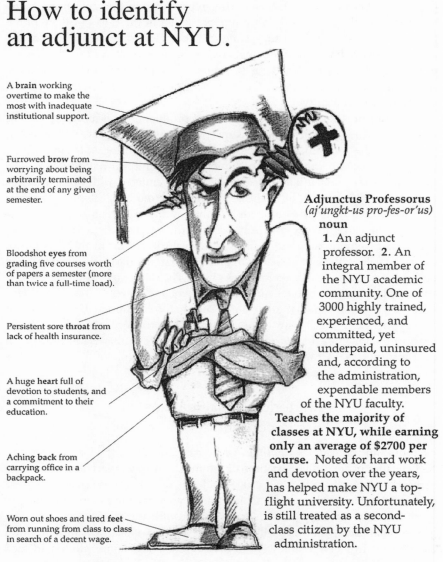

A **brain** working overtime to make the most with inadequate institutional support.

Furrowed **brow** from worrying about being arbitrarily terminated at the end of any given semester.

Bloodshot **eyes** from grading five courses worth of papers a semester (more than twice a full-time load).

Persistent sore **throat** from lack of health insurance.

A huge **heart** full of devotion to students, and a commitment to their education.

Aching **back** from carrying office in a backpack.

Worn out shoes and tired **feet** from running from class to class in search of a decent wage.

Adjunctus Professorus
(aj'ungkt-us pro-fes-or'us)
noun
1. An adjunct professor. 2. An integral member of the NYU academic community. One of 3000 highly trained, experienced, and committed, yet underpaid, uninsured and, according to the administration, expendable members of the NYU faculty. **Teaches the majority of classes at NYU, while earning only an average of $2700 per course.** Noted for hard work and devotion over the years, has helped make NYU a top-flight university. Unfortunately, is still treated as a second-class citizen by the NYU administration.

How to identify an adjunct at NYU. *(Image: James Levy; concept and copy: Andrew Boyd)*

(IRPE) on full-time–faculty composition, and figures provided by ACT-UAW Local 7902 on the composition of part-time faculty. However, the AAUP's published figures regarding NYU were for a single year (2005), and the statistics available from NYU's IRPE and ACT-UAW cover four years, allowing us to examine to the extent to which NYU's recent hiring practices have followed the model envisioned by its current administration.

TABLE 7.1   COMPOSITION OF NEW YORK UNIVERSITY FACULTY AND PROPORTIONATE
CHANGE, 2002–2003 TO 2005–2006 (EXCLUDING MEDICAL-SCHOOL FACULTY AND GRADUATE-STUDENT
LABOR)

TYPE OF APPOINTMENT	2002–2003		2003–2004		2004–2005		2005–2006		CHANGE 2002–2005	
	NO.	%	NO.	%	NO.	%	NO.	%	NO.	%
Tenured	962	23.43	976	21.95	1,022	22.75	1,027	21.23	+65	−2.20
Tenure-track, untenured	309	7.53	316	7.11	281	6.26	272	5.62	−37	−1.91
Total tenured and tenure-track	1,271	30.95	1,292	29.06	1,303	29.01	1,299	26.85	+28	−4.10
Full-time, non–tenure-track	552	13.44	630	14.17	707	15.74	744	15.38	+192	1.94
Total full-time faculty	1,823	44.4	1,922	43.23	2,010	44.75	2,043	42.23	+220	−2.17
Part-time faculty	2,283	55.6	2,524	56.77	2,482	55.25	2,795	57.77	+512	2.21
Total contingent (non–tenure-track part-time and full-time)	2,835	69.05	3,154	70.94	3,189	70.99	3,539	73.15	+704	4.10
TOTAL FACULTY	4,106		4,446		4,492		4,838		+732	

Data for full-time faculty composition are available from NYU's Office of Institutional Research and Program Evaluation. Data for part-time faculty were provided by ACT-UAW Local 7902. Figures for graduate-student labor were not available. Demographic data for NYU's full-time faculty for the academic years 2002–2003 through 2005–2006 are available online at http://www.nyu.edu/ir/demographics. Data for part-time faculty were provided by ACT-UAW Local 7902, who advise that these numbers grossly under-report the number of part-time faculty because they do not include faculty who teach fewer that forty contact hours per semester. Data for graduate-student employees were not available.

A review of these data (see Table 7.1) indicates that the administration's stated agenda of increasing non–tenure-track full-time faculty appointments is well under way. While the overall number of faculty has increased from 4,106 to 4,838, the proportion of non–tenure-track full-time appointments has increased from 13.44 percent of total faculty appointments in 2002–2003 to 15.38 percent in 2005–2006. The total number of faculty rose in all categories, with the exception of untenured faculty on the tenure track, where there was a real decline: Thirty-seven tenure-track lines were eliminated, which represents a proportionate decline of 1.91 percent for this category. While the total number of tenured appointments increased, the proportion of tenured appointments declined by 2.2 percent. In other words, while the actual number of tenured and tenurable lines has increased modestly, the proportion of tenure-track to non–tenure-track faculty (full- and part-time) declined by 4.1 percent, or slightly more than 1 percent each year, on average.

When it comes to reducing the ranks of adjunct faculty, the administration's practices have not followed the direction outlined in its policy statements. The use of adjunct faculty has increased, with the total number of part-time faculty who teach more than forty contact hours each semester (those who teach less are not included in the ACT-UAW bargaining unit and thus are not counted in the UAW's statistics) rising from 2,283 in 2002–2003 to 2,795 in 2005–2006. Part-time faculty also increased relative to all faculty: While they accounted for 55.62 percent of faculty in 2002–2003, by 2005–2006 they accounted for 57.77 percent of all faculty, a 2.21 percent increase. Between increases in the use of non–tenure-track full-time faculty and part-time faculty, the proportion of contingent faculty at NYU (excluding graduate-student workers) has increased by 4.1 percent over the first four years of the current university administration. If such statistical trends continue, tenured appointments will be eliminated in one generation.[22]

Although full-time non–tenure-track faculty currently account for only 15.38 percent of NYU's faculty, the rate of growth in this category was higher than in any other. While there were 552 non–tenure-track faculty lines in 2002–2003, the increase to 744 lines in 2005–2006 constitutes a 34.79 percent increase in the total number of non–tenure-track full-timers. By way of comparison, the addition of 512 new part-time appointments constituted only a 22.42 percent increase in total numbers of part-time faculty. ACT-UAW reports that, in the three years since the certification of the union that (between 2002 and 2005), 170 part-time faculty members in its bargaining unit had their appointments converted to full-time appointments. If all of these conversions were to non–tenure-track positions (which is likely), then part-time faculty who were promoted to full-time positions accounted for 170 of these 192 new non–tenure-track full-time appointments. Given that non–tenure-track full-time faculty constitute the fastest-growing type of faculty appointment, a closer look at the experience and subtypes in this category is useful.

Two Varieties of the Non–Tenure-Track Full-Time Experience

Not surprisingly, even among non–tenure-track full-time faculty members, there are nuances in the types of appointments that reiterate the bifurcation of academic labor into teaching and research and that further stratify the faculty. In researching this chapter, I spoke with a half-dozen people who currently hold or have held non–tenure-track full-time appointments. Those who are still employed as non–tenure-track full-timers serve at the pleasure of their department chairs, deans, or program directors, and their short-term contracts leave them vulnerable. As one pointed out, "An adjunct with six consecutive semesters at NYU has greater employment protection than a contract full-timer." Under the ACT-UAW contract, adjuncts with two classes per semester for three years have contractually enforceable job security, while non–tenure-track full-time contract employees have no due process with respect to contract renewal.[23]

If the stratification described here—tenured; non-tenured but tenure-track; non–tenure track; adjunct; and non–tenure-track full-time—were not divisive enough, the non–tenure-track full-timers are also readily parsed into at least two groups along the familiar teaching-versus researching divide: the *renewable contracted faculty,* usually called Master Teachers, who are, as their title announces, expected to be masters of teaching; and the *non-renewable three-year post-doctoral appointments,* the assistant professor and faculty fellows, who are expected to be up-and-coming scholars in their fields. While these assistant professorships cannot be renewed after their third year at NYU, their three years as full-timers can be counted toward tenure at another institution, should the hiring institution wish to recognize them.[24] The vagaries of these two types of appointments result in remarkably different experiences for individuals in each of these types of roles. The *habitus,* to use Pierre Bourdieu's term for the individual's interior experience of a particular social or professional field, for each of these jobs differs, despite their categorical similarities.

For the renewable teaching faculty, the professional emphasis is on teaching, advisement, and service inside the institution. Teaching loads of three courses per semester are typical. Scholarship and publications are expected but not required. For the non-renewable "research" faculty, the emphasis is on professional advancement within their discipline, but largely outside the immediate university. Teaching and departmental service are expected but will not be rewarded, as there is no possibility of contract renewal, and so they are deemphasized. Teaching loads of three courses per year—half the load for the renewable teaching faculty—are typical. Exceptional investment in either teaching or service would be a sign of a failure to comprehend one's place and temporary status within the institution. The renewable contracted faculty need local, intra-institutional advocates and support; the non-renewable "research" faculty need to advance their research and reputations within their scholarly and disciplinary communities, but outside the immediate institution, as their opportunities for advancement as faculty within the institution are negligible. (Occasionally non–tenure-track full-timers move into administrative appointments, and one with whom I spoke has moved to a visiting professor appointment, but these cases are exceptions.)

Not unexpectedly, there is greater approbation and respect within the institutional setting for the non-renewable junior faculty than for the master teaching faculty, for whom it would be most useful. The former may be thought of as junior scholars at the beginning of their careers, much as graduate students can be, while the latter are thought of as "super-adjuncts." Accordingly, a Master Teacher on the Faculty of Arts and Science at NYU reported that the non–tenure-track full-timers were not even invited to faculty events such as otherwise schoolwide receptions. More seriously, he noted, they have no representation in the Faculty Senate and thus no role in the official body of faculty governance. Another faculty member reiterated this concern, noting that tenure-track faculty shunned the new non–tenure-track full-timers recently incorporated into the Faculty of Arts and Science when NYU's General Studies Program, an undergraduate Liberal Studies program, was recently incorporated in the Graduate School of Arts and Science.

This avoidance and invisibility parallels a phenomenon that was widely observed by adjunct faculty members at NYU: While many full-time tenured faculty rallied to support their graduate students as GSOC was organizing, there was a marked lack of interest on their part for the adjunct-organizing campaign. Graduate students are one's intellectual progeny or successors, perceived in terms of future potential, while adjunct faculty may be regarded as pariah, perceived as limited, failed, or squandered potential. Graduate students and post-doctoral faculty fellows are potential future members of the blue team; adjuncts and contract full-time faculty are permanently relegated to the gray team.

These divisions play out in other ways, as well. Renewable non–tenure-track full-timers are frequently charged with extensive committee work, curriculum development, administration, and student advisement while their non-renewable counterparts are largely insulated from these responsibilities. However, it is important to remember that no matter how well the non–tenure-track junior research faculty may be treated in comparison with the renewable contract faculty, both groups are undercompensated when compared with tenure-track junior faculty. Starting salaries, though difficult to secure, are anecdotally reported to be 10–20 percent lower for non–tenure-track faculty than for beginning tenure-track assistants. Moreover, research funds for the non–tenure-track junior research faculty are markedly less, anywhere from one-fifth to to one-half of what tenure-track junior faculty typically receive. Moreover, by requiring triennial replacements through the nonrenewable appointment status, departments and programs save on the first year of retirement contributions. (Retirement contributions for non-renewable non–tenure-track faculty are not paid until the second year of employment.) In other words, the junior research faculty, like the "super-adjunct" non–tenure-track full-timers, are still a somewhat cost-effective means for the university to meet its need for full-time teaching faculty. But the real value of both of these groups of non–tenure-track full-timers is that they are easily dismissed, allowing the university to reduce its fixed liabilities. (Tenured appointments are, of course, ongoing liabilities—they are called "lines" because they are budget lines.) While all full-time appointments remain considerably more costly per course than adjunct faculty appointments, the advent of the adjunct union's contract has actually made the contingent full-timers a more flexible source of teaching labor.

Finally, there is the difference that one former non–tenure-track junior faculty member who has gone on to a tenure-track appointment at another research university described. At her new place of employment, she reported, she felt welcome. Her department chair checked in with her to ask how her publications were coming along and offered to make introductions that might help her place articles in appropriate professional journals. She described her work and her academic career as something she felt was "being resuscitated after three years in a desert" as a non–tenure-track assistant professor. At NYU, she said, she had felt as though she was "an academic orphan." Once she escaped from the realm of the non–tenure track, she experienced the very sort of support, collegiality, and sense of community that NYU's president imagines will be a feature of the "common enterprise university." Now she feels that her scholarly work is back "on track." Although she is working harder than ever, when she takes on committee assignments or additional student advisement she feels she is making a meaningful investment not only in her community but in her own future. Her own interests and those of her working community are structurally aligned. She is quite certain that this convergence of mutuality and self-interest could not have happened without the tenure track, without the sense of mutual investment that tenure can foster.

This former postdoctoral faculty fellow thought she was tired of academe, but she discovered that she was simply tired of feeling marginal and expendable. Her experience suggests that we should not be quite so ready to let tenure evaporate before our eyes. For those of us who have never experienced the shift in working conditions that this newly "on-track" faculty member describes, tenure may seem a tired anachronism. And if one subscribes to a belief in historical progressions, then a union for full-time faculty (tenure-track and non–tenure-track alike) may be a better way to align one's interests with the interests of one's colleagues. But one thing is certain: A fantasized resolution of competing visions of the university as market or commons should not be built on the backs of a new group of disenfranchised academic labor—the growing ranks of non-tenured full-timers who are asked to sacrifice job security in the interest of maintaining the institution's economic competitiveness.

If one were to take the rhetoric of true teacherhood seriously—if one were to genuinely subscribe to the belief that teaching is a sacred activity that shapes the next generation of scholars and leaders, as John Sexton seems to—then one would ensure that teachers are provided with optimal working conditions. Among these conditions would be the job security that encourages intellectual risk taking. Tenure has served that purpose for previous generations of scholars and teachers and continues to do so for a small group. In the current context, where non–tenure-track faculty constitute the majority of faculty at most American colleges and universities, there are two options: Tenure could be reinvigorated by the concerted efforts of faculty and administrators who are committed to the tradition of tenure and to the related principles of academic freedom and faculty governance, or job security could be mandated by another mechanism, through union contracts that preserve seniority, job security, and due process. Ideally, both of these strategies would be pursued, with faculty—whether contingent or tenure-track, part-time or full-time—united around their common interests in a working community where academic freedom and faculty governance are everyday realities rather than lofty principles evoked in rhetoric and reserved for an endangered minority. I am willing to speculate that at some level the NYU president actually shares this vision. Sports fans among us will remember that in 2000, when it was New York versus New York—the Mets versus the Yankees at Shea Stadium for the World Series—it was the gray team that won the day.

Notes

Unless otherwise noted, all websites were last accessed on March 5, 2007.

1. The *Contingent Faculty Index*, prepared by AAUP Research Director John W. Curtis, is available online at http://www.aaup.org/AAUP/pubsres/research/conind2006.htm. It is important to note that the definition of "contingent" used in the report is particular to academe, where the tradition of tenure makes all faculty who are not on the tenure track contingent, regardless of the duration of their employment with the university. Outside academe, contracts that are renewed on a triennial basis (as is the case of many contingent faculty at New York University) would not be considered contingent. For discussions of the definition of contingent labor, see Anne E. Polivka and Thomas Nardone, "On the Definition of 'Contingent Work,'" *Monthly Labor Review* 112, no. 12 (December 1989), available online at http://www.bls.gov/opub/mlr/1989/12/art2exc.htm; Steven Hipple, "Contingent Work: Results from the Second Survey," *Monthly Labor Review* 121, no. 11 (November 1998), available online at http://www.bls.gov/opub/mlr/1998/11/art2exc.htm.

2. For example, the Coalition of Contingent Academic Labor began holding annual conferences in 1999.

3. Karen W. Arenson, "Professors Teaching? NYU President Says It Isn't Such a Novel Idea," *New York Times,* September 3, 2003, B1; idem, "Two Unions Vie to Represent NYU Adjuncts," *New York Times,* May 27, 2002, B3 (Lexis-Nexis). My perspective on these developments has been firsthand as I served as an adjunct faculty member at NYU in 1989–1999, participated in the early stages of the adjunct faculty's unionization campaign, and then joined the NYU faculty on a temporary full-time basis as an assistant professor/faculty fellow in a three-year post-doctoral appointment from 2002 to 2005.

4. In his September 2002 installation address, Sexton called for the emergence of what he called the "enterprise university" that would face the challenges of rapid technological and political change—or what he called "hyperchange." Enterprise was foregrounded, and commonality was absent. Although the word "enterprise" appears fifteen times in the address, the words "common" and "commons" are nowhere to be found. Yet in March 2003, in the policy paper "The Role of Faculty in the Common Enterprise University," he refers to his installation address as the beginning of his formulation of the "common enterprise" university rather than simply as a formulation of the enterprise university. Both the inaugural address and the policy paper are available online, respectively, at http://www.nyu.edu/about/sexton-install.html and http://www.nyu.edu/president/faculty.enterprise.

5. Cristina Silva, "From Brooklyn to Bobst: John Sexton Revealed," *Washington Square News,* vol. 30, no. 99, May 2, 2002, 3, available online at http://media.www.nyunews.com/media/storage/paper869/news/1997/01/01/UndefinedSection/From-Brooklyn.To.Bobst.0151.John.Sexton.Revealed-2393654.shtml.

6. John E. Sexton, "Managing Austerity while Seizing Opportunities: A Report to the NYU Community," available online at http://www.nyu.edu/about/sexton-enterpriseupdate.html.

7. The *Yeshiva* decision was a 1980 determination by the Supreme Court in the case of the *National Labor Relations Board v. Yeshiva University.* The court ruled that full-time faculty are management and therefore not eligible to organize a union under the provisions of the National Labor Relations Act. For a detailed discussion of the implications of the *Yeshiva* decision, see Ellen Willis, "The Post-*Yeshiva* Paradox: Faculty Organizing at NYU," *Social Text* 20, no. 1 (Spring 2002): 11–25.

8. John E. Sexton's "The Role of the Faculty in the Common Enterprise University" was presented to the Trustees' Council on the Future of New York University for consideration at the June 12, 2003, meeting and is available online at http://www.nyu.edu/president/faculty.enterprise/faculty-enterprise.pdf.

9. One opportunity hire was recently provided with a penthouse apartment at the Pierre Hotel: Jacob Gershman, "NYU Professor Enjoys Peak Perk: An Apartment at the Pierre," *New York Sun,* August 25, 2005, available online at http://www.nysun.com/article/19144.

10. Sexton, "Role of Faculty," 28; idem, "The Common Enterprise University and the Teaching Mission," available online at http://www.nyu.edu/about/sexton-teachingmission04.html.

11. Sexton, "Common Enterprise University," n.p.

12. Ibid.

13. The 70 percent figure for the percentage of courses taught by adjunct faculty is from Arenson, "Professors Teaching?" while the 72 percent figure for the total number of contingent faculty is from AAUP, *Contingent Faculty Index, 2006.*

14. David L. Kirp, *Shakespeare, Einstein, and the Bottom Line: The Marketing of Higher Education* (Cambridge, Mass.: Harvard University Press, 2003) 85; idem, "How Much for That Professor?" *New York Times,* October 27, 2003, A21.

15. Another missive, the March 2003 "Managing Austerity and Seizing Opportunities," was designed to prepare the faculty for their individual financial sacrifices in a putative time of austerity. "Managing Austerity and Seizing Opportunities" is available online at http://www.nyu.edu/about/sexton-enterpriseupdate.html.

16. Thomas D. Snyder et al., *Digest of Education Statistics, 2005,* NCES 2006030, U.S. Department of Education, Washington, D.C., June 2006, available online at http://www.nces.ed.gov/ipeds (accessed October 14, 2007).

17. Traditionally women have been over-represented in the ranks of non–tenure-track full-time faculty and under-represented among the tenured and tenure-track full-timers. According to data available on the website of NYU's Office of Institutional Research and Program Evaluation, in 2002–2003 women accounted for 52.17 percent of all non–tenure-track full-time faculty appointments, while they represented only 33.12 percent of tenured and tenurable faculty members. Interestingly, by 2005–2006, the gender ratio of non–tenure-track full-timers had shifted quite remarkably, with women accounting for only 46.51 percent of this group. It seems plausible that, as this group is being expanded at NYU, and as the administration wants to provide greater credibility and status for this group, more men than women are being retained in these jobs.

18. See, e.g., Hannah Arendt, *The Human Condition* (Chicago: University of Chicago Press, 1958), 80*f.*

19. Although these sites have sometimes been misarticulated as private and public spheres (as Arlie Russell Hochschild and others have pointed out), the separate spheres of intimate and commercial realms were sites of contradictory values that operated as complementary, mutually reinforcing domains: Arlie Russell Hochschild, "The Commercial Spirit of Intimate Life and the Abduction of Feminism: Signs from Women's Advice Books," *Theory, Culture and Society* 11, no. 2 (1994): 1–24, republished in idem, *The Commercialization of Intimate Life: Notes from Home and Work* (Berkeley: University of California Press, 2003). See also Susan Gal, "A Semiotics of the Public/Private Distinction," *Differences* 13, no. 1 (2002); Linda K. Kerber, "Separate Spheres, Female Worlds, Woman's Place: The Rhetoric of Women's History," *Journal of American History* 75, no. 1 (1988); Joan W. Scott, "Comment: Conceptualizing Gender in American Business History," *Business History Review* 72,

no. 2 (1998). Similar to the Romantic ethic described by the sociologist Colin Campbell as operating in tandem with the Protestant ethic, or the anti-modernism that the historian T. Jackson Lears describes as functioning in reassuring counterpoint to the emergence of modernism, the intimate and commercial spheres allowed mutually contradictory values to operate with a minimum of conflict: Colin Campbell, *The Romantic Ethic and the Spirit of Modern Consumerism* (Cambridge, Mass.: Blackwell, 1987), 219; T. Jackson Lears, *No Place of Grace: Antimodernism and the Transformation of American Culture 1880–1920* (New York: Pantheon, 1981).

20. Duncan Waite, Susan Field Waite, and Sharon Fillion, "Duplicity, Democracy and Domesticity: Educational Leadership for Democratic Action," in *The Practical Critical Educator: Critical Inquiry and Educational Practice,* ed. Karyn Cooper and Robert White (Dordrecht: Springer, 2), 137–150.

21. See, for example, Micki McGee, "Hooked on Higher Education and Other Tales from Adjunct Faculty Organizing," *Social Text* 20, no. 1 (Spring 2002): 61–80.

22. The AAUP's figures show tenure-track and tenured faculty appointments nationwide declining from 56.8 percent of faculty appointments in 1975 to 35.1 percent in 2003, falling 21.7 percent in twenty-eight years, or at an average rate of slightly less than 1 percent (.76 percent) each year. NYU's rate of conversation, at slightly more than 1 percent each year, means that NYU will be leading the trend.

23. The ACT-UAW Local 7902 contract with NYU through 2009–2010 is available online at http://www.actuaw.org/contracts.html.

24. Technically, the assistant professor/faculty fellow appointments confound the categories as they are neither non–tenure track nor tenurable. As with other postdoctoral research and teaching appointments, these positions are not counted in the AAUP's *Contingent Faculty Index*; thus, the number of faculty who are, for all intents and purposes, off the tenure track at NYU is actually higher than what is reported in the *Index*.

Part II
GSOC Strike

Unions at NYU, 1971–2007

> *The first NYU building went up in 1835, and looked more like a gothic church than a university building. Prisoners from Sing-Sing Prison in Ossining, New York, quarried the marble without any pay, but unionized stonecutters organized against the practice, which was getting more and more common. In 1834, they rioted in front of one of the contractor's buildings at 160 Broadway, causing $2,000 in damages and the intervention of the New York State National Guard. This was the first labor riot in New York State history and foreshadowed NYU's turbulent relations with its unions.*
>
> —BRUCE KAYTON, *Radical Walking Tours of New York City*
> (New York: Seven Stories Press, 1999), 26–27

1971

Local 810 of the International Brotherhood of Teamsters, representing NYU's engineers and skilled maintenance workers, strike to protest the administration's refusal to meet their salary demands.

The strike lasts three months, the longest job action at NYU until the GSOC strike.

1972

Clerical workers at NYU's Washington Square campus begin a union drive, with the help of District 65 of the Distributive Workers of America.

During the National Labor Relations Board (NLRB) hearings to determine which workers are eligible to vote in an election for union representation, NYU argues that workers at the University Heights campus, in the Bronx, should also be included. The NLRB rules in NYU's favor. Isolated from the union campaign and subjected to anti-union messages from NYU leading to the election, University Heights workers largely vote no, providing the margin to defeat the organizing drive. Shortly after the election, NYU reveals plans to sell off its University Heights facilities and consolidate its campus at Washington Square.

(NYU Archives)

1973 and 1976

NYU faculty conduct union drives through the AAUP.

University President James Hester vigorously opposes unionization. Anti-union faculty, organized into the Committee for No Representation, support the administration's position. The vote fails both times.

According to Hester, an attorney who worked for NYU to oppose unionization later became the chief litigator in the *Yeshiva* case, which in 1980 put an end to faculty organizing in private universities. In effect, the *Yeshiva* case was modeled on the earlier argument of the NYU administration for the managerial status of full-time faculty.

1979

Clerical workers at NYU attempt to unionize again, this time affiliating with the American Federation of Teachers.

The *Washington Square News,* NYU's student newspaper, discloses that "Friends of NYU," nominally a group of anti-union employees, is actually a front for administrators' anti-union campaign. The scandal sparks support for the union, soon recognized as AFT Local 3882.

1988

UCATS-AFT Local 3882, the union for clerical and technical staff at NYU, strikes for an agency shop. The strike lasts three weeks and ends with UCATS still an open shop.

1997

NYU graduate assistants form the Graduate Student Organizing Committee (GSOC) and affiliate with the United Automobile Workers (UAW).

1998

GSOC/UAW signs up a majority of eligible graduate students in support of union representation.

1999

GSOC/UAW asks NYU for legal recognition of the union. NYU refuses, and the union files a petition with the NLRB seeking election for union representation.

The NLRB holds hearings to determine whether graduate assistants at NYU are employees entitled to collective-bargaining rights.

NYU Professor Joel Westheimer is denied tenure after testifying in support of GSOC at the NLRB hearings.

During a subsequent NLRB hearing for Westheimer's unfair labor practice suit filed against NYU, an e-mail from NYU Dean Anne Marcus, who overturned the unanimous recommendation to grant Westheimer tenure, is submitted as evidence. In the e-mail, Marcus refers to adjunct hiring policy this way: "We need people we can abuse, exploit and then turn loose."

2000

April 3

The NLRB rules that NYU graduate assistants are both students and employees, free to form a union. NYU appeals.

April 25–27

NYU graduate students vote on whether to be represented by the UAW. The NLRB seals the ballot boxes, pending adjudication of NYU's appeal.

October 31

UCATS-AFT 3882 ratifies a five-year contract, for the first time with agency fees rather than an open shop.

(Scott Sommer)

The prospect of a joint GSOC–UCATS job action helps lead to union security for UCATS, twelve years after striking unsuccessfully for it and following subsequent actions during the 1990s.

November 1

The NLRB dismisses NYU's appeal, reaffirming employee status for graduate assistants. The impounded ballots are counted. GSOC/UAW wins. NYU is put under legal obligation to bargain with GSOC/UAW.

November 2000–February 2001

NYU delays bargaining, threatening to take its case through the federal court system. Nearly three thousand undergraduates and two hundred faculty members protest in support of GSOC.

2001

March 1

Hours before a scheduled strike-authorization vote, NYU and the union sign a letter of agreement, under which NYU recognizes the union and agrees to bargain.

2002

January 28

GSOC/UAW ratifies the first union contract covering graduate-student employees at a private university. Its provisions are retroactive to the beginning of the 2001–2002 academic year.

(UAW Region 9A)

Adjunct professors at NYU and the New School form Adjuncts Come Together and begin a union drive. GSOC's unprecedented contract, the first for graduate employees at a private university, is recognized as a catalyst for the ACT campaign.

2004

May 20

The NYU chapter of ACT-UAW Local 7902 ratifies its first contract, in effect through the 2009–2010 academic year.

After twenty months of negotiations, the union calls for a strike vote. A tentative bargaining agreement is reached between the union's bargaining committee and university negotiators at dawn on April 21, hours before the strike deadline.

July 13

The NLRB rules that the primary relationship between graduate teachers and researchers and Brown University is "primarily" educative, not economic. *Brown* is written broadly enough to overturn *NYU.* The dissent in *Brown* points to GSOC, with one year remaining on its contact, as in jeopardy after the decision. NYU administrators refuse to address whether they will continue to recognize GSOC when the contract expires.

2005

April 21

GSOC presents a petition to the NYU administration demanding negotiations and signed by a large majority of its bargaining unit.

City Council President Christine Quinn (then council member for NYU's district) and Reverend Jesse Jackson address an assembled crowd of hundreds and demand to meet with administrators. They are denied access to Bobst Library, home to the university president's and provost's offices. Instead, university Vice President Jacob Lew accepts the petition from Quinn, Jackson, and members of GSOC's bargaining committee in the library's foyer.

June 16

NYU administration announces its intention not to negotiate a second contract with GSOC and opens a thirty-day period for notice and comment on this decision.

July 12

A Town Hall meeting is held by NYU as part of the notice and comment period.

August 2

The NYU administration sends a contract proposal to GSOC/UAW, giving the union forty-eight hours to take it or leave it.

August 4

GSOC/UAW requests a face-to-face meeting to negotiate elements of the second contract.

August 5

NYU administration announces its final decision not to negotiate with union. UAW officials are notified by telephone, while a press release is issued and a mass memo is sent to all NYU e-mail accounts.

August 31

GSOC's first contract expires. GSOC/UAW holds a rally that includes a peaceful act of civil disobedience outside the Bobst Library. Seventy-six protesters are arrested, including AFL-CIO President John Sweeney.

October 24–28

GSOC members vote to authorize a strike by an 85 percent majority.

November 1

UCATS-AFT Local 3882 ratifies a new contract after uncharacteristically swift and amicable negotiations.

November 9

First day of the strike.

November 28

University President Sexton announces in an e-mail to all graduate students a December 5 deadline to return to work, after which strikers face firing from their jobs for the next three semesters and the salary for that work.

(Stephen Rechner)

These punitive measures would be illegal if the graduate students were still recognized as workers by the NLRB (which prevents the intimidation of striking workers as well as retaliation for past union participation).

November 30

Graduate/Undergraduate Solidarity (GUS) Day of Action. GUS and GSOC members storm the Bobst Library and march on the president's office, demanding recognition for GSOC and for negotiations to begin immediately.

December 2

The renowned academic Judith Butler launches an online petition in support of striking NYU graduate students and condemning the administration's threats. The petition will soon collect more than seven thousand signatures from scholars worldwide.

December 5

The strike continues. An open letter signed by more than one hundred international GSOC members is submitted to President Sexton, condemning his threats for their impact on non-citizens in particular, and proclaiming that international students on both sides of the picket line support the union.

Faculty Democracy holds a mock funeral procession from the arch in Washington Square Park to the Bobst Library, following a coffin containing "Faculty Voice at NYU."

2006

January–February

Twenty strikers are fired in waves.

April 27

The American Arbitration Association certifies majority support for GSOC among eligible members. Fifty-seven members and supporters are arrested in an act of peaceful civil disobedience.

May

The spring semester ends, and GSOC ends the strike.

November

Elections are held for a House of Delegates, a new graduate-student group promoted by administrators to replace the union. Candidates run for forty-seven of a proposed fifty-three seats. Candidates running on a pro-union GSOC ticket win thirty-seven seats, including all twenty-six in the Graduate School of Arts and Sciences, the largest pool of graduate-student employees.

2007

January 31

A grievance by twenty teaching assistants fired for striking is denied a full year after it is filed. An appeal is pending.

February

The AFL-CIO and UAW submit a complaint to the International Labor Organization of the United Nations, encouraging that body to censure the U.S. federal government for its NLRB ruling in *Brown.*

The complaint highlights NYU as an example of how private universities in the United States are denying workers the basic right to form a union, in clear violation of international law.

Note

The editors thank the following people for help in compiling this timeline: GSOC members and alumni Emily Wilbourne, Kitty Krupat, Laura Tanenbaum, and Patrick McCreery; Bob Lesko, vice president of UCATS-AFT 3882; Steve Rechner, president of UCATS; Joel Schlemowitz, president of ACT-UAW 7902; and Cate Fallon, recording secretary of ACT-UAW.

The Administration Strikes Back

Union Busting at NYU

Susan Valentine

To write about the 2005–2006 GSOC strike is to offer a story *in medias res,* the second episode in a trilogy whose finale is unwritten. The first part of this epic saga has been documented by those who were involved on the ground as well as some who watched from afar, measuring the campaign's impact and implications for the future of the academic workplace.[1] A 2004 article, "Star Wars," chronicles NYU's transformation from commuter school to "number-one dream school," accomplished by attracting big-name faculty who add to NYU's reputation through the remaking of departments and running of institutes while leaving the teaching of undergraduates to untenured junior faculty, adjuncts, and graduate students.[2] That article ends on a hopeful note, viewing successful union campaigns by GSOC/UAW Local 2110 and ACT-UAW Local 7902, and the resurrection of NYU's chapter of the AAUP, as opening salvos to mitigate the worst effects of academic labor's increasing casualization at this university.

But that new hope was to be short-lived. Initial victories at NYU have given way to intense struggles simply to retain what was won. Even after the National Labor Relations Board ruled unanimously in October 2000 that graduate assistants at private institutions had a right to form unions, NYU's administration balked at recognizing GSOC/UAW and was compelled to the bargaining table only by the threat of a strike.[3] Nearly four years later, in the summer of 2004, an NLRB now dominated by George W. Bush's appointees overturned the precedent of NYU in a review brought by Brown University, splitting along partisan lines.[4] The NYU administration, leading up to and during the GSOC strike of 2005–2006, embraced this regressive ruling to intensify its control over NYU's academic labor force. This chapter presents an analysis of its tactics and a narrative of its campaign as it has unfolded since *Brown*. Classic techniques such as interference from supervisors (faculty, in this case) and the threat—and fulfillment—of firings come into play, but the most powerful weapons that the university employed were delay, deflection, and disinformation.

The academic year is both short and shifting, its rhythms requiring students and teachers alike to think in increments of weeks and semesters. NYU administrators, by contrast, consider fundraising, hiring, and development projects in terms of years and decades. At NYU, the decision to break the union from the safety of the post–*Brown* legal climate was likely made in a handful of high-level meetings of the "University Leadership Team (ULT)," presided over by John Sexton, a former law professor hand picked by the Board of Trustees in 2001 as NYU's next president.[5] The trustees themselves—or the handful of the most powerful trustee-donors—were likely consulted, along with costly advisers on public-relations and legal issues. The ULT had thirteen months between *Brown* and the expiration of GSOC's first contract to develop and roll out its plan to withdraw recognition of the union. This year of "deliberations" over whether to negotiate with GSOC, and the two months between the threats of teaching assistants being fired and their execution, are units of time that comfortably fit their long-term plans, but for those subject to the academic year, even a few weeks of uncertainty can feel like a lifetime.

Methods of deflection aided administrators' ability to sustain long periods of delay. For example, shortly after *Brown* the provost asked two governing bodies—the Faculty Advisory Committee on Academic Priorities and a joint committee composed of the Senate Academic Affairs Committee and the Senate Executive Committee—to consider the issue and report back at the end of academic year 2004–2005. The ULT would make the final decision based on this and other "input." This process had the guise of legitimacy and consultation, although it is no leap to assume that the ULT already had its plan, while "consultation" with these governing bodies offered a patina of campus dialogue. GSOC leaders begged for a hearing with both groups (one relented, one refused), after learning that NYU's human-resources boss, Terry Nolan, had made presentations to each. Furthermore, these groups absorbed a lot of the anger from GSOC members, faculty, and the outlying community while sowing confusion about who actually had control over the final decision.[6]

Disinformation, however, was the favored feature of the ULT campaign. Facts were distorted to characterize grievances over equal pay for equal work as "interference in academic affairs" and to make grads' own fight for self-determination into meddling by "Auto Workers."[7] Figures were distorted to make grads' economic situation appear like middle-class comfort, to make the numbers of people at a rally or on strike at a given time appear small, or to minimize the disruption we were causing on campus. Another, more subtle method of disinformation was the university's strategy of dissociating the gains of the contract from the collective-bargaining process that had secured them. Hoping to exploit institutional memory gaps, Sexton repeatedly assured graduates in public forums that they could trust the administration to preserve "competitive financial-aid packages." This phrase mystified where those "packages" came from: a year of contract negotiations after five years of organizing. As a result of the contract—and the organizing—pay rose an average of 40 percent and more than doubled in some departments.[8] Sexton and the ULT re-termed the money received by graduates "financial aid," articulating the money to student status rather than teaching and other labor. Further, terming this money "financial aid" created another history for the "competitive" amounts—one that NYU was invested in giving graduates to attract the most competitive candidates instead of hard-won rises in pay that NYU had fought back on and would not have increased if the union had not pressured it to do so.[9]

Benefiting from the August 31, 2005, expiration of our contract, the ULT planned to delay a final decision until that summer, betting that the gestures at community input and deliberation would placate the community who returned that fall to a *fait accompli*. By May, the two internal governance bodies charged with considering the decision recommended against negotiations.[10] Responding to NYU's continued references to the union's "interference in academic affairs," UAW officials decided to call the administration's bluff.[11] At a May 26 meeting, the UAW offered to drop all current grievances and accept new contract language that NYU preferred concerning academic management rights if NYU would sit down and bargain. Members of the ULT who were present said that they would consider this offer and made no comments to the university community, to GSOC, or to other UAW representatives for nearly a month.

Finally, on June 16, the ULT broke its silence in a memorandum regarding its "proposed decision" not to negotiate with GSOC/UAW. The memo, from Executive Vice President Jacob Lew and Provost David McLaughlin, explained that the university had always embraced the view stated in *Brown*, placed "reservations" about the impact of grad unionization in the mouths of an unspecified "many in the community," and returned again to those grievances, which they termed a "failure of the union to abide by the original commitment" and which they had determined could not be remedied by new contract language.[12] Lew and McLaughlin asserted the university's desire "to build on the positive impact of unionization," continuing their strategy to disentangle the gains of the first contract from the mechanism by which they were secured. The memo also announced a thirty-day "notice and comment" period and provided an e-mail address in addition to a Town Hall on the matter to be hosted by John Sexton on July 12. The constant pressure from GSOC for discussion had finally resulted in an open forum, but just four days before the decision was to be finalized.

July 12 is about as close to the dead of summer as one can get at a university campus, but GSOC members and supporters from all quarters of NYU turned out in full force, filling a large auditorium.[13] While other members of the ULT and the university's government- and media-relations teams hovered in the balcony or in the side aisles, Sexton stood center-stage with a hand-held microphone. When he indicated two microphones in the aisles, around fifty people lined up to speak. All but a few urged him to reconsider. It was clear from Sexton's tone at the event that he was unprepared for the amount of resistance to the ULT's decision. Despite his insistence at the outset that he was there to listen, not to respond, he quickly became angry and urged the crowd to cease talking about whether NYU should negotiate a new contract and instead focus on the suggested "alternatives" outlined in the June 16 memo.

Rather than announce the final decision after the end of the notice-and-comment period in late July, as promised, the ULT crafted a take-it-or-leave-it "offer" that it sent to UAW executives in Detroit, offering to let the UAW "represent" the unit if it accepted a set financial package as laid out in the letter, as well as two "poison pills"—no third-party arbitration and an open shop.[14] If the UAW could neither support us in negotiations—of which there were to be none—nor in any challenges to the contract through arbitration, exactly what representation would they be doing? The insistence on an open shop seemed a ploy to suggest that the UAW was more interested in GSOC members' paltry dues than our welfare. But an open shop would also ensure that if we were foolish enough to take this "offer," we would have much less ability to organize a resistance to NYU's next attempt to refuse negotiations. The UAW asked again to sit down at the table and negotiate a real agreement, but NYU refused.[15] The next day, Lew and McLaughlin again addressed the university community via e-mail to announce that "the University will not negotiate a new contract with the UAW and that we will implement the financial aid benefits and other proposals" as described in the June 16 memo.[16]

Once the semester began (and after a rally for negotiations that attracted more than a thousand protesters and featured the arrest of AFL-CIO President John Sweeney and seventy-five others for peaceful civil disobedience), the administration increased their efforts to undermine the union. Supportive faculty let GSOC activists know about oblique references to "consequences" that might befall any grads who participated in a labor action, messages from the administration disseminated through meetings of department chairs and directors of graduate studies. While this intimidation had to suffice in the majority of departments, where faculty were uncomfortable with NYU's tactics, if not outright supportive of grads' right to fight back, in the few departments where NYU's administration identified faculty allies, more direct threats ensued. Some directors of graduate studies sent e-mails to their whole departments, highlighting the support of the faculty for the administration's decision and warning against participation in any labor action. Some faculty told their advisees, teaching assistants, and research assistants about their anti-union position and explicitly warned that participation in a strike would harm their academic relationships. In October, as GSOC began gearing up for a strike vote, an e-mail to all students and a letter to parents worked to activate class prejudices about "Auto Workers," to spread misleading information about grads' economic conditions and predict failure, and to discourage potential supporters and intimidate the graduate assistants.[17] In the meantime, GSOC worked with Faculty Democracy, a group formed in response to the erosion of faculty governance at NYU, to secure agreements from faculty to remain neutral and refuse to act against graduate assistants.[18]

On October 24, the day GSOC's strike vote began, graduate assistants in the Graduate School of Arts and Sciences, by far the largest pool of teaching assistants and research assistants, received an e-mail from Dean Stimpson.[19] While none of the previous missives from the ULT had been addressed to us—the graduate assistants considering whether or not to strike—this was a personal plea asking us to vote "no." The "open letter" began with a dictionary definition of "responsible: 1. liable to be called to account (to a person or for a thing). 2. morally accountable for one's actions; capable of rational conduct." Though it prompted mocking responses among many grads, who were shocked to see a respected scholar and member of NYU's English Department employing a literary technique most often seen in high-school essays, the import of the letter was serious, including both a plea to a higher moral obligation and a threat:

> Graduate assistants or faculty, we are teachers, morally accountable for being with our students in their classrooms and laboratories. A vote for our accountability as teachers must trump a strike vote and a strike. If we are irresponsible, we are liable to be called to account.

Despite, or perhaps because of, this rhetoric, there was a strong turnout for the strike authorization vote, with 85 percent voting yes. The university's tactics had made many angry, but they had also begun to instill fear, especially in departments in which our organizers had not managed one-on-one conversations about our situation. For graduate assistants for whom contact with the union was composed mainly of e-mails, GSOC's was just one voice in the midst of a cacophony from the administration. In cases in which departmental faculty was adding a negative or threatening voice, the sheer weight and power of the anti-union rhetoric meant even committed union supporters were hesitant to strike.

Despite a crowd of more than a thousand, and an empty main building on the first day of the strike, NYU's spokesman John Beckman called disruption "minimal" and suggested that grads taught only 165 out of 2,700 classes at NYU on a given day, marshaling meaningless numbers to misrepresent our strength.[20] One hundred sixty-five seems to refer to the number of classes on a given day in which grads are the sole instructor of record, such as language courses and intro level classes in other disciplines. Yet Beckman knew well that graduate assistants were responsible for recitation sections and grading in hundreds more courses and for performing research or administrative work for departments, colloquia, or institutes. As part of a long-term strategy, however, this tactic would pay off: Although our members recognized these attempts at disinformation for what they were—especially early on, when energy was high—the lies could easily become reality for undergrads or faculty who were not paying close attention or for our members who did not come to the picket line for a week because of travel or illness.

The ULT's threats and disinformation and the pressure on faculty supervisors to warn or threaten were creating discomfort in the NYU community, but the next move would prove more disturbing. When faculty discovered on the first day of the strike that university administrators had been added as observers to their virtual classrooms on the Blackboard website, many faculty, at NYU and elsewhere, saw this action as flat-out spying and an unforgivable blow to the core of academic freedom.[21]

Unlike "Blackboardgate," the ULT's next move received little attention, yet it would prove decisive in breaking the strike. The administration could successfully ignore professors who grudgingly had to do their own grading or work without a research assistant, or undergrads who were not receiving help with papers or the explication of a lecture. The courses in which graduate assistants are the sole instructors—those 165 each day, at John Beckman's count—were another story. Courses in the language and literature departments and the Expository Writing Program led by teaching assistants make up a majority of these. Here is where NYU was hardest hit; here is where teaching assistants have strong claims against the "mentorship" rhetoric of *Brown*;[22] here is where they would have to break the strike.

On November 16, a memo to department chairs from deans Catharine Stimpson, Richard Foley, and Matthew Santirocco announced a "policy change" in language and literature departments.[23] The memo was not circulated broadly and included no reference to the now weeklong strike. The three deans had heard "concerns that the amount and kinds of teaching that graduate students do" in these courses "interferes with their academic progress and the goal of their teaching being an occasion for their development as teachers," and thus would reduce the workload from two courses per semester to one, beginning in spring 2006. The new policy appeared to be a belated attempt to render these jobs more apprentice-like and, perhaps, like a bribe to reassure these graduate assistants of the administration's goodwill. Not explicitly stated in the memo, however, was the directive to give the graduate assistants who had been teaching two courses in the fall a "free" semester in the spring, in which NYU would pay roughly the same without demanding teaching in return. This seemed to be the carrot before the stick, but it would prove to be both at once.

We expected the other shoe to drop on November 23, the Wednesday before Thanksgiving. When it had not, many of us welcomed the holiday, exhausted from picketing and the intense pressure of the campaign. Returning the next Monday, we heard it drop loud and clear. Buried in a three-thousand–word e-mail missive from President Sexton were the "consequences": We would not lose our pay for the three weeks that we had been on strike, as we might expect. Instead, we would be fired for all of next semester if we did not return to work in the next week.[24] The e-mail included a threat of firing for the following fall, too, if we dared come back now and strike again in the spring. As more than five thousand academics from around the world would quickly affirm through an Internet sign-on letter, this ultimatum was not simply punishment for our three-week absence from our work. It was retaliation and coercion.[25]

The threat of losing our livelihoods for up to one year had an immediately chilling effect, just as intended. But the ULT had played its trump card awfully early. If we could hold out past this, what else could they do? It behooved them to scare us but not to harm us. The potential for backlash was just too great, and firing each and every one of us who was on strike would be a logistical nightmare.

The picket line was already in a panic, however, and our first membership meeting that week demonstrated that the ULT had successfully deflected pressure back onto the union, as the fears of hundreds of people resulted in mistrust in every direction. At meetings later that week, however, many agreed with the organizing committee's assessment that we should call NYU's bluff. To discover who was on strike and who was not would be nearly impossible for the administration, as would forcing departments to deny those workers spring appointments, especially in light of faculty neutrality agreements and relative autonomy in hiring. The deluge of letters attacking NYU for these outsize penalties provided additional resolve. But the Faculty of Arts and Science "policy change" and a new bit of deflection by the ULT would serve to compound our troubles.

The teaching assistants who were teaching stand-alone courses in the affected departments faced a terrible dilemma: return to work and enjoy a spring semester free of teaching, with time to devote to neglected dissertations, or stay on strike and lose their pay when they were preemptively replaced. As ads seeking temporary "instructors" to teach three courses of Italian per semester appeared in the *Chronicle of Higher Education,* we realized that NYU was hiring replacement workers without scrutiny while convincing our members that their sacrifice would be meaningless. As many of the teaching assistants in language courses are international students whose visa status disallows them from working outside the university yet demands that they prove adequate financial support to live here, we could do nothing as loyal union supporters returned, reluctantly and tearfully, to work.

Despite assurances from the university that no one's visa status would be at risk, many international students felt too vulnerable, with the Bush administration's stance on immigration, to remain on strike. Others took the risk, and about one hundred international students wrote a letter to the university asserting their continued commitment to the cause of unionization and their disappointment in NYU's actions, regardless of whether they remained on strike.[26]

In the face of all of this pressure, hundreds of grads prepared to remain on strike past the December 5 deadline. Knowing that this was likely, the ULT took advantage of a new opportunity for delay and deflection. At 4 P.M. on Sunday, December 4, as we were planning picketing and fielding phone calls from the press about our plans for the next day, an e-mail from Brian Levine and Rodney Washington of the Graduate Affairs Committee appeared via NYU Direct, the e-mail system restricted to administrators.[27] They asked that the university extend the deadline until Wednesday to let both parties consider a proposal from the Graduate Affairs Committee, a "compromise" solution resembling a more fully formed version of plans to build on the "positive elements of unionization" from the ULT's July 16 memo. The Graduate Affairs Committee had never contacted GSOC and must have had the administration's approval or it would not have been able to use NYU Direct. The intended target of the e-mail could only be the NYU community. A few hours later, Sexton and McLaughlin agreed via NYU Direct, switching the new "deadline" to December 7.

Some undergrads, unclear about the relationship of the Graduate Affairs Committee to the striking graduate assistants, thought that we had called off the strike. The massive show of resolve planned for Monday's picket line, ripe for media coverage, was suddenly undercut as reporters called asking whether Wednesday was now the "new deadline." Our members had two more days to face their fears before they got over the hurdle of staring down the university. Members of the community who were already afraid for the graduate assistants started to consider whether a "third way" was a possibility.

By Wednesday, a group of faculty had adapted Washington and Levine's proposal and presented their refined version of a company union to the community via NYU Direct and introduced a resolution in a Faculty of Arts and Science meeting that called for an end to the strike and the removal of the threats. Faculty met with their union-supporting graduate students to sell them on the idea— openly in some departments and privately in others—prompting fissures where union support had run high.

The administration once again grew quiet, deflecting the pressure that we had so carefully built against it everywhere else. Publicly, it returned to minimizing the disruption that we were causing and directed press attention toward these proposals as the reason they hesitated to act on their outsize threats. Privately, they encouraged more concerned faculty, who were worried about their graduate students and about the labor of their departments come spring, to try and broker "compromises," all of which traded our union, which we had gone on strike to fight for, for the booby prize of no firings and some variation on a company union, bringing us no further than where we had started. Teaching assistants faced down their department chairs, their advisers, and respected scholars in their fields as these professors pushed one "deal" or another. Some graduate assistants had gone back to work before the deadline; some trickled back as the semester wound down. Hundreds remained on strike, But NYU's leaders again bet that they could fulfill their own prophecy. On December 7, NYU's spokesman Josh Taylor had told the *Washington Square News* that three-quarters of teaching assistants were back at work, perhaps the most egregious piece of disinformation of the whole campaign—at least in public statements—but by the end of the break, it was probably true.[28]

Winter break provided a welcome reprieve, but it also meant we were away from the mutual support that had kept us strong in the face of so much pressure. Members received e-mails—some innocent, some less so—from the professors to whom they were assigned in the spring, asking if they would be working, communications that would be illegal under the NLRA. A dean called for a meeting of all of the graduate assistants in her school, another instance of management interference. Teaching assistants were moved off of teaching rosters and into fellowship semesters against their will, for their protection. Organizers had little energy to work the phones and urge people to strike in the spring. Still, activists spent the beginning of January assessing the situation. About two hundred fifty people remained on strike.

Once we had begun the semester on strike, very few would return to work. Some sections were simply canceled by professors, preventing administrators from discovering whether their teaching assistants were striking. Although the administration maintained that disruption was minimal and the strike all but over, they followed through with their threats in a few cases, perhaps to scare a few more back to work or to prevent a resurgence later in the semester. In late January, a few stand-alone instructors received letters saying that they would be losing their spring pay. Clearly these were the easiest targets—if a few students reported that classes were not being met, the administration could act. Directors of graduate studies and undergraduate studies and department chairs were receiving e-mails phrased in the negative: "We have heard that So-and-So is not working. Please let us know if this is incorrect information." Other teaching assistants were not assigned spring jobs at all. Overall, twenty-three individuals lost their pay for the entire spring semester. If the firings were intended to scare others back to work, they had the opposite effect: My returning to work or GSOC's calling off the strike in February would not have restored my colleagues' salaries, as they had been fired for the whole semester. But the international outcry that had come when many were threatened did not return when just a few were harmed.

At a Town Hall Meeting on February 8 called by the Graduate Student Council, hundreds of GSOC members filled the room. Only three had been fired at this point, and one of these teaching assistants asked Provost McLaughlin why only three had been fired: Did he think there were only three people on strike? McLaughlin explained the policy: A report that a teaching assistant was not teaching began a process of investigation that could result in firing. If anyone in the room wanted to tell him that he or she was not working, he coolly stated, he would be happy to start the process.

We continued to pressure the administration by showing up at trustee meetings and public appearances by Sexton and other university leaders. When circumstances demanded, they reacted to our actions by painting us as a few misguided troublemakers, contrasting us with the majority who had returned to work, neglecting to mention the coercive actions that forced them there. The misrepresentation of our support reached absurd levels. Speaking at the United

Reporters from the NYU student newspaper were told that John
Sexton was away from campus on the "Day of Action," organized
by undergraduates to support the strike, but that morning a puppet NYU president encountered the real thing. (*Ben Janosch*/Washing-
ton Square News)

Nations to an audience that included about fifteen GSOC members, with more
demonstrating outside, Sexton reacted to our questions by explaining to the
assembled audience that the issue of graduate-student unionization at NYU had
been decided "democratically" and "the only people who disagree with that decision are in this room."

After spring break, we worked to counter these statements by once again
demonstrating majority support among NYU's graduate assistants. In just a few
weeks, GSOC organizers scoured the campus, collecting signatures for a petition
stating that, regardless of whether graduate assistants had returned to work or
stayed on strike, they still wanted a union contract. Before this petition drive was
public, another Town Hall with Sexton at the microphone demonstrated that the
ULT would simply switch rhetoric rather than respect the graduate assistants. He
told a room full of GSOC supporters that it did not matter if every graduate
assisant wanted a union contract. The issue had been decided.

On April 27, 2006, GSOC held a convention in which we unveiled our majority and gathered together, whether we had stayed on strike or gone back to work,
to say once again that the university leadership was busting our union against
our will. Fifty-seven people blocked traffic on Washington Square North and
took the trip to One Police Plaza in plastic handcuffs while hundreds more lined
both sides of the streets.[29]

Although our strike ended with the academic year, we are still struggling with the legacy of the university's anti-union campaign. Since the summer of 2006, we have grappled with what the university probably hoped would be the final piece of the campaign—replacing the union with an in-house body derived from that original GAC proposal, itself clearly an echo of the ULT's July 16 memo. In another instance of improbably coincident timing, the Graduate Affairs Committee released its final proposal to the *Washington Square News* on April 27, just as we were being released after the arrests.[30]

Understanding that the ULT would proceed with elections to this "House of Delegates" with or without the consent of the graduate assistants, GSOC members decided to run for seats on the body. Furthering the ULT's attempt to conflate wages for our labor with funding and financial aid, the Graduate Affairs Committee's proposal called for the conclusion of all "fully funded" graduate students, creating a membership about twice the size of the GSOC bargaining unit, meaning that in some cases whole departments that had not been in the union could both run and vote in the election. Despite these efforts at gerrymandering, GSOC candidates took thirty-seven of forty-seven seats in the December election.[31] As the democratically elected representatives of a majority of grads at NYU, we are continuing to fight for the rights and benefits of our members through this channel as we do through others.

Whether other universities will follow NYU's lead may depend on the outcome of the final episodes in this story. Whether it is another wave of labor action as part of a multifaceted campaign or a change in the political and legal landscapes or some combination of the two, a victory for GSOC will make it much harder for other private universities to follow the same playbook. Yale, Columbia, Brown, and the rest know this and have continued to pressure NYU, the "New Ivy," to stay strong. But the academic labor movement at NYU and elsewhere knows this also and is committed not just to regaining our rights here, but also to fighting back against larger trends in academe that we will continue to face as tomorrow's adjuncts, junior faculty, and even tenured faculty and as the colleagues of and mentors to future graduate students. The resistance at NYU is rebuilding, and eventually a final episode on the return of GSOC and collective bargaining for NYU's graduate-student employees will be written. The question is how long the fight will be and how bad the situation will get before that happens.

Notes

1. See, e.g., Kitty Krupat and Laura Tanenbaum, "A Network for Campus Democracy: Reflections on NYU and the Academic Labor Movement," *Social Text* 20, no. 1 (2002); Lisa Jessup, "The Campaign for Union Rights at NYU," in *Steal This University: The Rise of the Corporate University and the Academic Labor Movement,* ed. Benjamin Johnson, Patrick Cavanaugh, and Kevin Matteson (New York: Routledge, 2003).

2. Jonathan Van Antwerpen, "Star Wars: NYU," in *Shakespeare, Einstein and the Bottom Line: The Marketing of Higher Education,* ed. David Kirp (Cambridge, Mass.: Harvard University Press, 2004).

3. National Labor Relations Board, "New York University and International Union, United Automobile, Aerospace and Agricultural Implement Workers of America, AFL-CIO, Petitioner," case 2-RC-22082, October 31, 2000.

4. National Labor Relations Board, "Brown University and International Union, United Automobile, Aerospace and Agricultural Implement Workers of America, UAW AFL-CIO, Petitioner," case 1-RC-21368, July 13, 2004. The board's two Democrats wrote a vehement dissent, noting that the reversal was based not on new evidence but on a redefinition of the term "employee" to satisfy a policy decision, and that the reversal would disenfranchise a group of workers currently enjoying the benefits of a union contract. See also Steven Greenhouse and Karen W. Arenson, "Labor Board Says Graduate Students at Private Universities Have No Right to Unionize," *New York Times,* July 16, 2004.

5. During the union-busting campaign, key members of the ULT were vice presidents Cheryl Mills, Jack Lew, and Robert Berne, and Provost David McLaughlin. NYU announced the formation of Sexton's team when he became president: "The New University Leadership Team," NYU Today, November 19, 2002, available online at http://www.nyu.edu/nyutoday/archives/16/03/Stories/LeadershipTeam.html and http://www.nyu.edu/public.affairs/leadership (accessed September 17, 2007).

6. In late March 2005, Senior Vice President Cheryl Mills and Director of Labor Relations Terrence Nolan sent an e-mail claiming that, "ultimately, the University leadership will make a determination about whether to renegotiate with the UAW after listening to the thoughts, views, and recommendations of the community": Cheryl Mills and Terrence Nolan, "University Review Process Regarding Unionization of GA/TAs," March 31, 2005, available online at http://www.nyu.edu/provost/communications/ga/communications-033105.html (accessed September 17, 2007).

7. All of the official university communications on the issue remain on NYU's website in a section on the provost's pages titled "GA/TA issues," available online at http://www.nyu.edu/provost/communications/ga/ga.html (accessed September 17, 2007).

8. In response to the union drive, NYU announced that all entering Ph.D. candidates in the Graduate School of Arts and Science would receive MacCracken Fellowships, which governed not only the years in which students worked as graduate assistants but also awarded Ph.D. students fellowship years of funding at the same rate as assistantships, grouping both categories into "stipends." Other private universities, such as Columbia, raised their wages and funding to match, hoping to quell organizing drives on their campuses.

9. Private universities such as NYU have succeeded in some part in shaping a narrative that a competitive market, rather than academic labor organizing, has driven up wages for graduate assistants. See, e.g., Scott Jaschik, "Upping the Ante in Graduate Stipends," in *Inside Higher Ed,* February 8, 2007, available online at http://insidehighered.com/news/2007/02/08/chicago (accessed September 17, 2007).

10. "Recommendation from the Faculty Advisory Committee on Academic Priorities," April 26, 2005, and "Final Report from the Senate Academic Affairs Committee and the Senate Executive Committee," May 2, 2005, both available online at http://www.nyu.edu/provost/communications/ga/ga.html (accessed September 17, 2007).

11. Although future university communications would refer to this meeting and subsequent letters and calls between the two parties as "negotiations," this was not the case. The university had not decided whether to negotiate at this point and never agreed to sit down with GSOC's bargaining committee.

12. Available online at http://www.nyu.edu/provost/communications/ga/communications-061605.html (accessed September 17, 2007).

13. Audio recorded at the Town Hall meeting, along with a selective selection of e-mail comments received during the notice and comment period, is available online at http://

www.nyu.edu/provost/communications/ga/noticeandcomment.html (accessed September 17, 2007). See also Barbara Leonard, "Three Days before the Final Decision, Hundreds Rally for Grad Union," *Washington Square News,* July 15, 2005.

14. "Contract Proposal to the UAW," August 2, 2005, available online at http://www .nyu.edu/provost/communications/ga/ga.html (accessed September 17, 2007). The chair of NYU's Board of Trustees, Martin Lipton, is credited as the inventor of the "poison pill" as a defense to fend off mergers and acquisitions.

15. "Letter from UAW to NYU," August 4, 2005, available online at http://www.nyu .edu/provost/communications/ga/ga.html (accessed September 17, 2007).

16. Jacob Lew and David McLaughlin, "Final Decision regarding Our Graduate Assistants," August 5, 2005, available online at http://www.nyu.edu/provost/communications/ga/ communications-080505.html (accessed September 17, 2007).

17. "By now many of you are aware that the United Auto Workers is publicly discussing a job action involving graduate assistants . . . at NYU in the near future. In our opinion, the Auto Workers union is embarking on a regrettable and unfortunate course: regrettable because it fails to respect the significance of your efforts to pursue your education, and unfortunate because such an action will not result in recognition of the UAW to represent our graduate assistants": John Sexton and David McLaughlin, "Memo to Students from Sexton and McLaughlin," October 20, 2005, available online at http://www.nyu.edu/ provost/communications/ga/communications-102005.html (accessed September 17, 2007).

18. Faculty Democracy's website maintains a list of these resolutions at http://www .facultydemocracy.org/departmental.html (accessed September 17, 2007).

19. This communication, which does not derive from the ULT, is not collected with the others on the provost's website. See Emily Wilbourne, "The Future of Academia Is on the Line: Protest, Pedagogy, Picketing Performativity," *Workplace* 7, available online at http://www.cust.educ.ubc.ca/workplace/issue7p2/index.html (accessed September 17, 2007).

20. Beckman used these figures on several occasions. See, e.g., "On Strike," *Inside Higher Ed,* November 10, 2005, available online at http://www.insidehighered.com/news/ 2005/11/10/strike (accessed September 17, 2007).

21. David Epstein, "Digging In," *Inside Higher Ed,* November 11, 2005, available online at http://insidehighered.com/news/2005/11/11/strike (accessed September 17, 2007); Barbara Leonard, "Blackboard Access Infuriates Profs," *Washington Square News,* November 14, 2005; John Sexton, "A Letter to the NYU Community," November 14. 2005, available online at http://www.nyu.edu/provost/communications/ga/communications-111405.html (accessed September 17, 2007).

22. Language instruction is not training for being a professor of French literature. Instructors in Expository Writing Program compete with other graduate students and outside instructors in an application process to secure their jobs.

23. Catharine R. Stimpson, Richard Foley, and Matthew Santirocco to Faculty of Arts and Science chairs, "Re: A New Arts and Science Policy about Teaching Assistants and Stand-Alone Courses," memorandum, November 16, 2005.

24. Sexton referred to the time until the December 5 deadline as a period of "amnesty," which "represents a balance between our respect for the principled positions of those choosing to strike and our obligation to undergraduates": John Sexton, "A Letter to NYU Graduate Assistants," November 28, 2005, available online at http://www.nyu.edu/provost/ communications/ga/communications-112805.html (accessed September 17, 2007).

25. The petition, begun by the renowned gender scholar Judith Butler, remains online and ultimately garnered more than seven thousand signatures: see http://new.petition online.com/tosexton/petition.html (accessed September 17, 2007).

26. The blog on which this letter was hosted is no longer online. See the reference to the letter in David Epstein, "Conflicting Claims on NYU Strike," in *Inside Higher Ed*, December 12, 2005, available online at http://insidehighered.com/news/2005/12/12/nyu (accessed September 17, 2007).

27. The Graduate Affairs Committee is a subcommittee of the University Committee on Student Life, itself a subcommittee of the Student Senators Council, composed of fifteen senators elected through one of the notoriously undersubscribed NYU student-government elections, plus seven who are appointed by the Executive Committee of the University Senate, composed of one student, one administrator, one faculty member, and one dean. Brian Levine was then a student at the medical school, and Rodney Washington was a master's student at the Wagner School for Public Affairs. See "NYU Student Government: About Us," available online at http://www.nyu.edu/pages/stugov/about.html (accessed September 17, 2007).

28. Shayne Barr and Adam Playford, "Univ: ¾ of TAs at Work," *Washington Square News*, December 8, 2005. The supposed count of one hundred fifty to two hundred classrooms completed by the Office of the Provost on Wednesday, December 7, would produce a meaningless result: Only a minority of our jobs would have actually required our presence in classrooms on Wednesday. Many classes meet on a Tuesday–Thursday schedule, and Friday teaching is largely made up of recitations and labs led by teaching assistants. Even when teaching assistants returned to work, or did not strike in the first place, some taught off-campus.

29. Representatives from other local academic unions, and the Senate candidate Jonathan Tasini, UAW Local 2110's President Maida Rosenstein, and AAUP presidents Jane Buck and Cary Nelson (then newly elected), joined forty-seven GSOC members in the civil-disobedience action.

30. The resulting story is Brett Ackerman and Paige Glotzer, "Senate Group Expands Grad Rep Proposal," *Washington Square News*, April 28, 2006.

31. Demonstrating the general lack of interest and faith in this proposed body, six seats out of a proposed fifty-three had no candidates. By contrast, GSOC's active participation in the election in GSAS led to more than 40 percent turnout for the vote. The usual turnout in student-government elections at NYU is well below 10 percent. See Sergio Hernandez, "New Graduate Delegation Dominated by GSOC," *Washington Square News*, January 16, 2007.

Bad News for Academic Labor?

Lessons in Media Strategy from the GSOC Strike

STEVE FLETCHER

No strike is won on press coverage alone, but the opportunity to communicate a union message to the broadest possible audience of potential allies and supporters makes media coverage an appealing strategic goal for labor organizers. The maxim that any press is bad press for an employer in a labor crisis usually proves true. Even a dismissive news story with a strong anti-union bias signals trouble to an employer's current and potential investors, customers and allies. Throughout the GSOC strike, we attempted to disseminate our message through the media, despite the fact that the mainstream press routinely minimizes and mischaracterizes the few labor struggles it bothers to cover. This chapter reviews the press-related aspects of the GSOC strike to ask how activists can adopt strategies that use the biases of the mainstream press to earn media coverage that recruits support or adds pressure for employers.

The first significant obstacle activists face is that media consolidation and newsroom downsizing increasingly pressure reporters to cover more news with fewer resources. Though this problem is not unique to labor, one of the most consistent victims of such downsizing has been the labor-beat reporter, a position that has been eliminated at all but a few U.S. newspapers.[1] The result is that journalists increasingly receive news passively, responding to press releases and staged media events in the absence of time, resources, and specialized knowledge required to proactively seek out and analyze stories.[2] In light of this, I tend to follow Michael Parenti's suggestion that individual journalists do not carry the principal blame for the quality of coverage.[3] Rather, the journalists cited here produced work that reflected the corporate editorial positions and labor-relations strategies of their employers, although there were occasions in this case study in which individual journalists' personalities or biases played a limited role. Newsroom rationalization empowers organizations with established public-relations teams that are well connected with journalists from previous stories. My definition of "institutional bias" in the context of NYU is a departure from the term's most frequently deployed usage. Often, "institutional bias" implies insidious, direct relationships between the corporate owners of a news organization and the subject of its stories—for example, when the New York *Daily News* ran an anti–GSOC editorial without acknowledging that its chairman and publisher, Mort Zuckerman, is an NYU trustee.[4] I argue that such direct connections, while important to any media analysis, are not prerequisites for institutional bias.

The second obstacle for organized labor is that the remaining newsroom staff are under pressure to write for increasingly broader audiences in a consolidated media market, which Christopher Martin argues leads to a consumer-oriented approach to news selection. Organized labor is reduced, under this framework, to an organization with significant importance because of its large number of dues-paying members, in competition with other advocacy groups with similar or greater enrollments. For example, Martin notes, "A baseball strike idling about seven hundred unionized players is deemed much more worthy of national coverage because of inconvenienced sports consumers" than larger and longer strikes in less visible industries.[5] Because of their numbers and spending patterns, "baseball fans" merit greater coverage than "organized labor" in today's media. The combination of workplace speed-up and an orientation among editorial boards to a story's "consumer" base creates a significant institutional bias in the news media.

This consumer focus also leads the press to emphasize stories with dramatic narrative structure, making "drama . . . a defining characteristic of news."[6] I argue that this imposition of dramatic narrative expresses itself in two different registers simultaneously. Each story, especially stories that continue along a single story arc across multiple events on multiple days, must have some kind of dramatic question at its core. That framing question can set strict limits to the quantity and quality of media coverage labor activists will receive, especially during prolonged strikes or other impasses. At the same time, news outlets maintain long-term narrative arcs that develop cumulatively as a result of multiple separate stories about particular institutions. Those institutional narratives further confine news coverage to particular themes and story lines. For stories to be newsworthy, they must offer a dramatic story that engages (either by confirming or directly challenging) an institutional narrative. Decisions about whether to cover a particular event and what questions a reporter should pursue are made on this basis.

Since journalists at major news outlets rarely have the time to do thorough investigative work, they look to two sources of information: that from the institutions involved in the story, and coverage by smaller, more specialized news outlets—especially those that publish on the Internet. In the case of the GSOC strike, there were several occasions where stories in NYU's student newspaper, the *Washington Square News,* were picked up by larger media.[7] This created both an opportunity and a problem. GSOC organizers were able to develop relationships with *Washington Square News* writers and editors that sometimes resulted in positive coverage and editorials. However, the quality of reporting at a student newspaper such as the *Washington Square News* is extremely uneven and often created confusion through imprecise or inaccurate reporting; *Washington Square News* printed some of the best and most in-depth and some of the least accurate stories about the strike. Student reporters are insufficient substitutes for professional investigative journalists, but these unpredictable and inexperienced undergraduates were the only ones who even attempted the labor of ongoing, extensive investigation and coverage.

The GSOC communications committee, of which I was part, attempted to create the kind of streamlined information output typical of institutional public-relations organizations, with centralized press contacts and formal press releases. We referred journalists to easily reachable spokespeople for the strike so they could do their reporting by phone. We also attempted, whenever possible, to connect our story with the media's narratives of other institutions with larger consumer bases. We did not always get it right; we sent out press releases for far more events than earned coverage and probably earned less coverage than we could have if we had aligned particular events more accurately with popular media narratives. Still, we earned a sufficient quantity of coverage to support analysis that considers how institutional biases are identifiable in GSOC coverage and how those biases might be exploited by activists.

The school year began for GSOC on August 31 with a media-friendly event in which national labor leaders joined GSOC members to protest the NYU administration's refusal to bargain a second contract. The protest culminated in the civil disobedience and arrest of seventy-seven activists, including AFL-CIO President John Sweeney. The *New York Times* and the *New York Sun* both covered the rally.[8] Neither of those institutions would have covered the event, I argue, if they had imagined the several hundred GSOC members and supporters attending the rally as the story's subjects.[9] What attracted the papers was the apparent emergence of a battle between two established institutions that did affect the papers' readers sufficiently to merit coverage: New York University and the AFL-CIO. Martin's consumer model explains the coverage: AFL-CIO President John Sweeney as a representative of more than ten million dues-paying members nationwide represents a broad enough section of the *Times*'s readership to merit coverage when his actions are sufficiently extraordinary. For media outlets considering national audiences, the AFL-CIO is a newsworthy institution, if one that is competing with many other organizations with similarly significant constituencies. For local news outlets such as TV affiliates, the AFL-CIO and its leadership from other states are less directly relevant than local politicians and institutions. In any case, labor leaders have to be quite dramatic to compete with other powerful

Labor leaders lined up to be arrested in support of GSOC on the day its first contract expired. Pictured here, from left: John Sweeney, president, AFL-CIO; Robert Proto, president, UNITE-HERE Local 35 (with shops at Yale University); Phil Wheeler, director, UAW Region 9A; Elizabeth Bunn, secretary-treasurer, UAW; and Maida Rosenstein, president, UAW Local 2110 (with shops at NYU and Columbia). *(Padraig O'Donoghue)*

institutions for coverage. Were Sweeney simply giving a speech at a rally reaffirming the unsurprising claim that he supports labor unions, he is not likely to have earned coverage for GSOC. From the editors' perspective, he had to go to jail.

Despite their very different ideological approaches to the story, the *New York Times* and *New York Sun* appear to have made their decisions to cover the August 31 event in roughly the same way. Both papers frequently cover NYU because of its prominent position as a major employer, land developer, and cultural force in Manhattan. Neither paper, however, decided to cover this event because of NYU, because NYU was not taking dramatic action in that moment. Had the students of GSOC not been joined by national labor leaders, these papers likely would have waited for the strike to begin to cover NYU's role in the conflict. Since the AFL-CIO decided to make a dramatic action that signaled an unusually strong commitment to this particular struggle, the event had narrative force for institutional coverage of the AFL-CIO, which both the *Sun* and the *Times* determined was worthy of coverage, but local TV stations did not. The stories both papers wrote emphasized the AFL-CIO's role and introduced details of the labor situation: the National Labor Relations Board ruling and NYU's accusation that the union had interfered with academic affairs.

The differences between the two papers emphasize the importance of a paper's ongoing institutional narrative in determining the quality of coverage. The *New York Times* treats organized labor as a serious and legitimate institution in its coverage but appears skeptical about unions' attempts to branch out into knowledge work. Steven Greenhouse, labor reporter at the *Times*, was not assigned to the GSOC story, with the exception of one story six months into the strike. Instead, the paper assigned the education reporter Karen Arenson—who had routinely published positive stories about NYU's growth in the previous decade—as the primary correspondent on the story. The story as written by Arenson conveyed the *Times*'s skepticism, giving plenty of space to charges of interference leveled by Arenson's familiar contacts in the NYU administration.[10] The more explicitly conservative *New York Sun*, by contrast, routinely treats labor unions as an undemocratic form of coercive interference in the free market. Accordingly, the *Sun* reporter Jacob Gershman was most interested in providing data (inaccurately reported) that emphasized the role of labor leaders from outside NYU as compared with the small number of actual GSOC members participating in the civil disobedience.[11]

Once John Sweeney had been released from jail, media coverage shifted back to its institutional focus on NYU. The *Times* typically frames NYU as an institution striving to rise in status on the national academic scene. Stories in the *Times* tend to emphasize three major elements of those aspirations: recruitment metrics, including test scores and application data; resources such as alumni giving and endowment funds; and NYU's relationship with the surrounding Greenwich Village community, including issues such as campus safety and NYU's contested real-estate–development plans.[12] More locally focused media outlets tend to frame NYU solely in terms of its community relationships.[13] More conservative outlets such as the *New York Sun* emphasize NYU as a bastion of liberalism and political correctness, focusing on stories about provocative content generated at the university, particularly when the administration intervenes in controversial campus activities.[14]

The strike offered no shortage of material for any of those frames. The first day saw a swarm of press, including four TV news networks, multiple radio stations, the *New York Sun*, the *New York Times*, and the Associated Press. Of that coverage, the local news outlets' stories on the first day of the strike were most friendly to GSOC's intended message. TV stations reported on disruptions, interviewing a few of the undergraduates/consumers affected by the strike, and reporting the bizarre off-campus locations (such as billiard halls) that were accommodating professors who did not want to teach across picket lines. The stories were colorful, loud, chaotic, and cut together around short, simple sound bites. The local reporters were passive in their interview selection, typically allowing the GSOC communications committee to introduce them to GSOC spokespeople who had been trained by the union to provide concise soundbites.[15] Local television stations sought out apparently unaffiliated undergraduates for their consumer perspective rather than interviewing undergraduate activists who were actively engaged in the conflict.

The *New York Times,* by contrast, barely covered the strike at all on the first day. The reporter Alan Finder spent all day taking interviews with GSOC members, undergraduates, and faculty. However, the resulting article, published on November 9, was 182 words and included no quotes from those interviews, stating only that the strike had begun and "disruptions appeared to be modest."[16] This coverage is consistent with the *Times*'s institutional focus on NYU: November 9, 2005 was not a day in which NYU was undertaking significant, media-visible actions that would affect its own narrative. Rather, November 9 was a day of action for GSOC and was therefore not compelling to the *Times* editorial boards.

Instead, the *New York Times* covered the strike in moments when the story was driven by NYU's actions. It covered NYU's decision to withdraw recognition of the union twice. Both stories featured NYU spokespeople claiming that the union was harmful to their academic-decision making processes, and UAW Region 9 Director Phil Wheeler insisting that "the university was not harmed"[17] by the union and that the union "gave [NYU] 100 percent of what they wanted."[18] This framing question: "Is the union harmful or not harmful to the university?" notably elides discussion about ways that the union might be beneficial to the university. The institutional frame clearly defines the terms of discussion.

The *New York Times* did not run substantive coverage of the strike again until its second week, on November 17, 2005. That story identifies NYU's consumer constituencies in the first sentence, noting that "the frustrations of students, strikers, professors and parents were rising."[19] The members of GSOC were relegated to a role as merely one constituency of the story's institutional subject. The story focuses primarily on disruptions to education that might affect student/consumers as well as NYU's national reputation (and through that reputation, the much larger consumer base of parents and high-school students considering the college-application process nationwide). The selected quotes all frame the story in terms of the NYU administration's management of the situation.

By contrast, the *New York Sun* was virtually obsessed with the run-up to the strike, running stories about the conflict on the October 25 and October 31, as well as on November 8–10 and November 14. The strike enabled Gershman to seamlessly merge the *Sun*'s narrative about organized labor with its favorite story about the NYU administration's attempts to keep its out-of-control knee-jerk left-liberal faculty and students in check. The story in the *Sun* was that naïve, existentially leftist graduate students were mindlessly following the ruthless, manipulative United Auto Workers. In advance of the strike, Gershman tried persistently to get anyone to use the word "strike" so that he could run a story showing that the union had undemocratically predetermined the course of action for GSOC. He asked one GSOC member the same question more than a dozen times in an attempt to bait her.[20] Though he failed to secure an actual quote to this effect, he still began his October 25 article with his premise: "The Union representing NYU graduate teaching assistants is encouraging its members to stage a strike."[21] He also wrote in a great detail about the mechanics of the strike-authorization vote, casting vague aspersions on the fairness of the outcome.

Not content merely to malign the union's intentions and methods, Gershman also used the article to take aim at NYU's graduate students and faculty. Gershman advanced his thematic assertion that graduate students cannot think for themselves, reporting that the union "published a talking points memo on its website to help graduate assistants justify a strike to undergraduates"[22]— a detail not found relevant by any other reporter. His effort to trivialize graduate students' political actions probably culminated with the November 1 story, which put scare quotes around the word "strike" in the headline.[23] Gershman's story about courses that were held in off-campus locations also represents a particularly partisan swipe at faculty, deploying hyperbole to describe the Communist Party USA headquarters as "one of the most popular substitute classrooms" used by supportive faculty, and citing the Zagat restaurant guide's description of another temporary classroom location as "a 'dark' and 'sexy' nexus for 'cuddling up'"[24] to belittle faculty members' "symbolic gesture," which, he emphasized, "stop[s] short of canceling their classes and discarding their teaching responsibilities."[25]

Antagonistic and irresponsible though his reporting on the strike was, Gershman was one of only three professional reporters (and the only one working for a daily publication) who invested much energy in going beyond packaged stories to find fresh angles. Only Tom Robbins from the *Village Voice* and Scott Sherman at the *Nation* invested similar energy in actual investigative work. Robbins— himself a member of Local 2110 as a worker at the *Voice*—spent time on the picket line and around campus, verifying details for himself and producing an accurate and supportive story.[26] Scott Sherman produced more mixed results in the *Nation*, from our perspective. His long and detailed interviews produced a story that was mostly accurate and positive for the union, but it also included an inaccurate quote from unnamed "sources inside GSOC" to provide data we declined to provide about the number of people on strike. These "sources" told him that only one hundred fifty of our members remained on strike—a demoralizing number even lower than the NYU administration's estimate at that time.[27]

Although it did not yield entirely positive coverage, Sherman's and Robbins's willingness to look beyond institutional sources is refreshing because it produced news stories that were actually informed by conversations with striking members of GSOC, erasing one of the key factors responsible for the institutional bias reported throughout this essay. The more common scenario with most print and television media was that voices of GSOC members were ignored or heavily edited to fit a story about one institution or another. Thus, UAW Regional Director Phil Wheeler, not a GSOC member, was called on to comment on GSOC in newspaper articles leading up to the strike. Organizers at the regional and national level cooperated fully with the media's institutional focus. Rather than insist reporters interview rank-and-file members, Wheeler and others consistently complied with these interview requests. Regional and national labor organizers also collaborated with the media's institutional bias by organizing events that featured institutionally powerful speakers addressing an audience of strikers and press.

The default structure for institutionally coordinated labor events, regardless of the location or the union, is a rapid-fire "press conference" rally where several high-profile speakers get the megaphone for a very short amount of time to address an assembled crowd of strikers, supporters, and reporters. A quantitative analysis shows these were among the least successful press events organized by GSOC. At least seven events that year earned coverage in five or more news outlets; none of the three "press conferences" earned that quantity of coverage. The speakers at these events, I argue, did little to advance either their own media narrative or the strike's narrative. Politicians and labor leaders who are well-known labor supporters do not create news by avowing their support for striking workers. To a reporter who follows labor closely, there might be politics to parse about who did and did not show up; perhaps the actual strength of behind-the-scenes support could be measured in the number of City Council members or the presence of two frequently feuding union leaders on the same stage together. Very few of the reporters assigned to cover the story had such knowledge of labor politics or would have considered that knowledge newsworthy in any case.

These events, to be sure, are not held solely for the purpose of obtaining press coverage. The events are intended to inspire and reassure activists, and they were held at crucial moments (on the day before the strike deadline, and in the last week of January when the strike was looking particularly weak and strikers' pay was being cut). The rallies created spectacle not only for the cameras, but also for the attendees and the administration. We hoped at the time that the speakers and the attendees would walk away fired up to renew their energy and commitment to the struggle.

Those goals could have been accomplished more effectively without the constraints of staged media visuals. If the media is not the primary audience, activists are more able to design events that teach, that build relationships, and that inspire participants. A slew of people taking turns at a microphone or megaphone for short times demonstrates the quantity of a union's supporters but offers little substance. By the time each speaker performed the ritual acknowledgments and expressions of gratitude to the other speakers, he or she often had little time to say anything meaningful about the strike. Politicians and labor leaders who knew practically nothing about the strike did not sound substantively different at those events from genuine GSOC allies such as City Council Speaker Christine Quinn and UNITE-HERE's co-president, John Wilhelm, who both took the time to intimately learn and get involved with the details of the struggle. The troubling, unresolved question implicit in the suggestion to de-prioritize media for non-narrative events is this: Would the dignitaries still come to meet with strikers and supporters without the promise of media coverage? Undoubtedly, some of them would not. When choosing between an event that provides limited media exposure to a large number of supporters or a more thoughtful event for supporters to connect with the campaign more deeply, organizers need to make a pragmatic assessment of how little press the AFL-CIO's standard press rallies typically generate in the absence of major announcements or mass arrests.

Notably, the event that earned the most coverage—the December 5 return-to-work deadline set by NYU—was not a coherent event with prepackaged visuals. For every news outlet that had ever covered GSOC, the deadline clearly represented a narrative turning point in the strike that merited coverage. Each of those stories that reported the deadline seemed to promise future coverage when the deadline arrived. By setting a deadline, the NYU union-busting team took control over the narrative of the strike—from a media perspective and from the perspective of the NYU community. Once it had control, the administration played it to its advantage; it postponed the deadline by two days the evening before it arrived, simultaneously heightening the anxiety of strikers facing a tough decision and creating confusion for reporters looking for an event to cover. Some outlets ran brief stories announcing the change of deadline; others waited for the "real" deadline to run a story, and a few dropped the story altogether.

The *New York Times,* which had planned to run a piece about the deadline on December 6, posted a short story on December 8 that reflected this confusion. The December 8 article devotes one short paragraph each to several different events on campus: a faculty attempt to broker peace, a company-union proposal allegedly generated by two graduate students, NYU's unverifiable assertion (through spokesman John Beckman) that 75 percent of graduate workers were back at work, and a petition signed by more than five thousand faculty members around the world condemning NYU's threats.[28] The story summarized all of those events in fewer than five hundred words.

The remainder of that winter and spring saw a significant drop off in news coverage, with fewer consistent patterns to what coverage did occur. Behind the scenes, Karen Arenson at the *New York Times* wrote a piece in February describing the strike as a failure, which GSOC managed to convince the paper was premature. The story did not run that spring, but its existence indicated that the strike would be a very low news priority at the *Times.* The *New York Sun* assigned Bradley Hope, former editor of the *Washington Square News,* to cover the strike, which he did only once in January (with none of Gershman's vitriol).[29] The NYU administration cut strikers' pay a few people at a time, ensuring there was never one central event around which to focus media attention. Although there were isolated instances of good coverage that spring, the strike's narrative for almost everyone who had covered it intensely in November was that it was either dying or dead.

On April 27, 2006, GSOC held a rally and civil-disobedience action to announce that the union had reestablished majority support through a petition drive. For labor watchers, the achievement stands out as remarkable; it is very difficult, if not unheard of, to reestablish majority support for the union six months into a strike, after many people had returned to work. Unfortunately, news editorial boards failed to appreciate the significance. Were it not for the institutional power of GSOC allies, the only coverage would have been in the *Washington Square News,* in Columbia University's student newspaper, and in the education press (*Inside Higher Ed* and the *Chronicle of Higher Education*).

Arenson did not "see" a story, but supportive labor leaders were able to leverage their relationship with Steven Greenhouse (one of the handful of labor-beat reporters who still has a job) to get him to write the story and to persuade the editors to run it. The result was the first *New York Times* story about the strike in six months, the first story oriented around the union since the August 31 event, and quite possibly the only time that GSOC and not some larger institution will ever be the focus of coverage in the *Times*.[30] The year began and ended with *New York Times* coverage of GSOC civil-disobedience actions at NYU. Arenson finally ran her story declaring the strike dead on September 7, 2006, when the strike was unambiguously over.[31]

What is evident from all of this is that activists simply do not have the power to insert a new, surprising, radical message into the mainstream media. In discussions about media coverage, GSOC activists frequently named as goals "educating the public" and "changing the discourse" about academic labor. What my analysis suggests, however, is that these goals are possible only at media outlets that are sufficiently small in scope to consider a group an important constituency worthy of in-depth coverage. For GSOC, this meant that we had to become particularly adept at latching our struggle on to one of two readily available institutional hooks. In that regard, GSOC is a relatively privileged activist group compared with workers at less well-known institutions, or with activist groups organized around issues without obvious institutional hooks.

GSOC was also privileged relative to some similar campaigns because our conflict directly engaged NYU's media narrative. Because the *New York Times* and the local papers run coverage of NYU's attempts at community outreach in labor-friendly New York, the strike seemed to hold the potential to alter NYU's public image. The possibility of a narrative turning point in NYU's long-term institutional narrative put GSOC in the spotlight. In principle, other university administrations may be as vulnerable, but in practice, some are better protected than others. Yale University, for instance, which Steven Greenhouse writes "has developed the reputation of having the most acrimonious labor relations in American academia," has a tough institutional narrative that renders labor conflicts mundane and less worthy of coverage.[32] The narrative force of Yale's reputation closes off media possibilities, just as NYU's reputation opens it up to coverage of its labor disputes.

In light of this analysis, GSOC was relatively successful at using its resources to generate coverage but probably worried too much along the way about controlling who talked to the press and what they said. The content of quotes from GSOC workers mattered very little because *we were not the story*. The only bad message that could have changed coverage would have been a message of reconciliation or loss of resolve that closed off the narrative. As long as the sentence started with, "I'm on strike because . . ." (which was our press-training mantra), it mattered very little what we said next or who said it. What did matter was that reporters understood the narrative and institutional context in which they were going to use those quotes. To convey that understanding, activists must realistically assess the institutional narratives to which they can attach their stories and create systems to partner with news outlets in their streamlined production by feeding them easily digestible summaries of those institutional and narrative connections. In situations where workers can latch on to compelling institutional hooks, a heavily downsized, anti-union press still cannot be relied on to publish accurate, thoughtful coverage of academic labor conflicts, but they will cover the story. If all news is bad news for employers, then the bad news the mainstream press can be counted on to write still deserves a place in academic labor campaigns.

Notes

1. In *Framed! Labor and the Corporate Media* (Ithaca, N.Y.: Cornell University Press, 2004), Christopher Martin reports that there are "fewer than five" labor reporters, citing Robert McChesney's article "Why We Need *In These Times*," *In These Times*, January 18, 2002, available online at http://www.inthesetimes.com/issue/26/06/feature1.shtml (accessed September 11, 2007).

2. Herbert J. Gans, *Deciding What's News: A Study of CBS Evening News, NBC Nightly News, Newsweek and Time* (New York: Random House, 1979), 88.

3. Michael Parenti, *Inventing Reality: The Politics of the Mass Media* (New York: St. Martin's Press, 1986).

4. "Out of the Ivory Tower," editorial, *New York Daily News*, December 3, 2005, 34.

5. Martin, *Framed!* 53

6. David L. Paletz, and Robert M. Entman, *Media, Power, Politics* (New York: Free Press, 1981), 16.

7. For example, Karen Arenson of the *New York Times* cited Amanda Farah's November 28, 2005, article, "In Third Week of Strike, Some Classes Move Back on Campus." Barbara Leonard's November 10, 2005, article "Administrators Access Class Blackboard Sites" scooped other media outlets and drew attention to an issue that eventually earned mention by larger media outlets, as well.

8. Several additional news outlets decided to run brief stories based on wire reports later in the day when crime-beat reporters saw busloads of arrestees at New York Central Booking.

9. In the case of the *New York Times*, this is unambiguously accurate; a contact at the *Times* told a GSOC leader explicitly the paper would not have assigned a reporter were it not for John Sweeney's participation in the civil-disobedience action.

10. Karen Arenson, "76 Arrested Protesting NYU's Cutoff of Student Union," *New York Times*, September 1, 2005, B5.

11. Jacob Gershman, "Dozens Arrested at Rally to Pressure NYU to Negotiate with Graduate Students," *New York Sun*, September 1, 2005, 3.

12. For example, see Karen Arenson, "After Suicides, NYU Will Limit Access to Balconies," *New York Times*, March 30, 2005; "NYU Begins Hiring Effort to Lift Its Liberal Arts Standing," *New York Times*, September 27, 2004.

13. For example, see New York One, "Residents Angered by Bar Noise in Downtown Manhattan," broadcast, March 3, 2006, which singles out NYU as a source of noise; and "NYU Leads Applicants' 'Dream List,'" broadcast, March 22, 2006, which devotes most of the report on NYU's success to emphasizing reasons (tuition cost, lack of physical campus area) that NYU should not be so highly regarded by applicants.

14. For examples, see Jacob Gershman, "Sexton Takes on Issues of Tenure, Academic Freedom," *New York Sun,* December 3, 2004, 3, which includes Sexton's opinion about the ethics of inviting Osama bin Laden to speak on campus, and Bradley Hope's "Cartoons Discussed but Not Shown at NYU Event," *New York Sun,* March 30, 2006, which covers the scandal over cartoons offensive to Muslims.

15. The author's documentary footage shows that WABC, WNBC, and New York One conducted interviews for their November 9, 2005, stories with Michael Palm, Miabi Chatterji, Joanna Holzman, Elizabeth Loeb, Andrew Ross, myself, and Jenny Shaw, all of whom were on the communications committee's spokesperson list for that day.

16. Alan Finder, "NYU Teaching Assistants Strike," in "Metro Briefing: New York: Manhattan," comp. John Sullivan, *New York Times,* November 10, 2005.

17. Idem, "NYU Ends Negotiations with Graduate Students' Union," *New York Times,* August 6, 2005, B3.

18. Karen Arenson, "NYU Moves to Disband Graduate Students Union," *New York Times,* June 17, 2005, B2.

19. Idem, "Strike by Graduate Students at NYU Enters Its Second Week," *New York Times,* November 17, 2005, B4.

20. Communications team meeting, January 27, 2006, in the author's documentary video archive.

21. Jacob Gershman, "NYU Graduate Assistants Rally for the Strike," *New York Sun,* October 25, 2005, 3.

22. Ibid.

23. Idem, "Grad Students Plan To Go on 'Strike'" *New York Sun,* November 1, 2005, 2.

24. Idem, "NYU Class in Communist HQ," *New York Sun,* November 18, 2005, 1.

25. Ibid.

26. Tom Robbins, "The Nerds Are Pissed: New York University Opts for War With Its Best and Brightest," *Village Voice,* November 15, 2005, available online at http://www.villagevoice.com/news/0546,robbins,70018,5.html (accessed September 11, 2007).

27. Scott Sherman, "Bitter Winter at NYU," *Nation,* December 20, 2005, available online at http://www.thenation.com/doc/20060109/sherman (accessed September 11, 2007).

28. Karen Arenson, "NYU Graduate Assistants Keep Striking despite Penalties," *New York Times,* December 8, 2005, B4.

29. Bradley Hope, "Group of NYU Students to Resume Their Strike Today," *New York Sun,* January 17, 2006, 4.

30. Steven Greenhouse, "57 Teaching Assistants Arrested at NYU Sit-In for Union Rights," *New York Times,* April 28, 2006, B5.

31. Karen Arenson, "NYU Teaching Aides End Strike, with Union Unrecognized," *New York Times,* September 7, 2006, B2.

32. Steven Greenhouse, "Price of Labor Peace," *New York Times,* September 20, 2003, B4.

If Not Now, When?

The GSOC Strike, 2005–2006

Miabi Chatterji, Maggie Clinton, Natasha Lightfoot,
Sherene Seikaly, and Naomi Schiller

How do unions in the midst of struggle and crisis deal with structures of difference and power—race, class, citizenship, sexuality, and gender privilege? How do unions focused on winning an immediate strike relate their struggle to broader social-justice issues? How does union leadership at the heart of a crisis respond to determined criticism from the rank and file? During its 2005–2006 strike, GSOC faced all of these issues, as had many other unions and social movements. Its response was to defer discussions of difference in the name of solidarity and an imminent win. It bracketed broader social-justice issues, such as the U.S. wars on Iraq and Afghanistan, the Israeli occupation of Palestine, and immigrant rights in the United States, during the contract drive. It implied that members who critiqued GSOC's political practice were potentially weakening, even sabotaging, the movement's collective force by raising "divisive" issues.

There were several initiatives on the part of pro-union, striking graduate assistants to work within union channels to strengthen our movement by raising these issues and creating a more transparent and just struggle. International students wrote a powerful collective letter to the NYU administration, explaining their particular duress under strike-breaking sanctions, which implicitly revealed the union's marginalization of citizenship concerns.[1] Other union activists raised poignant concerns about the alienating and regressive heteronormative and sexist tendencies of the Organizing Committee as it was constituted in the spring of 2006. Others participated in what became known as the "Monday Meetings," which took place in February and March 2006 after numerous striking members collectively questioned whether the union leadership was indeed representing their best interests. A cadre of progressive students, some of color and some white, some U.S.-born and others not, who were deeply invested in the direction of our struggle sought to criticize constructively its strategy and tactics. A cohort of GSOC organizers, including authors of this chapter, actively engaged these concerns. The Monday Meeting discussions forced us to step back from the everyday maintenance of the campaign and assess GSOC's organizing successes and failures. These conversations were critical to the reorientation of our union activism and remain integral to our current organizing practice.

We remain committed to GSOC/UAW Local 2110's struggle for a second contract and to the right of academic workers everywhere to union representation. Our critique of the strike is intended to help present and future organizers avoid replicating structures of inequality and injustice. In the following roundtable discussion we respond individually to a series of questions, but our thoughts were forged through ongoing critical conversation with each other and many other comrades. Although some themes receive more sustained treatment than others, this reflects a limitation of space rather than a judgment about relative importance. The authors of this chapter, along with academic union activists everywhere, will continue to fight to equalize academe through unionization and to transform our own union through frank dialogue and mindful political practice.

How Did Axes of Difference and Power Affect GSOC's Struggle?

Natasha

Racial differences as well as GSOC's structural shortcomings underscored the exchanges between members and union organizers prior to and during the Monday Meetings. Many members had highly articulated critiques that were silenced because the Organizing Committee wished to appear as a unified front that showed no signs of internal dissent or self-critique. Many of us touted the "party line," however ill-defined that was beyond the stated goal of winning a contract. Many members both within and beyond the Monday Meetings noticed that the largely white Organizing Committee was privileged in terms of race, class, citizenship status, and access to education. There seemed to be little variety in the political positions and kinds of privileges held by Organizing Committee members, creating a culture that was exclusionary to GSOC's general membership. This culture seriously weakened the union and contributed to our campaign's disintegration at key moments.

Hearing certain students raise their concerns about GSOC, I realized that, to quote Miabi Chatterji, I had subconsciously "checked race at the door" every time I organized on behalf of GSOC—in phone banking, in face-to-face conversations, and in Organizing Committee meetings. I came to understand my own role in perpetuating the union's general silence on race issues.

Contradictions surrounding relations of gender and sexuality also plagued GSOC's struggle. Some female organizers began to notice the gender imbalance in the daily maintenance of the picket line. Women seemed to compose the majority of picketers, exhausting themselves on the line, yelling slogans, and cleaning up afterward. The men tended to congregate around the strike kiosk, appearing to assume a more official capacity. The significance of these relatively innocuous though troubling experiences was heightened after certain women on the Organizing Committee became subject to a more aggressive sexism and heterosexist behavior.

Naomi

The class issues surrounding our struggle were murky. Students whose families' historical experience with higher education was restricted due to race and class felt that students from families who had long had access to higher education did not appreciate or understand the stakes and the risks of the struggle.

When GSOC was finally called on to recognize issues of white and citizenship privilege in the union, what remained of the collectivity seemed to have little sustained commitment or capacity to confront these problems. People were frequently accused of looking for an "easy way out" of the strike by playing the "race card." Without an overt commitment to working against privilege from the beginning of the strike and a sustained collective dialogue around this issue, our collective could not weather the NYU administration's efforts to pressure striking graduate assistants to go back to work.

Miabi

GSOC's organizational culture was dominated by people who inhabit historically normative or privileged positions in the United States and in the academy: white, straight, middle-class or upper-class U.S.-born men and women, many of whom were new to progressive, or even liberal, political work. I do not think that any group that is majority-white, or majority-straight, etc., inevitably creates a culture inhospitable to people from other identity categories. What created problems was that privilege combined with a politics that sidelined issues of power and difference and that did not prioritize the challenges disempowered groups face within the academy. If we had been committed to anti-oppressive principles and practices, we would have created an entirely different culture from the one I experienced during the strike.

Maggie

In the months leading up to and during the strike, the GSOC leadership persistently deferred collective discussion on how race, class, sexuality, gender, and citizenship might inform a given member's understanding of the significance of a graduate degree and what she or he put at risk by striking. The material gains secured by a union contract that have made academe accessible to a broader group of people were indeed a constant talking point and rallying cry among the union leadership. Yet this did not translate into open, critical discussions of our own daily practices and the forms of privilege that were replicated within our ranks. An attitude of "trust us, we have your best interests in mind and know what to do about it" pervaded the leadership and helped to foster an atmosphere that many found both personally alienating and politically problematic, for it silenced members' experiences and lacked transparency and democracy. The disjuncture between means and ends, between the leadership's disinterest in examining the replication of privilege within our ranks and its simultaneous commitment to a contract that would contribute to the elimination of these same social hierarchies within the university at large, led many of us to question whether a victory, if achieved, could be meaningful and whether GSOC should secure our loyalty.

Sherene

In one spring 2006 Organizing Committee meeting, a number of organizers pushed for antiracism and self-critique as essential cornerstones of our union struggle. Some Organizing Committee members expressed their qualified agreement. Yet while they acknowledged that antiracism was an essential approach, they conjured up students who were not actually present at the meeting to make two troubling assertions. One was that graduate students in the sciences—as opposed to the humanities—were simply not interested in the "race" question. The second and all-too-common deferral mechanism was that an antiracist agenda would alienate our base and weaken our struggle. Our demands to overhaul political practice in what was, after all, *our* union were silenced in order to appeal to an allegedly broader base.

No doubt most people would have been as "uncomfortable" with the discussion of racism and antiracism as organizers and members in GSOC meetings and the Monday Meetings were. Yet these difficult conversations are the only way to forge a meaningful agenda in which people of color, immigrants, and antiracist activists could belong. Being accountable to, recognizing, and embracing difference was necessary to *build* solidarity, but time and again difference was deferred in the name of solidarity.

What Were the Challenges of Building a Collective Movement?

Natasha

Through eye-opening exchanges in the Monday Meetings, we engaged GSOC's broader potential to politicize the university in multiple ways by plugging into progressive struggles within and beyond the workers' rights movement. Our efforts to expand GSOC's political practice by highlighting the inadequate attention paid to differences in politics and lived experiences among our membership and the possibilities for expanding the scope of our struggle were criticized and ultimately sidelined in the name of maintaining "solidarity" in the union.

GSOC's lack of transparency and accountability also made it difficult to build a collective movement. GSOC called the strike without establishing a means for open communication with membership as our campaign progressed. The union's structure, organizing tactics, and strategy were ambiguous to members (and some organizers). As the strike extended into a second semester and the NYU administration's union-busting tactics further eroded membership support, members repeatedly questioned the structure of our union. How did the Organizing Committee come into being? Who determined GSOC's official strategy and who ultimately made decisions? What was our relationship to the UAW and Local 2110? What communication channels existed between the GSOC leadership and membership? And what would the union represent for students after a contract was won? Because of the rapidly changing nature of GSOC's leadership structure, as well as the ongoing crisis, the Organizing Committee did not offer definite answers to these questions.[2]

The Monday Meetings were one concerted effort to collectively discuss these issues with the broader membership. They strove to make GSOC more accountable to members who felt underrepresented politically by the union that was presumably all of ours to shape.

Naomi

For many of us, it was impossible to imagine a better moment to launch our fight. In the midst of intense feelings of powerlessness about the war in Iraq and the occupation of Palestine, a local struggle seemed to be a practical place to start. We were organizing, we were fighting, we were together. It seemed so clear in the beginning.

Yet one of the main difficulties we faced was thinking collectively when there was little material reality on which to base a collectivity. We lacked a collective work experience and collective history. Graduate students in different departments across the university face starkly different work environments, relationships with faculty, and teaching loads. What were our collective interests if what we risked was vastly different for each person? This disparity of experience, which is often true in collective struggles, was magnified by the fact that many members were ambivalent about claiming that we were workers, and many had little experience of working and thinking collectively in any environment.

A community of belief did indeed develop as the strike became increasingly polarized. Nonetheless, the people who spent time together on the Organizing Committee came to see our situation from a different perspective from those striking members who remained outside the union leadership. Many of us wondered who really had an informed perspective on the potential or numbers of our "collective" and on the reality of our situation—or our possibility for winning.

Miabi

I witnessed a change in our organizing techniques during the two years I worked on the Organizing Committee: They became increasingly heavy-handed and alienated many members. Our organizing had been relatively more flexible and dialogic in the year before the contract expired, but for several reasons, we organizers began to exhort people to do what we wanted them to do, to push past their concerns and doubt, rather than allowing for real dialogue between the "organizer/member" and the "member being organized." Why? In part this was due to the urgency of the contract-expiration date and what our leaders saw as a short window for an effective strike. In part the crisis at hand left little time and energy for broader discussions on organizing methods among the large influx of new organizers after our contract expired. Most importantly, in the fall of 2005 there was no transparent and accountable mechanism for feedback, input, and concerns, and this, in my experience, stymied even the best and more passionate organizers.

When some of the same people who had raised issues of difference also had concerns about the lack of structural transparency and process, they were treated as threats by a few key members of the union leadership. While some GSOC leaders listened to these concerns and acknowledged their importance, there was little institutional support to help bring these ideas to a broader group. Our efforts to raise issues of process faltered, and some people had reached a point of rupture with the campaign. This lesson was by far the most painful for me and haunts my memory of my two years working with GSOC. When I was an Organizing Committee member doing my work fairly quietly and without dissension, the union leadership wanted my presence and even sought out my public participation as one of the very few women of color on the Organizing Committee. Yet when some of us brought up legitimate, urgent concerns about the way that we were running our campaign, we were dismissed. It saddened and disappointed me that people who hold power in leftist movements are still using that age-old line that issues of race, class, gender, sexuality, or citizenship are "not relevant" to the supposed "core principles" of a campaign.

Maggie

What constitutes the grounds of solidarity in an organization with a non–self-selecting membership, such as a closed-shop union? Graduate-assistant labor at New York University is united by certain objective conditions—most immediately, those created by the administration's decision to employ contingent labor for the majority of its teaching. At the same time, graduate-assistant work for the university takes many different forms and is performed by people with widely diverging lived experiences. Although our first contract recognized and concretized the common objective conditions of our work, the subjective ties that meaningfully bind our membership into a collectivity capable of sustaining a strike remained elusive. At the beginning of the 2005–2006 strike, our greatest strength was the overwhelming support among graduate assistants and faculty for the renewal of our first contract. Our greatest internal weakness was and remained the union leadership's failure to assess adequately both the fragility of the ties that bound our membership into a purposeful collectivity and what individual members had at risk if they struck.

This weakness was exacerbated by the deliberately disaggregated nature of NYU, which has neither a centralized campus nor a single unpoliced common-area bulletin board. In the best of circumstances, it is logistically difficult to carry on the kinds of conversations necessary to render the connections between different kinds of graduate-assistant work meaningful to our membership. These conversations were actively thwarted by the administration's virulent anti-union campaign, a part of its broader neoliberal agenda.

Sherene

Standing on the picket line and sitting in long meetings, people engaged one another and exchanged life experiences. There was a tangible sense of togetherness and possibility that was at times powerful and binding. At other times, differing notions of what graduate students wanted and what they could hope for punctured this sense of a collective. Some students dismissed the very idea of self-identifying as workers while others saw a historic labor struggle at a private university as a primary site of struggle for broader social justice. The fault lines of political possibility became ever more clear as the strike wore on.

For those of us who came into GSOC from experiences of antiwar, anticolonial, and antiracist organizing, the idea of an imminent win was simultaneously appealing and alienating. Longtime union organizers, well established in the union movement with many years of labor-organizing experience, were particularly vested in relaying that a win was just around the corner. Our union struggle was appealing because it was a local battle that—unlike the antiwar movement or Palestinian solidarity, for example—was immediately winnable.

In December 2005, the NYU administration issued an ultimatum that included barring strikers from future teaching positions. Under duress, the majority of graduate students went back to work, and the possibility of a win became more fragile. Nevertheless, the ideology of an imminent win continued unabated. I remember telling leading organizers in the throes of a minority strike that I was ready to fight, but they needed to tell me how we would win. This question was never answered in a practical way. Most of the Organizing Committee seemed ever more convinced that we would get our contract by the end of the year. If they were not convinced, this was certainly not revealed in strategy conversations. For some, this relentless optimism coupled with a lack of clarity on how, exactly, we were going to win a minority strike provided another reason to step away from an increasingly embattled struggle.

Picket lines dwindled during the strike's second semester. *(Dave Rowland)*

How Did the Struggle for a Contract Influence the Broader Political Agenda of the Union? What Gains and Sacrifices Resulted?

Natasha

In August 2005, I abstained from participating in the pre-planned civil-disobedience action that concluded GSOC's late-summer rally to publicize the end of our first contract. Despite my disagreement with the planned arrests, I never publicly articulated my feelings about why, as a woman of color born and raised in New York City and witness to corrupt police tactics my entire life, I was reluctant to be voluntarily detained by the New York Police Department (NYPD) alongside my mostly white fellow union members. This was in stark contrast to April 2006, when, during an Organizing Committee planning meeting for the second staged arrest, I clearly established my perspective on the issue based on my lived experiences outside the realm of white privilege. Although the union struggle remained incredibly important to me, I could not prioritize it above my personal and political position regarding the racism embedded within New York's police state. Despite the sustained and vocal opposition of a few of us, GSOC went ahead with its plans to show support for the union through staged arrests and cooperation with the NYPD. I abstained a second time from arrest. The critique of police cooperation that I and other organizers raised during spring 2006 sparked provocative conversation in Organizing Committee meetings about the different risks members faced in a mass struggle. While we did not bring about sustained changes in political practice, those of us who worked in the Monday Meetings and beyond challenged GSOC's approach.

Naomi

Despite the important concerns raised about the unequal ability to participate in the planned GSOC arrest action and about the wider ramifications of complicity with the NYPD, it was deemed necessary by the majority of the Organizing Committee to go ahead with the staged arrest to regain waning press attention. This decision was alienating and deeply disappointing for many of us, because it signaled a tacit belief within the Organizing Committee that the participation of people of color and non-citizens was insignificant in the building of the graduate-student union. Race and citizenship were not recognized as everyone's issue.

Another critical moment occurred in mid-spring, when a busload of GSOC members, myself included, headed to Albany, New York, for a strange U.S. practice called "Lobby Day," where groups solicit help from state senators by pleading their case in less than five minutes. We were hoping to block a proposal in front of the State Senate's budget committee for funding to construct new buildings at NYU. In one of the many long corridors of the State Senate building I bumped into an undergraduate student from the class in which I had been the teaching assistant before going on strike. The young man was part of a group of students the NYU administration had organized to lobby state senators on behalf of NYU to ensure the granting of Tuition Assistance Program (TAP) money, which provides financial aid for working-class and poor students. I was part of a group of almost entirely white graduate students. My former student was part of a group of almost entirely Black, Latino, and South Asian undergraduates. When our eyes met, he quickly looked away, and there was a vast distance between us. I imagined what he might be seeing and how all my privilege may have looked through his eyes. Positioning ourselves opposite undergraduate students of color, albeit unwittingly, encapsulated so many of our missteps. We had no way to reach these students or build any common solidarity. By this point, we had already failed.

For many of us, being involved in union politics meant compromising some of our core political beliefs. Late in the Spring term, GSOC aligned with two of the U.S. Senate's most distinguished Zionists and friends of the American Israeli Public Affairs Committee, Hillary Clinton and Charles Schumer. The union celebrated when Clinton and Schumer finally wrote a letter to NYU President John Sexton supporting our right to unionize. From that experience, I realized that macropolitics, like the protracted international struggle for justice in Palestine, and micropolitics, such as a unionization campaign contained within a singular university campus, are inevitably connected. Activists often face moments when they are asked to compromise the broader spectrum of their political beliefs. Uncomfortable and outright contradictory political alignments are sometimes necessary. However, GSOC's alliance with pro-war pro-occupation politicians was made with little discussion among the union membership of the merits and problems of such a move.

Miabi

When I got involved in GSOC activism during my second year as an American Studies Ph.D. student, I had hoped that GSOC, if it called on the long traditions of progressive union activism and student activism in the United States, could be a place where issues of social justice affecting academic workers were seriously thought through and fought for. Such issues include the casualization of academic labor; the politics of race, gender, sexual orientation, class, and citizenship on campus; the increased political targeting of progressive faculty and of specific fields, such as Middle East Studies, by neoconservatives; the connection between universities such as NYU and oppressive regimes such as international sweatshop labor; and the decision of many universities to hand over the personal information of international students because of repressive and highly discriminatory post–September 11 laws.

Some unions and workers' rights centers do deal with such issues. In my opinion, we, as a union, would have stood a greater chance of sustaining our fight, albeit on different terms, after the strike folded if we had fashioned ourselves as a more collectively run group that addressed a greater breadth of issues and concerns. Calling off the strike in the 2006–2007 school year, I believe, has put GSOC in a position of having to acknowledge defeat, because the singular goal was the negotiation of a second contract; if there had been other, pressing issues of academic social justice for which we were also fighting, we could still be a thriving group. Unfortunately, GSOC was not a visible or growing group during the 2006–2007 school year. I do not have any illusions that a more diverse, multi-issue, collectively run body would have won the strike. We would, most likely, have acted more slowly and with less institutional pull from politicians and other labor leaders, for example. But I think we would have had a more sustainable organization—a movement rather than a singular campaign. Such a movement would be much more difficult to repress in our next instance of labor conflict.

Maggie

A union contract is not a fundamental solution to structures of inequality either within or beyond the ivory tower. A contract for graduate assistants simply seeks to equalize access to academe, to normalize the conditions of progression to a degree, and to remunerate teachers fairly for labor performed. Attaining this decidedly liberal goal required compromise with a liberal power structure that many of us were committed to critiquing and resisting. As striking graduate assistants began to return to work, GSOC's strategy relied ever more heavily on a leverage campaign that sought assistance from pro-war politicians and the

NYPD. Whether practical or not, this strategy further alienated people who had been critical of an organizing method that privileged the implementation of a predetermined agenda over feedback from the general membership. Given the force of NYU's anti-union campaign and the many other factors that prevented a GSOC victory, it would be unfair to attribute our setback solely to the actions and attitudes of the Organizing Committee. It is both reasonable and necessary, however, to insist that unions always engage in open and critical discussion about how our daily practices and our public strategy consciously and unconsciously reproduce the inequalities we claim to struggle against.

Sherene

In the face of the increasing intransigence of the doctrine of imminent win, several organizers became more committed to the transformation of GSOC's internal political practice. If we could not win the larger struggle with the university, we could make concrete and lasting changes inside our political community and develop it as a mutually supportive space for collective practice. This work, we hoped, would be one step of many to building a more sustainable, radical, and inclusive movement. Unfortunately, while these efforts were encouraged and supported, they were ultimately understood as marginal to the real struggle at hand.

We sought to foster a better sense of ownership and accountability, yet these efforts were subsumed time and again by the emphasis on an imminent win. Leading UAW representatives were particularly vested in insisting that we would win through lobbying state representatives and other allies to challenge NYU. These strategies moved away from collective labor action and toward mainstream political advocacy. This shift came into particular relief when UAW representatives assured us about the possibilities of lobbying state representatives—by securing Republican allies in the light of their eroding power. Were we now to place our struggle for a contract in the hands of Republican pundits? Was that supposed to give me hope or foster my sense of ownership? What say did I have in these strategies and our change of approach?

At the end of the spring semester, the Organizing Committee organized a "Convention" and a staged arrest as final performances of strength, even though we still had no contract. For me, the "Convention" was a disturbing reenactment of everything I had hoped to fight against in and with my union. At the "Convention," the reading of a letter from senators Hillary Clinton and Charles Schumer, expressing little more than empty promises and political opportunism, was the icing on the cake. It was a performance of union power—there were relatively few students there in comparison to the gathering of union activists from all over the city—that was defined by an alienating and unfathomable energy of triumphalism.

I did not enjoy being among the few dissenting voices in meetings, but it would have been insincere for me to continue otherwise. I did not conceive of this union as a place for empty optimism or some illusive middle ground. I understood it as mine, and for it to be mine, there had to be real conversations about social justice, racism, and U.S. wars on Iraq and Afghanistan. In fact, when historians look back on our movement, I expect that they will be struck by the absence of discussions about the context of heightened American empire, the wars on Iraq and Afghanistan, and the hegemony of American neoconservatism. A key exception was GSOC's participation in New York City's May Day immigrant rally, when a Latino immigrant GSOC member represented his experiences to the hundreds of thousands who rallied for immigrant rights and social justice that day. His role as the rally's GSOC representative was a small victory for our push for broader participation and political engagement.

Looking Forward: Lessons for the Future

Our union's ability to mobilize thousands of supporters in the face of extraordinary counter-force over the course of many months was one of the most powerful accomplishments of the strike. Our mobilizing flew in the face of the NYU administration's relentless neoliberal agenda, which works to divide and conquer resistance at every step. President John Sexton colloquially summarized this agenda in an April 2006 *Washington Square News* article:

> It's very hard for anyone here to view us as a sort of holistic community. . . . We're an aggregation of micro-communities. And that's really what the world of the 21st century is going to be, especially in New York. We're the world of microcosm—NYU is the university that embraces that. We try to build that into our student body. And this is one reason not to do big-time sports. Big-time sports, which gather people in a stadium all wearing the same colors, all singing the same song . . . that's kind of 1950s-community. And that's not a complex community. One of the things that we kind of make a conscious or unconscious vow to do . . . is to throw ourselves into a situation where it's difficult to find that community. And we have to work at it.[3]

Echoing Margaret Thatcher's assertion that "there is no such thing as society," Sexton suggests that twenty-first–century universities will provide no space for collective action and that their administrations will make finding it as difficult as possible. We are expected to either submit to the top-down division into "micro-communities" or blindly repeat an already superseded 1950s past. Neither of these options is acceptable. We draw inspiration instead from radical, interracial, internationalist, and anti-imperialist organizers who built their collectives and communities—on and off campuses—throughout the '60s, '70s, and '80s. Our actions of 2005–2006 demonstrated the degree and strength of discontent with the neoliberal formulation of academe. A different kind of university already exists in raw form. Exhilarating as our struggle was at times, the terms in which the union leadership undertook its mobilization effort unfortunately replicated structures of privilege that neoliberalism seeks to entrench and a union contract intends to help level.

Every campaign for social change has its share of problems and difficulties, and our small victories—and, we hope, graduate assistants' eventual victory in negotiation with NYU—are that much sweeter because of the extent of the challenges we face. Critique and dialogue with members of our communities (academic, political, and other) about our challenges are necessary for future progress. It is with the hope that other, parallel campaigns do not find themselves falling into the same traps in the future that we share some of the hard lessons that we learned from the GSOC strike at NYU.

Intellectuals are most certainly workers, subject to corporate and state power. The fight for collective power is a necessary condition for any sincere commitment to the life of the mind. It is the form and content of that collective work, which we must now imagine in radically different ways, that positions our labor battle in broader struggles for social justice.

Notes

1. The text of this letter is available online at http://nerdsforgsoc.blogspot.com/2005/12/international-students-respond-sexton.html (accessed September 20, 2007).

2. In spring 2006, the UAW International recommended that GSOC restructure its leadership as a strategic move toward securing a win. The strike had previously been directed by officers of Local 2110, the UAW chapter with which GSOC is affiliated. Upon restructuring, we were partnered instead with leaders from GESO (UNITE-HERE), the graduate union at Yale University, along with officers from the UAW International's central leadership. In mid-spring, the UAW International hired a dozen NYU graduate students as temporary staff organizers (including Maggie Clinton) to help bring the strike to successful completion. This radical shift in leadership in the midst of the strike posed further challenges to the task of clarifying GSOC's leadership structure to members.

3. Brad Clough, "Sexton: Football Too Much of a Risk," *Washington Square News*, April 24, 2006.

Which Side Are We On?

NYU's Full-Time Faculty and the GSOC Strike

JEFF GOODWIN

> As a group, American professors have seldom if ever been polit-
> ically engaged: the trend toward a technician's role has, by
> strengthening their apolitical professional ideology, reduced
> whatever political involvement they may have had and often,
> by sheer atrophy, their ability even to grasp political problems.
> —C. WRIGHT MILLS, *White Collar* (New York:
> Oxford University Press, 1951), 136

One of the great myths of the modern academy is that it is chock full of highly politicized "tenured radicals." In this view, a handful of besieged conservative faculty are valiantly defending traditional academic values such as civility, free speech, and the quest for objective truth. This fairy tale only makes sense if one believes that "radicals" include supporters of such far-left extremists as, say, Bill and Hillary Clinton—a notion that many conservatives, alas, actually seem to hold. Universities may indeed be bastions of a kind of centrist liberalism, much to the dismay of conservatives, but faculty radicals and especially radical activists are very few and far between. For that matter, political activists of any kind are exceedingly rare among university faculty today. This has considerable importance for the topic at hand.

While the "corporatization" of the university may yet foster faculty rebellions at elite universities—in defense of traditional faculty prerogatives, no doubt—that day seems very far off. One could even argue that the trend among faculty in recent decades, at least at elite universities, has been in the opposite direction: toward greater individualism, careerism, and practical political apathy. The fact that various forms of intellectual and theoretical radicalism have recently influenced a good deal of scholarship, if only in the humanities (for example, postmodernism, postcolonialism, radical feminism, queer theory, Gramscian Marxism, and so on) does not seem to have slowed this tendency and may even have reinforced it. (Alas, many theoretical radicals in the academy have no practical political commitments to speak of. Many have quite conventional and even conservative political views.) Consider this: In 1973 and again in 1976, NYU faculty attempted but failed to unionize. (This was before the Supreme Court ruled, in its infamous *Yeshiva* decision of 1980, that full-time faculty at private universities were not eligible to join unions—at least, not any union with which a university was obliged to bargain.) Today, by contrast, full-time NYU faculty seem more interested in negotiating a three-course teaching load with their deans (three courses *per year*) or an extended research sabbatical than in joining a union.

I exaggerate only a little here. The reality is that a surprising number of faculty at NYU were not actively involved one way or the other in the issue of graduate-student unionization, especially faculty who did not themselves work with teaching assistants. Of those who became actively involved, most supported the union and subsequent strike, at least initially, although this support was very uneven across and even within departments. Faculty petitions that supported the right of students to unionize and strike, or which decried sanctions against striking teaching assistants, were signed by two hundred to two hundred eighty faculty, mostly from the Faculty of Arts and Science. (NYU has a faculty of more than three thousand professors, of whom about six hundred fifty are in the FAS.) Anti-union faculty occasionally circulated their own petitions, which were typically signed by fifty to eighty FAS faculty. (Some anti-union petitions gathered upward of one hundred fifty signatures, although a very large number were from faculty in the medical and dental schools, whose students were not part of the bargaining unit.) Thus, while it is fair to say that a majority of faculty who worked with teaching assistants in the bargaining unit supported the right of students to organize and strike, a great many faculty were silent or actively opposed the union. This raises a number of questions: What explains faculty apathy? What were the sources of pro-union sentiment among the faculty? And why were some faculty anti-union? What follow are my own speculative answers to these questions, albeit based on fifteen years' experience at NYU and active involvement in faculty efforts to support the right of students to organize and strike, including the group Faculty Democracy.

Faculty Apathy

The social structure of academic life, especially at elite universities, encourages a type of political apathy that is only rarely overcome on a large scale. Many if not most university faculty today live in a cocoon of professional and job-related commitments, deadlines, anxieties, and fears. Lectures must be prepared, papers graded, research carried out, graduate students mentored, papers prepared for professional meetings, grants applied for, job talks attended, and so on. (Some of us also have partners and children who demand occasional attention.) One's income and status are closely yoked to these responsibilities. Junior (untenured) faculty live especially anxious and lonely lives, striving hard to please their elders and wisely avoiding departmental spats and university politics.

While collaborative research is certainly possible, the incentive structure of the university generally encourages highly individualized forms of research and teaching. Indeed, one of the main attractions of working at an elite research university is the opportunity it affords individuals to pursue their own, often highly specialized, research interests with little day-to-day oversight by their employer. If one wants to study the class anxieties expressed in Victorian literature, for example, and to do most of one's research between 9 P.M. and 3 A.M., then go to it. Professors don't punch clocks, and there is no functional equivalent of the foreman roaming the hallways of academe.

Alas, this lifestyle, while attractive in so many ways, has strongly antisocial aspects. It tends to breed a great deal of individualism, even narcissism, as well as a fair amount of petulance and eccentricity; it does not provide a strong foundation for sympathy or social solidarity with others, even with other faculty or department members (never mind graduate students); and it discourages civic and political engagement, even at the university and community level. What the academic lifestyle in the age of the corporate university encourages, above all, is careerism. Indeed, I would estimate the ratio of what we might call "tenured careerists" to so-called tenured radicals to be at least fifty to one.

Faculty solidarity is also discouraged by extensive stratification among professors. Especially at private universities, the pay and teaching loads of faculty vary considerably. This is aggravated by the "star system" of hiring and promotions, by which a relative handful of academic "stars"—essentially, scholars who can obtain a job offer at any number of elite universities—receive huge salaries and other amenities (one's own institute, for example, or a huge research budget). Even more corrosive of faculty solidarity are the star wannabees: For every academic star, there are at least twenty other faculty who aspire to such a status, with behavior to match.

Faculty solidarity is also made difficult by departmental and institutional divisions. Faculty are especially compartmentalized at NYU, which has a dizzying array of schools and programs. The FAS stands apart from the Steinhardt School of Culture, Education, and Human Development, the Tisch School of the Arts, the Courant Institute of Mathematical Sciences, the Stern Business School, and the Gallatin School of Individualized Study, all of which teach undergraduates as well as graduates. Undergraduates are also taught, mainly by adjunct faculty (who successfully unionized shortly after NYU's teaching assistants) in the School of Continuing and Professional Studies. This framework ensures that faculty who are capable of seeing beyond their own narrow career interests will rarely transcend departmental or disciplinary concerns.

All of which helps to explain, I think, why so many full-time faculty at NYU were not heavily invested one way or the other in the GSOC organizing campaign or strike, including some who regularly worked with teaching assistants. Even within the FAS, where faculty had many opportunities at least to sign a pro- or anti-union petition, nearly half never did so. And for many, signing a petition was the full extent of their activism on this issue, if we may call it that. But given the organization and incentive structure of the university, this should not be particularly surprising.

Faculty Support for GSOC

Despite the quotidian pressures that generate careerism and political ignorance among faculty, the right of graduate students to unionize and strike was supported by a significant number of NYU faculty—far more, certainly, than the number who opposed the union—including a majority of FAS faculty who actually worked with teaching assistants. Compared with Yale and Columbia, moreover, where teaching-assistant unions have confronted virtually uniform faculty hostility or indifference, NYU stands out for the extent of faculty solidarity with students. Whether this indicates an incipient trend remains to be seen.

Exactly how extensive was faculty support for the union? As noted earlier, between 200 and 280 faculty, mostly from the FAS, signed various public petitions in support of the right of teaching assistants to organize and strike. More than 220 faculty became involved in the group Faculty Democracy and signed up for Faculty Democracy's electronic discussion forum; again, most but not all Faculty Democracy members were from the FAS. Most of the faculty who relocated their classes off-campus during the strike—GSOC estimates that as many as six hundred classes were moved off-campus—were presumably part of this pool of union sympathizers.

As the GSOC strike unfolded, faculty support was expressed in three ways: at the individual level; at the departmental level; and through Faculty Democracy, which coordinated many support activities. At the individual level, many faculty agreed to move their classes off-campus so as not to cross picket lines—although the wisdom of this tactic, which inconvenienced faculty and undergraduates without directly affecting the university administration, was widely questioned. More important, many faculty also agreed not to take on the teaching responsibilities of their teaching assistants (e.g., leading discussion sections or doing the grading that teaching assistants would normally do), as this was tantamount to scab labor. At the end of the fall semester, however, virtually all faculty would submit course grades, although some quite belatedly.

At the departmental level, "neutrality statements" were formally adopted by more than twenty departments. These statements indicated that teaching assistants should be free to follow their own consciences in deciding whether to strike and that they would not be penalized by the department in any way for whichever course of action they followed. Some such statements also indicated that departmental officers would not reveal the names of striking students to university officials—although it was generally assumed that the administration would discover sooner or later, by one method or another, which teaching assistants were striking. In the aftermath of the strike, some departmental officers also worked very hard to overturn some of the harsher sanctions that the administration imposed on students.

Departmental neutrality statements were endorsed, among other activities, by Faculty Democracy, which brought together NYU faculty across a wide range of departments and divisions, although most members were from the FAS. (I use the word "member" loosely; the group did not have formal membership requirements.) Faculty Democracy was the most visible collective form of faculty support for the strike, although this support waned as the strike dragged on without resolution.

While a large number of faculty quickly gravitated to Faculty Democracy in November 2005, the group did not of course materialize out of thin air. At the core of Faculty Democracy was a small group of faculty who were already well connected, having been very active in the teaching-assistant–union issue beginning with GSOC's initial organizing campaign—or even earlier, in some cases. Many had also been active in NYU's chapter of the AAUP. Most faculty in this core group were based in the American Studies program or History department, including Andrew Ross, Molly Nolan, Adam Green, Lisa Duggan, Greg Grandin, Rebecca Karl, Harry Harootunian, and Walter Johnson. However, faculty from a range of other departments were also involved in this core group, including Jim Uleman (Psychology), Kristin Ross (Comparative Literature), and myself (Sociology), and several faculty were from divisions outside the FAS, including Stephen Duncombe (Gallatin), Marita Sturken and Nicholas Mirzeoff (Steinhardt), and Anna McCarthy and Dana Polan (Cinema Studies).

What glued together those of us in this core group? Most of us had a long-standing interest in labor issues and the labor movement, and some also had a prior history of political activism—as opposed to the purely theoretical radicalism that is more prevalent on university campuses. Together with adjunct faculty who were organizing at the time, some faculty from this core group—as well as the late Ellen Willis (Journalism), Christine Harrington (Politics), Kathy Hull (General Studies), Micki McGee (Draper Program), and Arvind Rajagopal (Culture and Communication)—had reestablished NYU's AAUP chapter, which flourished briefly in the aftermath of GSOC's initial organizing campaign. The AAUP's brief renaissance grew out of the sense among many faculty that the administration's opposition to the union campaign was undertaken without proper consultation with faculty or in direct opposition to the expressed views of many faculty. After the administration negotiated a contract with GSOC, however, faculty activism dissipated, and the AAUP chapter with it. The chapter's leadership subsequently decided to support Faculty Democracy, thinking that it would be a more effective vehicle for supporting the teaching-assistant strike. To a large extent, then, Faculty Democracy emerged from the previous activities and networks of NYU's AAUP chapter.

Faculty who participated in Faculty Democracy, as its name indicates, were concerned with the general lack of faculty power and administrative transparency at NYU. The great majority were full-time professors from the FAS, as opposed to adjunct faculty, and were generally senior (tenured) faculty. These were faculty, in other words, who were perceived, and generally perceived themselves, to have a stake in the direction and, indeed, "ownership" of the university, but whose interests were being thwarted by administrators. Many were angry that the administration's longstanding opposition to the union did not reflect the views of faculty who actually worked with teaching assistants. In fact, many felt that on a whole range of issues—including the selection in 2001 of John Sexton to become university president—faculty views were being ignored by the administration in contravention of academic norms and traditions.

Faculty interest in Faculty Democracy grew exponentially immediately before and after the teaching-assistant strike began. One important event that galvanized Faculty Democracy at the outset of the strike became known as "Blackboardgate." (Blackboard is a popular "electronic forum" through which faculty can post course outlines, documents, and links to articles, and engage in discussions with students in their classes.) On the very first day of the strike, some FAS faculty discovered that their Blackboard accounts had been surreptitiously accessed by two associate deans. Faculty suspected the administration of spying on courses to determine which teaching assistants were striking, the better to penalize them. The administration cited "inadvertent technological error," but many faculty were outraged by this event, which seemed yet another indication of the administration's disdain for faculty prerogatives—in this case, the right to teach however one likes without administrative oversight. The Blackboard incident was one of the key complaints in a petition signed by more than two hundred faculty in November, a petition addressed to President Sexton that stated that "faculty trust in the administration's good faith has been irreparably damaged." (Some faculty wished to go further than this petition and pass a resolution of no confidence in President Sexton, but most balked at that move.)

What exactly did Faculty Democracy do? Shortly before the strike began, a group of about twenty-five Faculty Democracy members met with President Sexton, urging him to avoid a strike by returning to the bargaining table with GSOC. But Sexton would not budge. He suggested that it was GSOC's choice to "suffer a slow death or a quick one." After the strike began, Faculty Democracy served primarily as a discussion forum that galvanized various collective actions. Courses of action would be discussed at group meetings or online, but it was left to individual faculty members to decide how, or whether, to act. Faculty Democracy members participated in strike rallies and marched on picket lines; circulated several petitions in support of the strike; set up a website; encouraged scholars outside NYU to sign a petition supporting the striking teaching assistants (nearly five thousand would eventually do so); put together a well-attended teach-in on the strike for undergraduates; and organized a protest march that mourned the death of faculty democracy at NYU.

As this summary suggests, a good deal of faculty involvement in Faculty Democracy (beyond its core), and much faculty support for the strike—as well as for the earlier unionization campaign—may have had less to do with the faculty's political beliefs or sympathy for teaching assistants than with a fear that their own professional autonomy was under threat from the administration. In any event, it was the administration, not GSOC, that really mobilized the faculty. For to attack the teaching assistants' union, the administration had to either ignore or shamefully misrepresent faculty views on the union issue. This provoked a faculty reaction that made the administration's effort to squash the strike that much more difficult.

Faculty Opposition to the Strike

It is difficult to gauge the full extent of faculty opposition to the teaching-assistant union and strike. As noted earlier, about fifty to eighty FAS faculty generally signed anti-union petitions. But, of course, there was much less need for faculty activism on this front since the NYU administration amply represented, in effect, anti-union faculty. Also, some faculty no doubt hesitated to sign public petitions that aligned them with a minority viewpoint and would perhaps alienate most of their colleagues and students.

Faculty opponents of the union and strike generally came in three flavors. First, there were those who opposed the union because they felt it would be practically harmful or simply made no sense in a university context. (Some conservative faculty opposed the union on strictly ideological grounds, but this was fairly rare—or, at least, rarely expressed.) Many opponents of the union were concentrated in the natural sciences and feared (groundlessly, as a matter of fact) that union rules would prohibit graduate students from putting in the long hours in the laboratory that were necessary for scientific training. Many from this group also felt the union had won certification in the first place only because of the exclusion ("gerrymandering") of certain groups of science students from the bargaining unit. (Of course, the bargaining unit was decided by the National Labor Relations Board, not by GSOC.)

NYU's Philosophy Department was also a center of anti-union sentiment, standing out from the other humanities disciplines in this regard. Professor Paul Boghossian was an especially energetic opponent of the union, arguing on technical grounds, albeit with surprising fervor, that it made no sense to regard teaching assistants as "primarily" workers. Less surprisingly, most faculty in the Economics Department also opposed the union and strike, feeling that unions, if they were necessary at all, were certainly not necessary for graduate students. In fact, faculty diatribes against GSOC would commonly begin with the words, "I'm not anti-union in general, but . . ." or "I've always supported the labor movement, but. . . ." For many faculty, in fact, the presumptive middle-class origins and aspirations of graduate students seemed to disqualify them from the category "worker" and hence from union membership. Some faculty seemed to feel that graduate students could only play act as trade unionists, a category that included steel and auto workers but certainly not biologists or philosophers. I recall vividly how one of my colleagues initially balked at signing a petition in support of the teaching-assistant union. Having supported the civil-rights struggle, how could she get all worked up about the plight of a few middle-class students?

A second group of faculty who were overtly hostile to the union sprang, not surprisingly, from the ranks of faculty with conspicuously close ties to the administration. This group included some department chairs, former chairs, former deans, and aspirants to chairs and deanships. For example, a few faculty participated on two committees, charged by the administration to report on the union issue, that recommended against continued recognition of GSOC after the expiration of its first contract. These were the University Senate's Academic Affairs and Executive Committees (acting jointly) and the Faculty Advisory Committee on Academic Priorities. Despite their names, these were not independent faculty committees that were elected and responsible to faculty members. Both included deans or other administrators as well as faculty from professional schools and other NYU divisions whose students were not part of the union bargaining unit. Faculty from the FAS, which was the core of the bargaining unit, were severely underrepresented on these committees: The joint Senate committees included only two FAS faculty among fifteen members, and the Faculty Advisory Committee included only six FAS faculty (including a recent dean who had vigorously opposed teaching-assistant unionization) among its twenty members.

Connections with the university administration and to President Sexton in particular also presumably explain the unexpected anti-union stance of Law Professor Derek Bell. Bell would seem to be a model political progressive. He quit Harvard Law School because of its failure to hire more minority faculty and ever since has held a long-term visiting professorship at NYU. However, in response to Scott Sherman's article in *The Nation*, "Bitter Winter at NYU" (January 9–16, 2006), which was sympathetic to the strike, Bell wrote a strongly anti-union letter that mainly rehashed some of the staler propaganda points that the administration had been circulating. Bell seemed especially upset that Sherman portrayed President Sexton as "the bad guy." To be fair to Bell, it should be noted that the law faculty (whose students do not belong to the teaching-assistant bargaining unit) stood solidly behind Sexton, who was their dean before being appointed president. So Bell's antipathy to the union was, in this respect, merely exemplary of faculty opinion at the law school.

Finally, there were the "third way-ers." About six weeks into the strike, some faculty began looking for a means to end it by finding a "third way" between the administration and GSOC. Not all of these faculty were anti-union at the outset, but they came to feel (along with many others) that the strike—which they now thought had virtually no chance of winning—was hurting undergraduates, NYU's reputation, and vulnerable teaching assistants from poor and generally minority backgrounds. And so several proposals were set forth, publicly and privately, mainly from faculty in the Sociology, History, and Anthropology departments, to set up an alternative to GSOC to represent teaching assistants' interests. From GSOC's perspective, these proposals amounted to setting up a phony "company" or "yellow" union. In any event, the administration did not act on any of these initiatives. But the tide of faculty sentiment was clearly turning.

In fact, as the strike moved into December, and visible teaching-assistant support for it seemed to wane (picket lines had all but disappeared), a growing number of formerly sympathetic faculty began to doubt its wisdom. Messages began to appear on the Faculty Democracy discussion forum that questioned continued faculty support for such a doomed effort. Some faculty felt the union was placing the students who remained on strike at great risk for no plausible reason. Even more felt that undergraduates were bearing the costs of the strike, which was having no tangible effect on administrators. The responsible action, accordingly, would be to end the strike. Statements in support of the strike were attacked as wishful thinking. In this hostile context, the core group that had helped establish Faculty Democracy began to hold more and more discussions "off-line." Faculty Democracy was splintering. By the spring, it was a shadow of its former self.

Near the end, the solidarity of Faculty Democracy was severely strained by a series of misinformed allegations about an alleged "witch hunt" to expose and punish faculty opponents of the strike. Faculty Democracy was accused, in short, of a type of left-wing McCarthyism. In reality, a small group of Faculty Democracy members, including myself, had simply volunteered to listen to students who wanted to speak to Faculty Democracy about how they had allegedly been harassed or threatened by faculty for their union sympathies. (In the end, we never actually met with these students.) When word of this spread—it had been openly discussed at a Faculty Democracy meeting—a number of professors denounced the idea as a flagrant violation of academic freedom. One professor likened our actions—never mind that we had not met with any students nor accused any professors of anything—to the terror of the French Revolution. This entire imbroglio, however, highlights the way in which a kind of fundamentalist commitment to academic freedom may stand in the path of solidarity with others.

Lessons?

Whatever their aspirations, white-collar people have been pushed by twentieth-century facts toward the wage-worker kind of organized economic life, and slowly their illusions have been moving into closer harmony with the terms of their existence. They are becoming aware that the world of the old middle class, the community of entrepreneurs, has given way to a new society in which they, the white-collar workers, are part of a world of dependent employees.

—MILLS, *White Collar*, 301–302

Assuming that the corporatization of the academy continues apace, we are likely to see in the years ahead more unionization campaigns, and more strikes, on university campuses, especially by teaching assistants and adjunct faculty, the least powerful academic laborers. Public-sector faculty who are not already unionized will not be far behind, one assumes, and—who knows?—even we faculty at elite private institutions may one day put aside our illusions, discover that we too are dependent employees, and enter the fray. In the meantime, many full-time faculty will face the question of how to relate to teaching assistants and adjunct faculty who are organizing and striking. In short, which side are we on?

What lessons might be drawn from the role of NYU's full-time faculty in the GSOC strike? First, it is important not to exaggerate this role. At the end of the day, the role of faculty was just one of many factors that influenced the outcome of the strike. The strike collapsed for many reasons, no doubt, but it failed primarily because the teaching assistants who struck were unable to impose sufficient costs on the university administration and thereby drive it back to the bargaining table. Instead, administration threats drove many teaching assistants back to the classroom. Had many more teaching assistants struck, and held out much longer, the strike might have had a chance. But in most cases, teaching assistants did not decide to strike, refuse to strike, or discontinue striking primarily because of faculty attitudes or actions. These decisions were the result of a great many concerns. Of course, this does not mean that faculty attitudes and actions did not matter at all or that they will not matter in future strikes. But future teaching-assistant strikes will be won or lost mainly because of the solidarity and institutional leverage—or lack thereof—of teaching assistants themselves, not because of the actions of faculty.

A second lesson is that graduate-student organizing and strikes need not always confront across-the-board faculty opposition. The case of NYU demonstrates that even at elite private universities, with faculties who are generally uninterested in their own self-organization, a significant number of professors can be persuaded to support graduate-student unions. The core supporters of such unions will generally be found among faculty with a prior interest in labor issues and the labor movement—hence, primarily in labor-studies programs, History and American Studies departments, and social-science departments. Supporters are also likely to be found among faculty with a prior history of political activism or who grew up in households with a union member or political activist. Union organizers will want to locate and reach out to such faculty to build faculty support groups and to encourage these faculty to pull still more pro-union faculty into the group through their own networks.

Third, faculty support for teaching-assistant unions and strikes is likely to become especially vigorous when large numbers of faculty feel that administrators are acting against teaching assistants without proper concern for faculty views and prerogatives—in other words, when the faculty's guild privileges, if you like, are being threatened. Faculty sympathy for graduate students, it seems, is generally less robust than faculty concerns for their own putative professional privileges. If and when the latter are trampled in the course of an anti-union campaign, faculty are especially likely to mobilize. It follows that teaching-assistant unions should attempt to yoke faculty concerns with administrative aggrandizement to their own struggles with administrators. Appealing to the guild interests of faculty is more likely to win their support than pleading for such support out of political or moral principle.

Faculty support for graduate-student strikes, however, may be very difficult to sustain for more than a few weeks or months, even when faculty are broadly unhappy with administrators. As mentioned earlier, some faculty grew concerned that the strike would ultimately harm the most vulnerable teaching assistants—namely, graduate students from poor and minority backgrounds, some of whom were the first in their families to attend university. For example, many faculty in the History Department who initially supported the strike quickly came to feel that a prolonged strike in the face of threats from administrators would place these students at disproportionate risk. A fourth lesson of the GSOC strike, then, is that teaching-assistant unions need to reassure faculty as well as their own members, through both words and actions, that they are especially concerned with the needs of the most vulnerable strikers.

The GSOC strike also suggests that faculty who might be inclined to support graduate students in a simple confrontation with university administrators are nonetheless loath to encourage a strike that seems to harm undergraduates. Many NYU faculty grew resentful of striking teaching assistants for imposing costs on undergraduates in the form of relocated classes, canceled classes, canceled discussion sections, withheld grades, and so forth. As the strike wore on, a common faculty complaint was that undergraduates, not administrators or trustees, were mainly suffering the consequences. The fact that, at least initially, teaching assistants had not lost any of their own benefits by striking only added to the resentment. With considerable encouragement from the administration, many faculty came to view the strike as selfish and insensitive to the educational needs of undergraduates, including seniors who would need grades to graduate and financially needy students who required a certain number of credits to retain their scholarships.

Of course, most faculty fully realize that the point of a strike is to bring pressure to bear on employers by withholding labor. In the service sector of the economy, however, clients as well as employers suffer when labor is withheld and a service is not provided. In higher education, undergraduates are the main "clients"—and they cannot simply relocate to another institution in the event of a strike. Thus, a graduate-student strike imposes direct costs not only or even mainly on employers or administrators but on undergraduates. Any faculty strike would do the same.

Thus, a final lesson of the GSOC strike is really a challenge for graduate-student unions—namely, to discover creative ways to pressure employers directly, in the strongest possible way, while minimizing harm to other members of the university community, especially undergraduates. If such harm turns out to be unavoidable, then unions will need to work hard to prepare undergraduates to assume these costs. And undergraduates in turn will need to assure faculty that they are bearing such costs willingly. Otherwise, faculty will likely blame striking teaching assistants for disrupting the education of undergraduates—a responsibility that most faculty take very seriously. From the perspective of many NYU faculty, including pro-union faculty, this was the Achilles' heel of the teaching-assistant strike. GSOC did mobilize undergraduate support but not enough to dampen faculty concerns about the disruption of undergraduate education.

Undergraduate Participation in Campus Labor Coalitions

Lessons from the NYU Strike

Andrew Cornell

In the flood of commentary that followed the historic shutdown of the 1999 World Trade Organization meetings in Seattle, no slogan was invoked as frequently as the now famous, "Turtles and Teamsters, Together at Last!" With its breathless promise of a green–blue alliance, it served as a placeholder for broad hopes about the potential for building "unity in action" among the famously balkanized U.S. left at the end of the millennium. Transforming that hopeful sentiment into concrete action, however, would require more than finding common ground in the agendas of the AFL-CIO and the Audubon Society. It would mean creating respect for serious tactical differences and a search for ways to harmonize organizations with very different internal organizational structures—small anarchist affinity groups and million-member–strong international unions, for example—into functional coalitions. Both the difficulties and the importance of this sort of coalitional work became evident in the series of mass actions that occurred in cities across the United States in the years immediately following Seattle.

In this search for collaboration, the student anti-sweatshop movement offered some hope. Students had forged working relationships with mainstream labor, most notably the garment workers' union UNITE! two years prior to Seattle, and their collaborative efforts to expose abysmal labor standards in the offshore production of collegiate and name-brand apparel was responsible for much of the anticorporate sentiment and growing awareness of "globalization" in the lead-up to the Seattle actions.[1] Afterward, these activists' fluid connections to student environmentalists and their overlap with militantly minded youth in some parts of the country positioned them to act as a potential hinge. The student group–union relationship was certainly not seamless—tensions over the students' autonomy from unions that funded them and disagreements about "protectionism" and other policy issues emerged early on—but the alliance had, at least, produced tangible results.[2] However, many of the efforts to cement a Global Justice partnership were put on ice following the September 11 attacks, the increased repression of social movements, and the redirection of organizing efforts that came in tow.

The union of graduate-student employees at New York University, GSOC/ UAW Local 2110, won recognition in the exhilarating period between Seattle and September 11, aided significantly by undergraduates enthusiastic about partnering with unions on local, as well as international, campaigns.[3] As GSOC's contract expired at the outset of the fall 2005 semester and NYU declared its refusal to bargain, the union again looked to undergraduate labor activists for support. Though the focus of campus organizing had shifted to antiwar work in the intervening years, GSOC found a cohort of undergraduates, still heavily influenced by Global Justice sensibilities, willing to collaborate when the union declared a strike to maintain recognition as the legal representative of NYU's teaching and research assistants.

Despite the efforts of thousands of people, the strike was ultimately unsuccessful. Undergraduates, as a central constituency on campus, affected this outcome in a variety of ways. Voicing a common perception of how the conflict unfolded, the NYU student activist Sarah Dell'Orto recalls that "toward the beginning of the strike there was an incredible amount of undergrad support. As the year wore on, some undergrads got bored, while I think others were either alienated or simply annoyed with the strike." An examination of why and how such broad undergraduate support swung rapidly toward apathy or hostility raises important questions about the union's overall strike strategy. It also indicates that tensions and disagreements that developed during the campaign between student activists and union leaders are reflective of differences at the national scale. By providing a case study of undergraduate–union relations during the 2005 strike at NYU, then, I hope to help develop a more coherent praxis of student involvement in academic labor struggles, but also to refocus discussion on ways to overcome barriers to building a networked, coalitional Global Justice movement.

Preparations

GSOC had to start nearly from scratch in developing awareness, credibility, and political capital among undergraduates when it began organizing to force NYU to negotiate a second contract in 2005. Member organizers worked to provide information to, and win the support (or, at least, neutralize the opposition) of the student body as a whole. In addition, GSOC sought to develop close working relationships with undergraduate social-justice activists who were eager to participate in the campaign on a deeper level and who viewed the success of the fight as tied to their larger political goals. GSOC looked to these undergraduate organizers to take on much of the work necessary to build union solidarity among their classmates.

Grad/Undergrad Solidarity (GUS) was initiated in the spring of 2005 when GSOC members contacted undergraduate student activists who had participated in other labor campaigns on campus, including a successful effort to ban Coca-Cola products from NYU.[4] These students were amenable to meeting due in part to the contributions GSOC organizers had previously made to the undergraduate-led campaigns. Students with little or no labor-activist experience joined this core in September and October, after being recruited by their teaching assistants, professors, or members of GUS. The group ranged in size from ten to thirty active members over the course of the campaign and included a few law students and graduate students who fell outside of GSOC's bargaining unit.

In the month prior to the strike, GUS members worked to educate the student body about the causes and stakes of the dispute and to publicize ways to support the teaching assistants. Many volunteered to deliver short presentations, developed in collaboration with GSOC members, to classes taught by faculty who supported the strike, resulting in conversations with more than a thousand students. GUS members argued that having a graduate-student union improved the quality of education undergraduates received and helped to make the university more democratic and responsive to its various constituencies. As the GUS member Canek Peña-Vargas put it, "We kept alive an alternative to the message that the administration was pro-student in the process of being anti-union. I think our presence in classes and [later] on the picket line reminded strikers that they were not victimizing their students, that they were in fact struggling with their students for a cause that would benefit them both."

Strike: The First Semester

When the strike began, GSOC's Organizing Committee, counseled by staff members of its parent union, the United Autoworkers of America, urged undergraduates and faculty members to show support by holding and attending classes off-campus as a means of honoring the picket line but did not attempt to shut down the university or to physically restrict access to the buildings it picketed. GSOC asked faculty to petition and lobby the administration; urged undergraduates to display their sympathies using pins, stickers, and armbands; and encouraged everyone to join in the daily pickets. Although undergraduate activists and union staff alike knew that obstructive acts of civil disobedience undertaken by students had proved effective in recent campus-labor conflicts, the possibility of actions of this sort were never directly discussed.[5]

These tactical decisions were based on a set of beliefs firmly held by union leaders that were rarely voiced comprehensively, but that fundamentally shaped the campaign. Union staff and many Organizing Committee members believed that GSOC organizers would be unable to persuade sufficient numbers of their members, along with students, faculty, and staff, to willingly cease all nonessential campus activities or to physically impede university operations on a large scale. On the contrary, building broad support from other on-campus constituencies depended on being less disruptive and asking fairly little of them, while winning support from politicians, the labor movement, and the "general public" required the use of only non-obstructive, "respectable" tactics. Those developing strategy believed that the labor withheld by union members, coupled with the support of these other on- and off-campus constituencies, would provide sufficient pressure to crack NYU. Graduate-student union strikes for recognition at Columbia and Yale in recent years had been premised on nearly the same set of assumptions, and these strikes had not proved successful. Union leaders believed they could achieve a different outcome by mobilizing greater staff and faculty support and carrying on the strike longer than previous ones.

During the early weeks of the strike, more than a thousand students signed a pro-union petition, while hundreds attended teach-ins and wore union pins, stickers, and armbands. Students encouraged professors to move classes off campus and attended classes that were moved without complaint. GSOC staff members found off-campus locations for more than five hundred classes during the fall semester. The *Washington Square News,* NYU's student newspaper, editorialized that "increasingly, [a] gulf exists not only between the administration and the Graduate Student Organizing Committee, but between the majority of our campus and the administration, which is supported by a vocal minority."[6] Student support, of course, was not universal. However, resentment never hardened into an organized anti-union student group or campaign, as had happened during previous academic labor strikes.

GUS members picketed regularly and worked assiduously to create a positive visual presence for GSOC on campus. They covered bathroom stalls and lampposts with thousands of stickers, détourned NYU promotional materials, created and distributed "GSOC LOVE" t-shirts, and produced a twenty-eight-page 'zine (homemade, photocopied magazine) analyzing the conflict. A week into the strike, GUS began to organize a large-scale "Day of Action" that would provide a forum for undergraduates to collectively demonstrate their support of the union. Organizers called for a class boycott, a lunchtime rally at the center of campus, and a joint teach-in and concert to follow. The class boycott proved a flop, but hundreds of students joined the rally as morning lectures let out. Organizers made the rally open mike to allow students the opportunity to express whatever opinions *they* had about the then three-week-old strike. Students were overwhelmingly pro-union but spoke from their experience and opinions, making their comments qualitatively different from those that had been offered by strikers and guest labor leaders over the preceding weeks. A GUS member closed the rally by explaining that the group had a letter to present to NYU President John Sexton and a banner they planned to unfurl inside the university library, where NYU administrative offices are located.

"What do we want? Contract!" Members of Grad/Undergrad Solidarity lead the charge into the Bobst Library to demand that NYU President John Sexton recognize GSOC. *(Juan Monroy)*

GUS members led approximately three hundred students to the picket line, then called for the assembled crowd to enter the library, and hundreds did. After administrators claimed Sexton was unavailable to meet with student representatives, GUS encouraged the crowd to read its letter aloud in unison. The demands of hundreds of students indignantly ringing throughout the sacred, usually hushed space of the library was a powerful, even transformative, event. Still energized after delivering its letter verbally, the group climbed ten flights of stairs to demand a meeting with the president. An hour long sit-in ensued when security guards blocked demonstrators from continuing past the tenth floor, ending with students chanting, "We'll Be Back!" The action put administrators on notice that students placed responsibility for the strike on NYU's shoulders and were growing impatient. Undergraduates had stretched the tactical envelope and injected a sense of excitement into the conflict that inspired union supporters and forced the university to react defensively.

Strike: The Second Semester

The second semester of the GSOC strike was experienced nearly unanimously as a very difficult time for union members and allies alike. Rebuilding excitement and resolve after the month-long semester break proved even more challenging than organizers had anticipated. As the semester began, many graduate students returned to work, and the enthusiasm of those who remained was put to the test by an apparent deadlock with the administration and gray, frosty mornings on the picket line. Frequently, no more than a half-dozen picketers represented the union, where forty or more had before the break. Faculty members moved classes back to campus with little opposition from students. Undergraduate support diminished sharply, sometimes turning to bitter resentment.

Statements on the op-ed page and comments made by undergraduates indicate that students saw themselves as a party to the conflict that demanded constant, concerted attention. A January 23 *Washington Square News* editorial claimed, "If GSOC wants to consider itself a viable, active organization, it needs to show the undergraduates that it is. Right now, GSOC appears weakened and complacent, self-assured that its cause is self-explanatory."[7] Reflecting on the strike months later, the GUS member Anne Rudnick concurred with this diagnosis. In her opinion, "Undergraduate support wasn't earned in the second semester and was often taken for granted." Such sentiments led GSOC to question the degree to which it needed to "perform" its strike for undergraduates. While members felt that having large and boisterous picket lines every day was not their top priority—since energy spent by members on other aspects of the campaign, such as lobbying, would likely do more to pressure the administration—they understood that many students judged the strength of the union primarily on the vibrancy and consistency of the picket line. The willingness of many to support, or even tolerate, the union depended on how strong they perceived it to be. Dave Hancock, a member of GUS, states, "I know that folks got tired of the withering picket lines, tired of the same old arguments and tired of tactics that seemed less to affect the administration and more to just bother and inconvenience students."

The second semester of the strike was also hard on GUS. Feeling the flagging morale on campus, members of the group thought concerted efforts were needed to demonstrate that union members and their supporters were still committed to winning the strike. Members of GUS met with a group of strikers interested in engaging in a building occupation or other obstructionist tactics. When GSOC staff members found out about these efforts, however, they moved to quash them, arguing that efforts of the sort were out of sync with the overall strategy and might look desperate. Disappointment with having its action rebuked was compounded by other frustrations for GUS members. GSOC faced mounting criticism from its members for its nontransparent decision-making process, its inattention to the specific concerns of international students and students of color, and its unsatisfactory handling of complaints about sexist and homophobic remarks made by members. GUS members began to feel disillusioned about the "structure, secrecy, and hierarchy of the union," as one member put it. Though GUS members rededicated themselves to winning the campaign after GSOC underwent significant internal reorganization, undergraduate support never rebounded to its first-semester heights.

In all, it seems that undergraduate support for the strike declined in the spring semester because (1) the negative effects of the strike on their lives and studies were dragged out and piled up over a long period without visible signs of progress in winning the strike; (2) undergraduates were not sufficiently organized; and (3) they were not inspired. In a campus strike, the union not only has to keep the entire bargaining unit organized, but it needs to keep a substantial number students and faculty, on whom it depends for moral support and supplementary action, involved with and supportive of the campaign. GSOC decided to request a certain kind of sacrifice from striking graduate students and their supporters; it asked them to make a low-risk sacrifice of time and energy for a long period of time. An alternative strategy might request a different kind of sacrifice—risking greater personal consequences but having to devote considerably less time. One serious, perhaps overriding, problem with the first strategy is that it does not marshal excitement, energy, and passion, making it extremely difficult to build a sense of real momentum in the hearts of union supporters.

The Challenge of Organizing Undergraduates

A few months after the strike recess, GUS members celebrated their positive contributions to the campaign and tried to assess the mistakes or shortcomings that they felt had contributed to the inability to win to date. The undergraduates did not have a solid organizing orientation. In the lead-up to the strike, GSOC and GUS viewed the group's main task as educating their fellow students about the union and strike in the hope that they would decide to support the campaign. Less attention was paid to expanding and solidifying GUS itself, and implementing an organizing model was never strongly considered by members of either group. While GSOC offered some GUS members training in how to deal effectively with media, they were not encouraged or trained to methodically pursue and develop the interest, participation, and skills of potential activists. In a campaign with more resources, the union might offer a weekend-long organizing institute for students or even consider hiring some to work part time as paid organizers.

However, the reticence to organize more systematically also stemmed in part from concerns raised by GUS members. Some expressed a hesitancy for the group to get too large and a concern that union-style organizing techniques were authoritarian. As discussed earlier, GUS initially took shape around a core of activists who had worked successfully as a small group in previous campaigns. The GUS member Kristin Campbell explains, "From the beginning, most of the core members of GUS were serious about creating a non-hierarchical, anti-authoritarian structure based on a modified consensus decision-making model. Most of us entered into organizing at a moment where this kind of model was deemed the *only* acceptable model." At one meeting, some members of the group argued that working with substantially more members made it difficult to make decisions using the consensus process, which privileged extensive discussion and attempts to incorporate the perspective of everyone involved. They believed the group could get more done if it remained a small unit. This hesitancy to grow seemed to stem from the experience of previous campaigns in which student groups could garner only a handful of dedicated participants. In those campaigns, the members of the core group had to assess whether their time was best spent recruiting or simply taking on heavier workloads for themselves. They were caught off guard, then, by large numbers of volunteers in the first week of the strike. In some ways, the structure made it difficult to incorporate and empower these new recruits. Campbell explains, "Spouting terms like 'non-hierarchical' and 'anti-authoritarian' came to stand in for many *organizing* basics like tactical outreach, making real connections with folks, delegating responsibility to others, and solidly building with other groups." Reflecting on the organization, Campbell also believes that GUS operated with an "ambiguous and implicitly seniority-based structure"—wherein some members held more clout even if they did not hold formal positions of power—that resulted from the friendships and working relationships some members had developed during previous campaigns. Combined, these issues "made it hard for GUS to keep up its momentum."

If it was challenging for GUS to retain members, part of the difficulty lay in finding ways to involve newcomers, which quickly instilled a sense that their time and energy was valuable. GUS was most successful at integrating newcomers during the build-up to the Day of Action. This was a large, tangible effort, controlled by students, that required a number of different skill sets. Students organized themselves into a variety of subcommittees, including ones that drafted the letter to be delivered to the university president, a publicity committee that created and wheat-pasted original artwork, a committee to create a guerrilla-theater skit for the event, and a committee to recruit speakers and help with the logistics. This variety gave newcomers a choice of activities where they could best use their skills, and having the larger tasks broken down made it possible to see how individuals' contributions were important to the success of the whole project.

GSOC and GUS were never able to establish mass picket-line participation, even though they tried several tactics, including publicizing a specified time for undergraduates to join in each day and giving out free food on certain occasions. Part of the problem, Dave Hancock believes, was that "no undergrad wished they were fighting the GSOC fight as a GSOC [member]. They wanted to fight it as an undergrad." One apparent reason for the success of the November 30 Day of Action was that it was billed as an opportunity for undergraduates to participate on their own terms. In retrospect, Hancock states, "I feel like there should have been less conventional ways for undergrads to get involved designed to demonstrate that we had power as unique stakeholders in the community that could be exercised through alternative channels and mechanisms."

The Student Group–Union Relationship

The relationship between members of GUS and GSOC began amicably amid a shared sense of dedication and excitement about the campaign. Not surprisingly, frustrations and divisions developed over the course of the year of collaborative action. The relationship that developed between GUS and GSOC can be used to discuss more generally challenges that arise in partnerships between unions and student groups.

Unions and Student Organizations Have Different Organizational Structures

During its strike, GSOC functioned similarly to a union in an organizing drive. It was organized on a three-tier approach with staff and a small, shifting coterie of members driving planning; an Organizing Committee that elaborated and attempted to carry out organizing; and the general membership, which the Organizing Committee sought to motivate. GUS, as we have seen, attempted to create a "flat" organizational model. Neither group clearly elaborated its organizational structure to the other, and, Campbell explains, for most of the campaign "we never had any real idea about the specifics of how decisions got made." This made it difficult for GUS to bring ideas, suggestions, and concerns—especially about interactions with undergraduates—to the union.

These different approaches to creating organizations are not necessarily irreconcilable. They reflect two attempts to organize collective action in a way that balances values of participation, equality, and efficiency. Over the course of the campaign, each group had to face shortcomings of its approach and ended up recognizing valuable aspects in the other's structure. It seems clear that a discussion at the outset of the collaboration clearly outlining the organizing and decision-making principles of the organizations would have created more clarity and common ground. The groups would not have to fully endorse each other's structure, but they would have had a much better sense of the terms on which they were entering into coalition.

GSOC Leaders Held Contradictory Impulses toward the Amount of Independence GUS Should Be Given

GSOC sought to send a clear and consistent message to the broader undergraduate community about why it was striking and what students should do to support the strike. It also worked hard to control its "messaging" to the press to win the support of politicians and the public and bruise NYU's image. To achieve these goals, GSOC sought a significant amount of control over GUS to keep student activists "on message." In this regard, GUS members were envisioned as auxiliary organizers of GSOC itself. Yet GSOC also hoped for and was happy to reap the benefits of independent actions taken by undergraduates (such as the library occupation) that it did not feel union members could be involved in planning. In these instances, undergrads were more usefully portrayed as wild cards inspired by the struggle to take action outside the union's hands—a symbol of the unknown and uncontrollable forces sure to break out in reaction to the campus crisis caused by administrative intransigence. This tension played out, among other situations, in questions of resource allocation. GUS depended on use of the UAW's copy machine to produce leaflets, and the UAW staff required approval of all materials that were being run off on the union's dime. This is understandable, but it delayed turnaround time on written materials and led to a reduction in student voice. After editing, undergraduate communications took on the tone of union communications.

Students Were Not Offered a Place in the Strategic Planning of the Campaign

Instead, plans were established by union leadership, and undergraduates were asked to help out or "plug in." One GSOC member, and sometimes a few members, attended all GUS meetings and reported back to the union organizing committee. GUS members often went to the union office to carry out work but were not invited to attend union Organizing Committee meetings. Most members of GUS accepted the political principle, established during the civil-rights and feminist struggles of the 1960s and '70s, that those who were negatively affected in a direct way by institutions or policies should determine the contours of the struggle opposing them. Yet working in a support or solidarity role for another constituency is something of an anomaly for many student activists, who are used to serving as the primary agents of change in campus-based campaigns for social justice.

Kristin Campbell now feels that undergraduate activists had a right to help establish strike strategy. "First of all, we had been through fighting the administration in earlier campaigns," she says. "We were putting in a lot of hard work and energy—more than many members of the union who were able to attend meetings. On top of that, we had a much better sense of undergrad opinion on campus. I feel that since we were willing to put ourselves on the line so much, and commit so much to the strike, that [gave] us the right to be in there strategizing and helping to make decisions." Union members may claim the right to full decision-making power in their own campaigns. But in doing so they risk alienating allies who feel their opinions or potential contributions are being neglected and disrespected. The union needs to evaluate how useful those allies' contributions are, in the short and long term, and whether it can afford to lose them if it is unwilling to open planning to those who offer significant support to the campaign.

Should Allies Take Greater Risks than Members?

Undergraduate opinion about strategy diverged most sharply from the GSOC leadership's over the importance of increasing levels of obstruction and confrontation on campus through civil-disobedience and direct-action tactics. GUS members with years of experience challenging NYU policies were "coming from a perspective where direct action seemed like the only way to get things we wanted," explained Campbell. The group was surprised, then, when it began to "seem like direct action wasn't on GSOC's mind, or something that wasn't wanted." In its initial contract campaign, GSOC actively encouraged undergraduates to partake in obstructive actions, but in 2005 the union's position was less clear.[8] Since it was assumed the strike would not be won through disruption, direct action was not prioritized. Still, staff members acknowledged that student actions had been beneficial to previous campaigns. "There are things that others will do, that we won't even know about, and that's fine," explained one staff member. By implication, GSOC members were not to be involved in actions of that sort.

The fact that GSOC encouraged students to engage in direct action in 2001 and celebrated the brief building occupation by undergraduates in 2005, and yet actively discouraged its members from participating in similar activities, raises an important question: Is it fair to encourage allies to engage in actions in which members of the union will not? An ethical affirmative answer to this question has to be based on the assumption that such actions involve fewer repercussions if carried out by non-members. Either the allies will be punished less severely by authorities, these consequences will be easier to bear by those receiving them, or the actions will not reflect as negatively on the credibility of the union. It appears that GSOC organizers and GUS members assessed these risks differently.

Campbell explains that GUS members did not attempt more actions autonomously because "we were not going to be the forerunners of some kind of occupation if the constituency that is actually striking isn't even thinking about doing something like that. We were waiting for the energy to come from grad students on strike." In the students' eyes, GSOC members were as able to engage in direct action as they were. When asked whether the situation would have been different if the people striking had filled a structural position accorded less privilege—for instance, if the striking workers had been immigrant custodial workers with families and a higher chance of being fired—Dave Hancock said, "Definitely. I think we wouldn't have expected them to take the lead in that situation." While in other aspects of the campaign, undergraduates were expected to follow the lead of union members and leadership, they were expected to take on the risks of direct action on their own accord. Here again, clearer conversations about what GSOC and GUS expected of each other would have been productive. This was hindered by GSOC's disinclination to have undergraduates attend Organizing Committee meetings and the insistence that potentially illegal actions not be discussed openly at union meetings.

Lessons Learned

The graduate-student–employee union movement cannot afford to ignore the strategic lessons learned by GSOC over the course of the 2005–2006 school year. Member and ally organizing is fundamental. Tactical creativity and variety, boldness, and a willingness to escalate are necessary not only to tighten the vise on administrators, but also to maintain the attention and support of non-strikers whose support helps to maintain the strikers' resolve. It is possible to mobilize undergraduate support, but maintaining such sympathy requires consistent, concerted effort and substantial resources. As coalitional work requires skill sets and relationships different from those that many student activists are accustomed to, clear and direct communication—along with a mutual willingness to negotiate over certain issues—is essential. While such a commitment to mutual understanding, dialogue, and appreciation cannot be expected to solve all conflicts, it has the potential to significantly reduce tensions and misunderstandings between the parties. It is my hope that these observations contribute to strategic conversations that move the labor movement toward more wins and a stronger progressive presence on university campuses and elsewhere.

Notes

1. Lisa Featherstone and United Students against Sweatshops, *Students against Sweatshops* (New York: Verso, 2002).

2. See Bhumika Muchhala, "Students against Sweatshops," in *A Movement of Movements: Is Another World Really Possible?* ed. Tom Mertes (New York: Verso, 2004).

3. Lisa Jessup, "The Campaign for Union Rights at NYU," in *Steal This University: The Rise of the Corporate University and the Academic Labor Movement,* ed. Patrick Kavanagh, Kevin Mattson (New York: Routledge, 2003); Charlie Eaton, "Student Unionism and Sustaining Student Power," *Social Text* 70 (2002): 51–60. Kitty Krupat and Laura Tanenbaum, "A Network for Campus Democracy: Reflections on NYU and the Academic Labor Movement," *Social Text* 70 (2002): 27–50.

4. See Michael Blanding, "The Case against Coke," *Nation,* May 1, 2006, 13–17.

5. Kristian Williams, "The Sweatshop and the Ivory Tower," in *We Are Everywhere: The Irresistible Rise of Global Anticapitalism,* ed. Notes from Nowhere (New York: Verso, 2003); Krupat and Tanenbaum, "Network for Campus Democracy," 43.

6. "Ignoring GSOC Abandons Education," *Washington Square News,* November 9, 2005, 4.

7. "Move It Along, GSOC," *Washington Square News,* January 23, 2006, 4.

8. Eaton, "Student Unionism," 53; Jessup, "Campaign for Union Rights," 168.

Village Hospitality

Matthew Osypowski

Even surrounded by the diverse sprawl of Manhattan, the impact of a strike involving the community's largest employer resonates beyond the walls of the workplace. The co-dependent relationship between smaller institutions and the central behemoth plays out in all manner of ways—economic, social, and political—and neither unions nor employers can afford to neglect the interests and opinions of the wider community without being called to account. While the power may seem to be held exclusively by the central institution, such is rarely the case, and many strikes are won or lost by the actions of these peripheral players.

During the GSOC strike, sympathetic small businesses and nonprofits took in hundreds of classes, often free of charge. These moves offered a unique opportunity to examine the complex relationship that exists between New York University and the diverse population of Greenwich Village. NYU is the single largest employer in downtown Manhattan, and the relocation of classes—to drafty basements, theaters, churches, restaurants—had the potential to be a decisive statement, one that simultaneously illustrated vast faculty support, disrupted the functioning of the university, and brought the community into the conflict in a direct, physical way.

It didn't quite happen. While the disruption was substantial, the university did not budge. The vast majority of classes were back on campus by the beginning of the strike's second semester—the halls full, the picket lines vastly reduced, the stampede of faculty rebellion safely corralled. What was achieved during those early months, and what lasting footprints were left behind in the larger Manhattan community? Who were these people who had opened the doors to our union? What did the students and professors bring back on their return?

We visited the host locations and conducted a series of interviews with owners, employees, faculty, and students. These interviews took place in the spring of 2006, near the end of the second and final semester of the GSOC strike. What follows is an exploration of our findings.

Liz Roberts is an activist to the core, critical and pragmatic but still very much a believer in meaningful dialogue and old-fashioned socialist revolution. She is an administrator at the Brecht Forum, a newly remodeled Marxist educational venue overlooking the Hudson River, an airy space with potted plants and a communal kitchen, no interior doors, loose lumber still leaning against some of the walls. Roberts described the Brecht Forum as "a refuge for radical faculty at higher-education institutions" established in the late 1960s "for non-sectarian dialogue . . . when sectarianism was tearing the left apart." The space hosts classes and workshops in topics ranging from socialist history to avant-garde jazz and is often used by professors who are looking to test pilot projects, host book-release parties, or teach courses with material deemed too radical for mainstream universities. Many of these "radical faculty" have tenure at NYU. When the strike began in November 2005, the Brecht Forum was quick to open its door.

Keith Vincent's "World Cultures: Japan" was one of many courses that relocated to the Brecht. It was a large class, enrolling 120 freshmen, and Vincent was scheduled to teach it in a relatively plush lecture hall at NYU equipped with stadium seating, PowerPoint projections, a polished space that screamed of professionalism. The transition to Brecht was abrupt.

"All of a sudden we moved to a very cramped space," said Vincent. "We were all on one level—I was sitting among them and lecturing." It is a long trip from NYU to Brecht, either on the subway or by foot, and the wind off the river makes for a cold walk. Not all of his students were eager to embrace the inconvenience. "I think you should know that I don't support this strike at all," wrote one in the course of a heated e-mail exchange. "I think it's a colossal waste of the undergrads' time and money for the [teaching assistants] and supportive staff to be acting this way. I have a hard time understanding any undergrad who supports such a strike, as they are essentially supporting a cause that will be detrimental to their grades and to their overall learning experience. I realize you feel you are being very righteous in withholding our grades from the registrar, but I see this action as nothing more than further arrogance on your part." Although this student was not alone in his frustration, such anger seemed to be the exception rather than the rule. "I (along with countless others from the class) truly admire you for informing us of what we couldn't hear and never giving up on what you believe," wrote another student in reply, expressing what seemed to be the opinion of the majority.

For her part, Roberts discussed the strike with the sympathetic air of an organizer who has been on the losing side of many such battles. Although only in her early thirties, she told me, she has been involved in "leftist politics" for fifteen years and has thought of herself as a socialist since she was fourteen. She described both GSOC and the Transport Workers Union strike of the same year as "surges that spark a renewed sense of hope" in the direction of American society, but generally acknowledged that "things have been pretty abysmal" for labor in recent years.

Roberts had very little personal contact with NYU faculty or students. The Brecht Forum was always hosting classes, and these felt no different from the others. NYU was, in her eyes, a "gentrifying, corporate force that continues to grow and creep all over the neighborhood." Teaching assistants represented "just another sector of labor," and it was clear to her that our cause was very much in line with the Brecht Forum's larger mission of "developing class consciousness and solidarity across different sectors." I found Roberts's casual empathy to be somewhat disconcerting. On the one hand, the Brecht Forum can be so easily placed within the current political climate as a representative of a familiar, idealistic, increasingly marginalized, almost antiquated fringe of the liberal left—a group with which I identify very closely but which, in recent decades, has lacked both the solidarity and the influence to significantly slow the rightward march of America. On the other hand, the diversity of those who teach and organize at the Brecht, and the obvious passion they bring to their work, made me ashamed of my cynicism. This split between ideological sympathy and pragmatic cynicism was, I realized, exactly what I saw and was frustrated by in many of my peers' reactions to the strike itself.

A struggling artist by trade, I was a bit more comfortable descending into the Village basement that houses the Millennium Film Workshop. It is situated beneath a relatively quiet block of East 4th Street, the space consisting of a reception area (which doubles as an art gallery), a small office, and a vast, cavernous room for film screenings, empty space dwarfing both the screen and the tiers of office chairs set up inside.

Howard Guttenplan, the Workshop's director, is a middle-aged man with slicked-back salt-and-pepper hair, cowboy boots, a sweater over a collared shirt, and a thick black goatee. He grew up in Brooklyn but has spent more than twenty years in the East Village, most of that time spent at the Millennium. He described the venue as a "haven for young and international filmmakers"—one that is constantly struggling to make ends meet, especially in the face of recent cuts in funding from the National Endowment for the Arts and rising bills. The Millennium is a small organization with a staff of five teachers and three film editors, along with a handful of part-time projectionists who double as site managers. It produces a magazine, offers editing workshops, and shows independent films.

Like many older Village businesses, the Millennium came of age alongside NYU. Before the university upgraded its editing equipment, many of its film students rented space and equipment here, and many current film students use the space to screen their projects. Oliver Stone did some of his early splicing in the back room. During the strike, the site was used by history, sociology, and film classes, mostly reserved for courses that relied heavily on multimedia. It was a perfect relationship, from Guttenplan's point of view—the daytime courses both brought in much needed income and exposed a large group of NYU students to the facility, while the Millennium in turn provided high-tech equipment that is difficult to find on short notice anywhere in the city. One technician worked extra hours to facilitate the classes; the work was more than welcome, since the Millennium relies on part-time labor and has more employees than hours to fill. Guttenplan was supportive of the union but had only a general sense of the issues at stake in the strike. He described unions in general as "a very important element in maintaining a balance," but added that they are much weaker than they once were.

Guttenplan had a more direct interest in the university's effect on the larger Village community. A longtime resident, he had been watching NYU's growth with some discomfort. "I think NYU is taking over a lot of real estate," he said. "They've created a bit of an imbalance." He told me about beautiful homes torn down to make room for dorms and offices, adding that the old charm of the East Village rested largely in low-density buildings and a "sense of the sky." Both are being lost, and now most artists cannot afford to live in the area at all. He noted that it is not a new phenomenon, nor is it not entirely NYU's fault, but "the pattern is accelerating."

The feeling was shared by James Solomon Benn, the administrative assistant at St. Mark's Church on East 10th Street. While he felt that NYU students make the Village "a vital place to live in," he saw something sinister in the behavior of the school's administration, a group that is behind "a process of gentrification that is not best for the neighborhood, not a good match for the architecture or the community. They don't have the community's interests at heart."

St. Mark's is a Gothic building, beautiful and barren in the rain. The main entrance is framed by two stained ivory statues of long-haired men leaning forward with their eyes closed, either listening to something or pushing their hair back behind their ears. There are rose bushes and gray pillars with flaking paint, a gravel peace sign just inside the gate, a cobblestoned courtyard marked with ancient grave markers, and a sinkhole that had opened the night before my interview, revealing layers of catacombs beneath. Benn described St. Mark's as "an activist church"—it was once a favorite hangout of Allen Ginsburg and the other Beat poets and now hosts everything from classical concertos to political meetings. St. Mark's and UAW Local 2110 came into contact during the 2004 Republican National Convention, when the church provided protestors with sleeping spaces, medical help, and entertainment. During the strike, it hosted a wide variety of courses, renting out a large, mostly empty room with stacks of chairs, a piano, a wood floor, bare white walls, and carvings of Mary and an angel in white set against a circular blue background. Like the Millennium, the feeling of the common room at St. Mark's could hardly have been more different from the halls of NYU—less polish, more history, and, between the two, a clear juxtaposition of the old Village and the new.

Jimmy Fergosa, the church sextant, did the work of setting up space for the classes. He said that the daily rearrangements of fourteen tables and a hundred chairs was "extra work," but it is work that he is paid to do and helpful to a cause that he fully supports. He found the students to be very respectful, and his thoughts on the strike were refreshingly blunt: "Everyone has a union these days, so what's NYU's problem? They own half of Manhattan. Don't tell me it's a money issue."

"We wanted to be in solidarity with the graduate students," said Benn. "Their grievances are meaningful and should be supported." He spoke about the strike with a certain calm detachment, recognizing such struggles as skirmishes in a much larger war.

I moved on to more secular waters. Fat Cat Billiards is a dim underground playhouse, a haven for musicians, gamers, and late-night wanderers. Half jazz room and half preadolescent fantasy, it offers music every night from ten until five in the morning and a large front room packed with pool and Ping-Pong tables, chess sets, Scrabble boards, black ceilings, yellow lamps, and African sculpture. A dog roams freely across the floor. Noah Sapir, the club's owner, employs mostly down-and-outers, musicians or artists passing through and out of money. He is a big man with a neat beard and a baseball cap cocked sideways above his forehead—a high-school dropout, a pianist, a former professional chess player. He grew up in New York but isn't "much of a city person anymore," living on Long Island four days a week and sleeping on a couch in the bar the other three. He was eager to talk, speaking of business and politics with an identical air of self-assured authority.

Sapir interested me in part for what he has done with his life and in part for the opportunities he has rejected. His mother is a former dean of the medical school at NYU. Years ago, she helped Sapir land a job in the school doing grant proposals and lab work—he told me it was a good salary for a dropout and gave him a chance to "pursue science without jumping through all the hoops." He used his connections to enroll in the Gallatin School for Independent Study at NYU but lasted only six weeks. It was not independent enough for his liking, and mandatory courses annoyed him. His preferred educational vision is embodied in the offerings of Fat Cat—buffet-style instruction in jazz, salsa, chess, Ping-Pong, and martial arts. "It's a drop-in alternative arts education. A chance for students to get their feet wet without the $30,000 price tag," he says. "Parents come here with their kids. They can do something cerebral, then something physical."

Sapir's connection to GSOC was an indirect one. A professor who was a good friend of his mother's went to the bar for a birthday party and told him about the strike, mentioning that Fat Cat's might be a good venue to host courses. Sapir agreed. He did not charge and seemed surprised when I asked. He told me that the courses "weren't a tremendous imposition" but wishes he had bought an espresso machine beforehand so he could have turned a bit of a profit. He hosted smaller classes, many of them at the graduate level, offering them a ring of cush-

Some of the six hundred fifty classes moved off-campus were hosted by Fat Cat, a pool hall, jazz venue, and counter-culture haven on Christopher Street in Greenwich Village. *(Andrew Ross)*

ioned couches and chairs in a carpeted area near the center of the larger room. Unlike the other sites I visited, there was no physical separation between the class space and the business—some students stuck around to have a drink or play pool after class, while a couple of professors complained about the noise from the Ping-Pong tables. "Too bad," says Sapir. "It's free space in Manhattan."

He is at heart an individualist, seeing the function in organizations such as unions but finding nothing ideologically compelling about their existence. "Unions can be as prosaic as providing enough money so that graduate students can afford to live in New York," he says. "Groups in general—religious factions, gangs, unions—all serve the same purpose: to gain something for their members." While he supports our need to fight collectively for decent living conditions, he thinks that group allegiance in general is "something that mankind needs to transcend." In our case, this critique spans both union and university memberships. Sapir says that he "has misgivings about the exclusivity and expense of education" and sees it as part of a larger cultural disease that fuels our misdirected aspirations toward "wealth and excess." He observed in passing that "change necessitates a humility on the part of everyone"—simple and familiar wisdom, but it rings with a certain profundity after long months of a stagnant strike.

Others I spoke to were more reticent. Larry Schulz, co-owner of the Sandra Cameron Dance Studio, emphasized that his relationship with the union was strictly professional. He spent decades in TV news and survived two long strikes but now struggles to keep his head above water on the ownership side of the labor divide, employing three full-time workers and thirty-five part-timers, and wishes he was bringing in enough money to offer more benefits and steadier hours. His may have been the only space rented simultaneously by GSOC and NYU: He was careful to let me know that he had nothing but positive experiences with NYU classes on either side of the labor dispute and had nothing to say on record regarding his stance on the strike. (He did, however, rent the space to GSOC at a 50 percent discount while charging the university full price.) This was a quiet place of mirrors, obsidian floors, and tall, beautiful women—a space with little use or tolerance for overt conflict.

Jill Raufman's Dallas BBQ restaurant is loud and equally apolitical, at least on the surface, the environment a hodgepodge of cheap drinks, dance music, checkered floors, and bright banners draping from ceiling and walls. It is located just across the street from NYU's largest academic building, a couple blocks from the central picket lines, and Raufman offered the basement banquet room to the union free of charge. She is a proud alumna of NYU but was upset with the administration's handling of GSOC: "Teaching assistants weren't being given rights they were entitled to. The administration was not being very understanding." I asked her if she had heard much talk about the strike among her clientele, and she seemed surprised by the question.

"They come here to drink," she replied with a shrug.

She was happy to help the union, though there was occasional tension. Professors would sometimes go over their allotted time and only grudgingly clear out for the Happy Hour rush, and one class moved back to university grounds at the heavy insistence of the students. It was a struggle for the professor, but he ultimately thanked her for the space and heeded the will of the class.

This professor was one of many to return to campus before final exams, citing increased student resistance, shortages of tables or chairs, unsatisfactory multimedia equipment, an excess of noise, or an unwillingness to force students to take the exams in less than ideal conditions. Even in December, momentum was slipping away from the union. The break between semesters proved decisive. Fatigue set in at every level, from undergraduates and teaching assistants to professors and department administrators. It was a time of press silence, cold weather, vastly reduced picket lines, and a population that was simply tired of a debate that felt both increasingly familiar and increasingly abstract. Come January, the halls of the academic buildings at NYU were once again packed with students, and those professors who chose to remain off-campus were an increasingly marginalized minority.

A foreign-language professor moved a class of six graduate students to her apartment in the fall, teaching her course around her dining-room table. "I'm not sure everybody appreciated it," she said, "but they put up with good humor." When the spring semester began, she told her advanced undergrad class of twelve students that they would meet in her apartment. All but three students dropped the class. "None of those who left talked to me," she said. "It did not reflect well on me. I can't tell you how terrible I felt." While her class in the fall was willing to put up with some inconvenience for part of a semester, her new students rebelled when faced with another semester of disruption.

Many undergraduates felt they were being asked to pay a concrete price for abstract reasons. There were younger students who had never before taken a city bus or explored beyond the NYU campus, relying heavily on the university to shelter them from the mass of the city. While many professors said class visits by striking GSOC members helped provide some understanding of the underlying issues, many felt that these visits did not do enough to establish a sense of personal connection and responsibility among the undergraduates.

"A lot of the time people would come to our classes to talk about how this is kind of fun, get yourself involved . . . but there was no necessity, no sense of responsibility put upon us by the grad students," said Professor Vincent Schipper, who said the union needed to make the case for how the lack of a graduate-worker union would affect students personally.

The anonymous language professor blamed herself for the collapse of her class. "Instead of using it as a teaching experience—with a vote, perhaps—I just simply announced that we were going to go off-campus," she said. This unilateral decision reflected a broad trend: While the union and the university did their best to convert the undergraduates to their way of thinking, neither was particularly responsive to undergraduates' concerns. "I felt like it was my decision, and if they had voted against it I think I would have felt angry," said an anonymous professor in the Gallatin School of Independent Study, who said a vote to remain on campus could have forced her to cross the picket line. Torn between conflicting loyalties to her undergraduates and to her fellow teachers, she was one of many professors who struggled to find a fair way forward. On the one hand, the underlying values of the strike included democracy and fair representation—ideas not upheld by a professor's unilateral declaration that class must move. On the other hand, many felt that they had a moral responsibility to support their fellow teachers, one that could not simply be turned over to their students for a vote.

For some professors, the proper middle ground lay in acknowledging that education is not limited to the material on the syllabus. In his "Urban Experience and Modern Japanese Literature" course, Professor Kota Inoue framed the strike as an urban event: "Corporations, business, workers—those things become invisible in classrooms and I want to put them back in. I think that it helped me drive this point about university education being—in my view, anyway—something that should tell them about the society they live in, no matter what they study, even foreign literature. This is something that's going to be part of your education, too."

There was a sense that the chaos of the strike shook students awake, freeing many of them to take a more active role in their classes. Holding class off campus created an environment that was "highly relaxed, highly informal," said Robert April, a graduate student. "It stimulates discussion. Everybody gets very chummy, and everybody lets their guard down and speaks their mind." In the same vein, the Gallatin professor said that students "who had been quieter . . . started talking. When you're on a campus, somehow you have institutional authority provided by the campus. There is a way in which moving off the campus changes that, as well. You relinquish some of the institutional authority of the university, and I think that that also is not a bad experience for students to have."

Back on campus, she asked not to be named for fear of retaliation.

"We were able in an indirect way to bring up making a living as a cultural issue," reported Greg Sholette, a professor of visual culture and art theory. "We talked a lot about literally what does one do to actually get by. For some of them I think it was kind of a wake up from what's often avoided."

Indeed, the venues mapped a wide range of intersecting points between the educational and professional worlds. For undergraduates who are not headed directly to high-level corporate positions, time spent in the Fat Cat, the Millennium, or the Brecht could offer a glimpse of where their own private passions might lead. The moves brought these students into contact with members of a diverse Village community increasingly threatened by the homogenizing effects of large real-estate interests such as NYU, many of whom watch warily as the university expands. The homogenizing process taking place in physical space mirrors very closely the increasing centralization of administrative power within the university; indeed, conflicts of ideology are rarely far removed from the concrete realities of space. The strike offered an opportunity for students, professors, and community members alike to pay new attention to the simple realities of buildings and sidewalks, to consider consciously the ever present political dimensions of walls, windows, and doors.

There was certainly the potential for a more unified front. Union organizers could have found ways to join with the community groups opposing NYU real-estate projects, blurring the dividing lines between the school and the city, potentially bringing outsiders such as Liz Roberts and James Solomon Benn into the mix, further threatening the autonomy of the trustees and their chosen administrators.

Randy Martin, an associate dean at the time of the strike, used the phrase "between comfort and crisis" to describe the atmosphere on campus. The greatest challenge faced by union organizers within an institution such as NYU may be that the vast majority of academics feel sheltered by the walls that separate them from the mass of the outside word. NYU students and faculty need to flash an identity card every time they set foot in a university building, and most are heavily invested in these rites of passage. Many want the doors closed behind them, and want to leave with a degree that is a key to new doors, new levels of access, higher perches above a world ever farther removed. Outside (and occasionally inside) the walls are the activists and individualists who would argue that the teaching and learning that takes place in other venues—a Marxist workshop on the Hudson, the basement of a jazz club, the editing room at the Millennium—is every bit as valuable, and should be valued every bit as highly, as the work done within the elite institutions of formal higher education.

Professor Bertell Ollman is a Marxist theorist who has been tenured at NYU since 1974 and has been involved in "free university" spaces (such as the Brecht Forum) for even longer. He felt that the process of moving classes off-campus forced students to actively take sides, to identify themselves either with the leaders of the university or the teachers who do the university's daily work. While the conflict itself remained abstract to many undergraduates, the physical act of moving away from campus into more public, less exclusive spaces mirrored the shape of these abstractions. For some, this shift was liberating; for others, it was profoundly discomforting.

Professor Keith Vincent concluded that the strike was a liberating experience. "It was not disillusioning but kind of helpful for me personally to stop thinking of the university as my superego—how corrupt, poorly run, and blind this place can be. It made me feel a little bit more confident that I have something to offer it." He contemplated the risk of not getting tenure, then started not to care.

It would be far too simplistic to end this article with the implication that the movement of classes of campus during the strike represented a privileging of alternative education over the dominant university paradigm. The two exist side by side, and will always exist side by side, and in the best of times the work of one should supplement rather than compete with work of the other. Professor Ollman's identification with both NYU and the Brecht Forum is one example of intellectual energy flowing between the two, and there are countless others: musicians moving between formal training at NYU and informal jam sessions at Fat Cat, NYU film students participating in the community at the Millennium, NYU writers organizing readings at the KGB Bar in the East Village. This fluid exchange between city and university is nothing new. The class moves merely forced undergraduates through doors that were always open, leading in some cases to frustration and hurried retreat and in others to an increased solidarity with the strikers, a humbler understanding of the university's place within the context of the city and a heightened awareness of the lessons to be learned beyond its walls.

Part III

Lessons for the Future

The State of the Academic Labor Movement

A Roundtable with Stanley Aronowitz, Barbara Bowen, and Ed Ott

MODERATED BY KITTY KRUPAT

W ith union density at a relatively healthy 25 percent, New York City can still call itself a union town. But for how long? That question preoccupies Ed Ott, executive director of New York City's Central Labor Council. "At this point," Ott says, "we're a series of fiefdoms. Everyone's hanging on to their piece. But if we want to grow and have real power, we have to act like a cohesive movement. We need to pick a fight we can win and all jump into it together. I thought NYU might have been that fight. I was clearly wrong." Ott was referring to the ten-month strike of graduate teaching and research assistants that ended in September 2006. Although the graduate students returned to work without a union contract, their strike—together with a three-year contract battle at the City University of New York—had put academic labor on the main stage of labor struggle in New York City. On October 10, 2006, Barbara Bowen, president of CUNY's Professional Staff Congress (PSC), and Stanley Aronowitz, Distinguished Professor of Sociology at CUNY and a member of the PSC Executive Council, joined Ott and Kitty Krupat for a conversation about contemporary academia and the prospects for an academic labor movement. Excerpts of that conversation are recorded below.[1]

KITTY KRUPAT: Stanley, you once famously said that you had "the last good job in America."[2] What did you mean by that?
STANLEY ARONOWITZ: I didn't say that was true of every academic job. To be a professor—even a tenured professor—is not the same on every campus or even within a single university. For example, at CUNY, which has

about six thousand full-time people, you have tiering, which goes from people like me—I teach one course a semester, whether I need to or not—to faculty at the community-college level, who teach multiple courses a year. Those people are working end to end, and most of their courses are introductory. They're under severe constraints. Sometimes textbooks are mandated. When I said I had the last good job, I was talking about academic jobs like mine. I'm one of the few people in the academy, or any other workplace, who has control over her or his time. I have a lot of autonomy. I can decide what I want to teach and when I teach it. Today, there are fewer and fewer people with that last good job, and most are in big research universities. But even for them, things are changing. Job listings, for example, now say, "Record of getting grants desirable." Humanities or social-science scholars can no longer simply teach their courses, write their books and articles, and work with graduate students. To get jobs and promotions, the university expects them to raise money or give service to the university over and above the usual academic functions.

KK: Despite what Stanley says, there are plenty of people who think that work in the academy is privileged or inherently different from work in other sectors. Is it?

BARBARA BOWEN: I wouldn't make that claim. But I *would* point out how deeply privatized academic work is. I didn't see this so clearly when I was a full-time professor, but I see it now. Academia rewards individual efforts. It fosters the illusion that everything you get has come your way because of your own brilliance. It also fosters the illusion that you operate independently. Despite the fact that you're working with students, you are encouraged to think that almost all of your work is your own product. When you walk into that classroom and close the door behind you, you're either the facilitator or the king, however you want to think about it. That's your classroom. And when you do research—even if you collaborate—you still have that sense of ownership and an intense feeling of privacy. That contributes to the illusion that academics don't need a union; that there's no reason for collective action; that in fact while other people—people who are not as *smart* as we are—might need collective action, we do not. Also, academic work, especially teaching, is atomized, which makes it difficult both conceptually and physically to organize. In most workplaces, people are physically together. Proximity may sound like a small thing, but it's not. In an office, for example, people can hang their union T-shirts outside their cubicles; they can talk over the tops; they're connected. Academics, you have to hunt them down, because they're all over the place. So even the physical arrangements of academia contribute to the idea that we're different.

KK: When I entered the academy after many years of office work and union work, I was intoxicated with a sense of collegiality that seemed to exist among students and teachers. I felt intellectually independent in ways I hadn't before. You know, even in the most progressive union, you learn to craft your ideas—

and your words—to suit organizational imperatives. As a member of the scholarly community, I wasn't constrained by that obligation. Despite the elitism and exploitation that I saw, I believed—and still do—that the academy is a relatively safe space for the exchange of ideas.

BB: Yes, you feel that very much. That's why you want to be in the academy. The official view is that academia is a very collegial enterprise. I thought that myself when I was teaching. But it's delusional. In reality, the academy encourages individualism and that can impede organizing around conditions of work.

SA: If you look at virtually any New York-area faculty, you'll discover that many of them come out of elite universities—the Ivies, Berkeley, and so on. They were socialized there. What they learned is that you either have it or you don't. It's all about you. They don't think of themselves as workers.

ED OTT: In that respect, academia is probably unique. But in the overall, academic work is not so different from other kinds of work. And organizing in the academy is not that different, either. If it's hard to organize in academia, look at the context. We're spectacularly unsuccessful in organizing *all* categories of work. We're not breaking through in either private industry or the nonprofit sector. We do not set the standard. In that sense, academia is in the American mainstream. But as Barbara points out, there's a specific culture in academia that needs to be addressed. You probably can't organize successfully in academia doing what Al Shanker tried to do in his years as president of the American Federation of Teachers (AFT).[3] In the end, Shanker reduced all questions of pedagogy to wages, hours, and working conditions. In general, the labor movement has not been very sensitive to specific workplace cultures. Nor have we been very good about building *any* culture of organizing that breaks down notions of individualism.

BB: I agree with Ed. But it's worth noting that higher education has changed dramatically in the last twenty years. In that time, we've had some success in organizing. Academic workers have actually had a better rate of unionization than many other professional groups—despite what I said about the difficulties. That bears examination.

SA: If you look at the successes, one of the things you'll discover is that they are not across the board. There are community colleges, state colleges, and elite universities. With some exceptions, in the New York area, the private nonprofit schools that got organized were third-tier universities—for example, Adelphi and St. John's. Elite research universities—even the second-tier schools—are almost nowhere organized.

KK: Except for graduate employees.

SA: Yes. About fifteen years ago—and much earlier at the University of Wisconsin—graduate students began to realize that their options were limited.[4] You may have a passion for Renaissance art, but you're likely to end up teaching writing or introductory courses. So grad students say, if I'm going to do that—and especially if I'm doing most of the teaching at my university—then I've got to make a living at it. Grad students are no longer simply teachers' assistants. In many cases, they are the main educators. They're beginning to say, "What the hell. We're entitled." They want a living wage, health-care benefits, and other things.

EO: The disappearance of those good jobs Stanley was talking about has created a whole workforce that at one time was considered privileged but is now mainstream. I think there's a growing sense among people who work in intellectual fields that this is the work that's left to us; we have to make something of it. We better define it. Industrial jobs were terrible. We made them better jobs. These jobs in academia can also be made better. It's not horrible work. It's clean; it's in a good setting; in certain times, it's stimulating. But it's low paid, without decent health care or other benefits. If you're an adjunct, you can't make a life out of it unless you have more than one job. This degrading of academic work has been a process. This is the work that's left to us? Holy shit. Now what? The idea of organizing in academia has taken hold, but it's not going to be easy. The son of a guns who run these universities are pretty bad. They've caught on to the corporate style of management.

SA: The corporatization process has been dramatic. In 1991, CUNY's chancellor, Joseph Murphy, quit and went back to the ranks. He became a university professor again. He was at the top of the scale, but at that time the salary of a full professor was not that far away from the chancellor's wage. Today the difference is astronomical. The current CUNY chancellor earns $395,000 a year, plus a housing allowance that allows him to live on East End Avenue. And this is in a public institution. College presidents in private universities earn much more—sometimes over a million, if you count the perks. These people are never going back to the ranks. They have become a distinct class. They're not in our class anymore—not only because of income but because of power. The trustees in both public and private universities are recruited from corporate boardrooms and from the political elite. The presidents and chancellors see themselves as part of that world. Their aspiration is to sell themselves as much as possible to the corporations. Today, that extends even to the curriculum. Huge corporations such as Verizon, for example, contract with universities to provide tailor-made training for their employees. The university gives the associate's or the bachelor's degree; but the company essentially controls the curriculum. College administrators are operating in a business milieu, and they see themselves in that light.

EO: There's always the potential among professionals to identify with the corporate structure. I observed that in the medical profession. Nurses and doctors—particularly medical students just coming into hospitals—were looking around and realizing, "We are not the power; we don't really run these places anymore. We used to make all the decisions, and now there's this thing called utilization review down the hall that monitors everything I do." Doctors were reduced in status in the hospitals. There are clear parallels here to the erosion of faculty governance and other aspects of corporate management in the university. People draw the conclusion that the road to advancement is not in the profession but in the business side of the institution. So it's not good enough to have a Ph.D, you better get an MBA or you're going to starve.

KK: Picking up on the class question: I like to think that the business model of higher education, with its new breed of administrators, has spawned a cadre of class-conscious intellectuals and activists, ready to challenge the academic establishment. Am I naïve; or is it possible that academics could organize on the basis of class politics?

EO: There's a basis for it, but we don't know how to capitalize on it. At this point, religious fundamentalists in this country fill the anticorporate void better than the labor movement does. At least they're willing to say, "We're not them; we offer you something else." We're not ready to say either one. We pose no serious ideological alternative—nothing that allows people to believe that, if they take certain risks, there are positive outcomes. I'm not sure workers see trade unionism as an instrument of progress anymore. We need to help workers—including academics—understand the socioeconomic and political conditions that define their lives so they can see the path out. But we don't raise the issue of class. Labor leaders don't sit around the table, asking the basic question about work and workers—where do we fit in? If we do that, I think we can develop a new class-conscious leadership.

KK: Aren't workers in the academy well positioned to raise the sorts of questions Ed is talking about? I think we missed an opportunity to do that at NYU. When we began organizing graduate students, we made a conscious decision to focus on bread-and-butter issues, which we saw as unifying. We avoided discussion of political and social issues, because we were afraid it might be divisive. We said, "We'll do that *after* we've won our union election." Not only did we lose an opportunity; I think we may have lost some *people* who envisioned their union as a venue for political engagement and a space for ideological debate.

BB: Our experience in the Professional Staff Congress may address your question. In 2000, Stanley and I were part of the New Caucus, a group inside the PSC that was challenging an incumbent leadership whom we saw as conservative and unwilling to take a stand on broad issues of social justice. Our slate was elected. But in the 2006 PSC election, *we* were challenged. We faced a strong opposition that wanted us to focus very narrowly on bread-and-butter collective-bargaining issues. They saw our involvement in broad social and political issues as a distraction from that. They were very vocal. They criticized us for taking a position on the war, for taking a position on union solidarity. They criticized me for standing next to Roger Toussaint, who led New York City's transit workers out on an illegal strike. How dare she be photographed next to that renegade union leader?[5]

SA: I think the debates we had to take on were good. They kept us thinking and listening to members.

EO: Your opposition was not without ideology.

BB: No, they were not. They had an articulate conservative ideology.

SA: We won, but we had a hard fight. The opposition got 46 percent of the vote. That says something. Generally speaking the academic unions—whether it's the AAUP, the NEA [National Education Association], the AFT, or even the UAW—we are organizing on the bread-and-butter model. We are saying to people, "You have interests as workers: You need health care; you need higher salaries; you need job security." With few exceptions, we are not negotiating over matters of academic principle. We are not saying, for example, that we want to be involved in discussions about curriculum. To some extent, the PSC is an exception. We've made some progress in those areas because we were able to integrate members of the Faculty Senate into our discussions. Many on the Faculty Senate, including the chair, are also on the PSC executive board; some are officers. That doesn't mean we've taken a firm hold of curriculum issues and faculty governance. That's very rare in academic unionism. In many cases, academic unions have even renounced a concern for those things.

KK: When grad students were negotiating a first contract at NYU, the administration insisted on a clear distinction between academic affairs and administrative affairs. I don't think we ever "renounced" a concern for academic issues, but we agreed to set them aside in bargaining. The problem comes in practice. Academic issues and administrative issues often overlap as conditions of employment, and where they do, the union has to take that on. I know a teaching assistant who was required to write the instructor's syllabus; teach all but two class sessions; and edit students' final papers for inclusion in a manual produced by the instructor. Imagine the hours of work required to complete that academic assignment. If we'd had a union then, that teaching assistant would have filed a grievance. In doing so, she would have raised important ethical questions about the instructor's responsibility to students and to the institution. But even after we won our union, the administration resisted grievances of that sort, repeatedly accusing us of trying to cross the line between academic and administrative affairs. Ultimately, it used that charge as a justification for refusing to negotiate a second contract.

BB: The PSC has taken a firm position that there are some things the union does and some things faculty governance does, and we do not try to duplicate what they do except to support them. But it's mythical that there is no bleeding across the line of academic prerogative and conditions of employment. Things that one side may claim are not union issues are often about how we do our jobs. In our campaign for union leadership, we spoke about issues of curriculum; questions about students—who's being admitted to the university; who's being excluded? For many of us, discussions of those and other questions that might be described as academic issues were the most exciting and most motivating. I think those issues are also terms and conditions of employment. The administration could say the number of students in a course is academic policy, right? Well, the number of students we have to teach is clearly a condition of employment.

KK: What about intellectual property?

BB: We've gone to court on that. The university claimed it did not have to negotiate with the union over anything to do with your rights to own what you create—a course description or a book. Our position was and is that creating such material is a fundamental part of your work, as fundamental as your teaching. At the bargaining table, the administration sat there and said, "We will not negotiate." The administration's lawyer said: "I will not allow the chancellor to negotiate on this subject." So we took them to court. We've won at several levels. It's one of our key victories, though some issues are still in debate.

SA: But there's a battle looming. Many public and some private universities are offering online baccalaureate degrees—online—you don't have to go to a class. At CUNY, our members are going to be doing the online tutorials. Who owns the syllabi used in those tutorials? Can the university simply take them and lend them to somebody else, standardize them, and so forth? These are important questions. And they are terms of employment. "No child left behind" and much of the New York City curriculum in elementary and secondary schools is driven by the aspiration for a teacherless curriculum—or, more precisely, by the idea that anyone can teach the curriculum. We're getting dangerously close to that when it comes to the baccalaureate and community-college degrees, as well.

BB: This has serious implications for organizing. If managements are successful in outsourcing teaching, not only will there be no physical place where faculty meet, there will be no permanent faculty.

EO: There will always be workers who say, "Look, pay me—that's all I care about; the content, I don't give a shit." That's much less the case among intellectual workers. But with online education, I think you may see more tension around questions of quality and quantity, so to speak. Online education is cost-effective. There are no illusions about it. The degree becomes a product. The student is isolated, and so is the faculty. They have no common ground of solidarity. That's very strange territory for organizing.

KK: Does academic work require new models of organizing? Or, to put the question another way, can academic work, as it is currently constructed, provide a new model for organizing? I sometimes wonder, for example, if a craft-union model would be useful in organizing adjuncts, who often work at several schools simultaneously.

EO: The old industrial models don't work in a whole lot of settings. Given the nature of academic work, some of the models that actors and other creative workers use may become more relevant. In those models—especially with actors—there's a distinction between work and a job. Actors never ask each other if they have a job. They ask, "Are you working?" That distinction elevates the profession to a kind of universal realm and lends itself to the craft-union structures actors and writers built in the 1930s. I see academic organizing going in that direction. Does that model have to take new forms? Absolutely. University managements—particularly on the business side—can't do what they want to do without denigrating the profession. Unions then have to become guardians of professional standards as well as preservers of workplace standards. Who will defend the profession if the people in it won't? To do that, they will have to have power. They certainly have the intellectual power. Institutional power might come from the craft-union model of organizing on a professional basis rather than shop by shop.

SA: Some years ago. I floated the idea of a hiring hall, which might be a model for organizing part-timers. You want a sociology teacher to teach intro? We have one.

EO: Doesn't that lend itself to their view, though? It kind of says to management, "You guys are right. Top of the list, he can come down and teach the class." I'm not sure that's what you want.

SA: I wouldn't do it universally, but you're talking about adjuncts, very few of whom, in any of the public universities and most of the private universities, get a chance to teach what their heart desires or even a subject in which they have a degree.

EO: But even so, there's a difference. Technically, a skilled-trades union is a guarantor of the work. The assumption is you take a journeyman carpenter from the union hiring hall; you give him the plans; and you walk away. He or she is supposed to be able to do the job. How do you become the guarantor of intellectual quality? Do you test? Do you do what Shanker did at the end of his career—hammer his own members to get more professionalized in order to elevate standards?

SA: The problem is the alternative: You turn it over to them.

BB: Right. And that's where it is already. Even temporary agencies are starting to place academic workers. So one way of thinking about it is, let Kelly Girls do it or do it ourselves. But I agree with Ed. It raises some serious issues. We don't want to guarantee quality of work or subject someone to a test before that person can teach one course in his or her field.

SA: But Barbara, the presumption today is that if you have a Ph.D. or some other credential in a field, you are skilled.

BB: That's the presumption, but skill is not the question that usually comes up. The issue is, well, we don't have the money to hire a full-time person, but we desperately need these students to be taught. So we reach in and take somebody. The issue of credentials is often secondary, and I think it's some measure of contempt for students that the question of credentials is *not* constantly there. I don't mean to say that people don't have credentials or that they should be checked, but I think the lack of concern for credentials shows an indifference to students and to pedagogy. They're lucky at CUNY. They get incredible quality without doing very much to demand it.

KK: The phrase "academic labor movement" has been used loosely to define a range of organizing activities on campuses from undergraduate anti-sweatshop and living-wage campaigns to graduate-student unions and faculty support groups such as the Faculty Democracy movement at NYU. Do these activities amount to an academic labor movement, and is that movement sustainable?

EO: I believe labor movements are reflective of a set of conditions people find and try to come to terms with. The particular forms those movements take change with the times. Right now and right here in the academic world, there's something going on. Is it an academic labor movement? I think so. Are its characteristics unique to universities? Not necessarily. They can apply to any large institutions. Look at the history of 1199SEIU, the hospital workers' union in New York. Some of 1199's biggest battles were fought in the big teaching hospitals. It started organizing the service workers and ultimately pulled in the skilled workers, the technical staff, and the nurses and doctors. Universities are similar. They are among the largest institutions in any given community, and they employ huge numbers of skilled workers, who are ripe for unionization.

BB: I'm not as confident that there *is* an academic labor movement or that it is known and accepted as such in the wider labor movement.

EO: It's known and accepted by those who are *aware* of it and who *understand* its implications. There are too many people involved for it not to be important. That said, there's still a sentiment among some people in labor leadership that universities are not a great thing to organize. They say, "OK, if the service units on the campus want to organize, go ahead," but they don't fully support the academic staff. I saw that during the NYU strike. They wouldn't articulate it, but a few labor leaders withheld support because they bought the university's line that the graduate-student union was somehow interfering with the privileges of the university. There are also people in the labor movement at all levels who think that anyone who teaches in higher education is very privileged.

KK: Does anti-intellectualism have anything to do with it?

EO: There is a degree of anti-intellectualism in the labor movement, but that's not why [those labor leaders] didn't support the NYU strike. I think they didn't support the strike because they didn't see it as important in the economy. They don't understand why you would strike an academic institution. What impact does it have? The fact is, academic jobs are here, and they're not going anywhere—except maybe online. What's important here is not the number of labor leaders who *don't* get it but the growing number of those who *do*. This is a badly crippled movement that is beginning to realize that its future lies in a new global structure. The academic labor movement has the potential to bring into that structure a new generation of workers.

SA: Ed is on to something very important. If you're going to build solidarity around organizing in academia, there has to be a reexamination of what the

One of the many Washington Square rallies featuring individual GSOC members alongside labor-movement leaders. Pictured here are Roger Toussaint, president, Transport
Workers Union Local 100 (hand to face), and John Wilhelm, co-president, UNITE-HERE
(applauding, without hat). *(Maris Zivarts)*

workforce looks like. Besides the immigrant population, the other big thing
is public employees and other service-sector workers. The service industries
are huge, and academia is among the major ones.

BB: There are people working in higher education who are ignited by the idea
of an academic labor movement. And they are doing serious, committed
organizing and political work against considerable odds. That's real, and we
shouldn't dismiss it. However, we don't have a well-defined set of principles
we're fighting for or a mass of people committed to making fundamental
change. I wouldn't say it's nowhere, but looking at the big picture, I wouldn't
call it a movement.

EO: Would you say you have the makings of a movement?

BB: Yes, potentially. The percentage of academic workers who have either a tenured or tenure-track job or any form of job security is less than 30 percent.
We are an industry that has 70 percent contingent workers. That to me is
shocking and forms the basis of a movement for change. Yet the issue of
wages and benefits for people in our industry is largely invisible. Management has been able to get away with it, and you're right, Ed: Too many labor
leaders don't have sympathy with professors. They think professors work
nine hours a week, wear tweed jackets with little leather elbow patches, and
smoke a pipe. So what are academic unions and other unions doing together

to change that perception? One thing could be joint legislative campaigns to address the problems of that 70 percent who do most of the work and also to stop the erosion of permanent jobs for the 30 percent. That's one way to advance some new thinking and to change the conversation.

SA: You have to add this to the conversation: If the Ph.D is a standard against which to measure credentials in academia, how long does it take to get a Ph.D? How much income is sacrificed? You do four years of college and then an average of seven or so for the Ph.D. During that period, you're working part-time and teaching here and there. You're talking about people who have given up conservatively $200,000 in that period of time. And they've accumulated an awful lot of debt. If they're lucky enough to get a tenure-track job, they get $50,000 or $55,000. I think we have an education job to do in the labor movement to tell the executive boards of the central labor councils, first, what it is that we do, and second, what we've sacrificed to get where we are.

KK: What have graduate students done to advance the academic labor movement?

SA: Today, many graduate students who become professors come out of graduate-student unions. They know what organizing is; they know what a movement is. Some of them came out of the anti-sweatshop or antiwar movement. Like a lot of student activists in the 1960s and '70s, they don't see the distinction between the antiwar movement and identity politics and the labor movement. It's all part of the same thing. Those with an activist history have a sense of themselves as subjects—some sense of history about themselves. I hung out at the NYU strike and talked to graduate students on the picket line. They were a different breed. They were fired up. These are people who have union-consciousness. Do they have class-consciousness? That's another question.

BB: There's also a convergence between what people are studying and writing and the idea of movement. That convergence explains in part why the movement has been so viciously attacked. There's a connection between reform in the social sciences and humanities in the last twenty years; the opening up of new subjects of study and new methods of study—the development of African American studies, queer studies, women's studies; globalization. Students are more likely these days to be studying Negri or Foucault or someone else who is challenging us to rethink power structures, rethink Marxism. Students are doing that, and when they look at their own conditions of labor, they see how horrible they are. They experience their own agency right there on the campus, and they have incredible energy. That's what makes those picket lines so exciting. It's one of the reasons that academic labor is exciting—because there can be a convergence between the hope and the political desire that you experience in what you study and the incredible discovery that you can act on that political desire in your own workplace. I mean, it's thrilling.

KK: How do you assess the NYU strike? What lessons did we learn from it?

BB: The strike itself was tremendous. It was impressive to see that there was top-level union support and support from all those City Council people. But with a few exceptions, what there was *not* was organized rank-and-file support from unions around town. And that's what I noticed in the transit strike, too. Major leaders came out, but most didn't mobilize their members on any scale. I think there's an important lesson in that.

EO: I remember calling someone from the picket line and saying, "You ought to get your ass down here. It's absolutely inspiring. I haven't felt this good in years." There was something about it—an energy and a vitality to what was going on there. The NYU struggle is one of those battles that had to be fought. Whether or not it's won or lost will be determined later. The question is, did the strike lay a basis to win down the road?

Notes

1. The roundtable discussion was organized by Kitty Krupat especially for inclusion in this volume. Krupat prepared the interview questions and conducted the session in the offices of the New York City Central Labor Council. The excerpts presented here were transcribed from a tape recording of the meeting; the introductory text and the notes were written by Krupat.

2. This phrase is also the title of Aronowitz's book *The Last Good Job in America* (Lanham, Md.: Rowman and Littlefield, 2001).

3. Albert Shanker was president of the AFT from 1974 to 1997.

4. Teaching assistants at the University of Wisconsin organized and won their right to union representation in 1969. They were the first graduate-student employees to unionize successfully in either the public or the private sector.

5. A controversial figure throughout his tenure as president of Local 100 of the Transport Workers Union, Roger Toussaint authorized a transit strike in December 2005, defying New York State's Taylor Law, which prohibits public employees from striking. As a result, he was sentenced to ten days in jail, and the union was heavily fined.

Global U

Andrew Ross

As universities are increasingly exposed to the rough justice of the market, their institutional life is distinguished more by the rate of change than by the observance of custom and tradition. Few examples illustrate this better than the rush, in recent years, to establish overseas programs and branch campuses. Since September 11, 2001, the pace of offshoring has surged and is being pursued across the entire spectrum of institutions that populate the higher-education landscape—from the ballooning for-profit sectors and online diploma mills to land-grant universities and the most elite, ivied colleges. No single organization has attained the operational status of a global university, after the model of the global corporation, but it may be only a matter of time before we see the current infants of that species take their first, unaided steps.

The World Trade Organization (WTO) has been pushing trade-services liberalization for several years, of which higher-educational services are a highly prized component, with an estimated global market of between $40 billion and $50 billion (not much less than the market for financial services).[1] Opponents of liberalization argue that higher education cannot and should not be subject to the kind of free-trade agreements that have been applied to commercial goods and other services in the global economy. After all, WTO agreements would guarantee foreign service providers the same rights that apply to domestic providers within any national education system while compromising the sovereignty of national regulatory efforts. Yet the evidence shows that, just as corporations did not wait for the WTO to conclude its ministerial rounds before moving their operations offshore, the lack of any international accords has not stopped universities in the leading Anglophone countries from establishing their names and services in a broad range of overseas locations. The formidable projected growth in student enrollment internationally, combined with the expansion of technological capacity and the consolidation of English as a lingua franca, has resulted in a bonanza-style environment for investors in offshore education.

As with any other commodity good or service that is allowed to roam across borders, there has also been much hand-wringing about the potential lack of quality assurance. Critics argue that the caliber of education will surely be jeopardized if the global market for it is deregulated. Much less has been said in this debate about the impact on the working conditions of academics or on the ethical profile and aspirational identity of institutions. How will globalization affect the security and integrity of livelihoods that are closely tied to liberal educational ideals such as meritocratic access, face-to-face learning, and the disinterested pursuit of knowledge? Will these ideals wither away entirely in the entrepreneurial race to compete for a global market share, or will they survive only in one corner of the market, as the elite preserve of those who are able to pay top dollar for such hand-crafted attention?

No slouch when it comes to entrepreneurial conduct, NYU has eagerly sought recognition as a global player. In the course of the 1990s, it established itself as the national pacesetter in sending students abroad. Currently, 25 percent of its vast student body, many of whom refer to their alma mater as Global U, enrolls in one of its eight study-abroad programs—in London, Paris, Madrid, Berlin, Prague, Florence, Shanghai, and Accra. The administration has mandated this student number to rise to 50 percent by 2011, new programs are being set up in Buenos Aires, Tel Aviv, and an additional one is likely to resume operations soon in Mexico. Its faculty ritually bemoans the quality of offerings in many of the overseas "island" programs (in which students study with other Americans on campuses abroad) or laments that students spend their time abroad in an edu-tourist bubble, cosseted from any authentic contact with a non–American culture or environment. Much less discussed is the financial reasoning behind these and other NYU offshore operations or the overall logic behind the rapid expansion of the university's existing global network in recent years. Some of this neglect is due to the lack of fiscal transparency at a private university and to the eroded state of faculty governance over academic affairs. But to approach the topic adequately requires familiarity with the larger picture of how and why American, British, and Australian institutions, in particular, are going global. This chapter charts some of the dimensions of that aggregate move, assessing NYU's profile in a sector that, for all its mercurial growth, is not well documented, let alone widely understood.

Greenwich Village in the Desert?

At some point in the course of the GSOC strike, the NYU administration was approached by representatives of the United Arab Emirates (UAE) with a proposal to set up an NYU branch campus in Abu Dhabi. The campus would be built from scratch with UAE money, and a donation of up to $100 million, according to some estimates, would be made available to NYU on signing the agreement. The degrees would include a full range of liberal-arts subjects and would be on offer, primarily, to UAE nationals. For colleges with prestige names, this kind of offer from the government of a developing country is increasingly common. As long as the source of the offer is not wholly disreputable, the prospect of acquiring an overseas facility at minimal cost and administrative energy is welcomed as an invaluable revenue "opportunity." The emirates and neighboring Qatar have been especially successful in attracting foreign colleges with such generous offers and are engaged in a bidding war to outdo each other to add cultural cache to their portfolio of corporate brands. The Louvre, Sorbonne, and Guggenheim had all been approached by Abu Dhabi government representatives before NYU was asked to set up a branch campus.[2] Dubai hosts a complex called Knowledge Village for offshore branch campuses from Pakistani, Russian, Canadian, and Indian universities, in addition to select British, Australian, and American universities, In Qatar, several top-brand American universities, including Carnegie Mellon, Cornell, Georgetown, Texas A&M, George Mason University, and Virginia Commonwealth, are already established in Doha's 2,500 acre Education City, with all expenses paid for by the royal family's Qatar Foundation.[3]

Students in the Middle East have every reason to feel they may not be welcome in the United States after 9/11, while the philosophical world-view associated with the War on Terror has provided administrators with an additional set of arguments to justify their newfound presence in the region. Many of their faculty are no doubt persuaded by Thomas Friedman-style reasoning that aspiring Middle Eastern students would be better served by a Western, liberal education than by the curriculum of a glorified madrassah. Yet those with a modicum of knowledge about the region are all too aware that the host countries in question are quasi-feudal monarchies that ruthlessly suppress Islamism, among other belief-systems, and are in no small measure responsible, as a result, for the flourishing of terror in the Middle East and beyond. So the debate falls along familiar lines, as it did at NYU: Is it better to try to influence the political climate in illiberal societies by fostering collegial zones of free speech, or is the instinct to engage student elites in such societies a naïve or, at worst, colonial instinct?

Notwithstanding the politics of any university's overseas mission, it is not at all easy to distinguish some of the new offshore academic centers from free-trade industrial zones where outsourcing corporations are welcomed with a lavish package of tax holidays, virtually free land, and duty-free privileges. Indeed, in many locations, Western universities are physically setting up shop in free-trade zones. In Dubai, the foreign universities are basically there to train knowledge-worker recruits in the Free Zone Authority's other complexes—Dubai Internet City, Dubai Media City, Dubai Studio City, DubaiTech, and the Dubai Outsource Zone. In Qatar, the colleges share facilities with the global high-tech companies that enjoy tax- and duty-free investments under that country's free-zone law. Some of China's largest free-trade locations have begun to attract brand-name colleges to relieve the shortage of skilled labor that is hampering the rate of off-shore transfer of jobs and technology. The University of Liverpool, the first to open a branch campus in Suzhou Industrial Park (which attracts more foreign direct investment than any other zone in the People's Republic of China), adver-tised entry-level positions at salaries beginning at $750 per month.

By the summer of 2006, the NYU administration had attracted widespread criticism—reinforced by events surrounding the GSOC strike—about the chronic lack of faculty consultation in decision making. Consequently, it felt the need to circulate the Abu Dhabi proposal to members of Faculty Senate Council. (A deci-sion the year before to enter into a collaborative venture with the American Uni-versity in Paris at a new site on the Isle Seguine was reached with minimal faculty consultation.) Even so, the faculty representatives were enjoined by President Sex-ton himself not to talk about the proposal beyond the confines of the council and, in particular, not to mention the location of the proposed site. Though he placed a quasi–gag order on faculty senators, President Sexton himself took the liberty of discussing the proposal publicly during conference presentations elsewhere. In the interim, he formed a branch campus committee under the leadership of a friend and outsider, Tom Jackson (a bankruptcy law specialist who had just served eleven years as president of the University of Rochester), to advise on this policy decision. Committees were also formed by the provost and by Faculty Senate Council, and a delegation of faculty and senior administrators was sent to Abu Dhabi to research advanced details of the proposal.

From the outset, faculty input about the Abu Dhabi proposal was highly cir-cumscribed, and, given the administration's record of non-transparency, few expected that the circle of consultation would be notably widened over time. Some regional specialists with close ties to the administration were invited to serve on the top-level branch-campus committee, but they distanced themselves after learning more details about the planned site. For those few, and for other faculty who ended up accepting the invitation (select faculty senators were sent on a site visit), the primary skepticism about the proposal focused on the limits to academic freedom that might be imposed by the host country.[4] Would slides of nudes be permitted in art history classes? Would queer students be allowed to organize their interests? What if the students ended up espousing radical versions of Islamism? Concerns were also raised about the opportunism of the proposal and about the likely student constituency in a country where a huge service class (up to 80 percent of the effective population) of low-wage, indentured migrant workers caters to the needs of a small citizen elite. There were no firm legal grounds for assuming that the royal sponsor could be wholly trusted to follow through on details of an agreement; nor ultimately was there any guarantee that the venture would not turn into a vast money pit.

On the face of it, the Abu Dhabi proposal put NYU on the threshold of a decision that other colleges had already made about whether to offer degrees abroad to local nationals. Would the reasons to make this move be fully debated in light of the experience of other colleges, and how would such a decision affect the character and resource map of the institution? Open deliberation on this question might help redress the ailing condition of faculty governance. It might also pressure the administration to observe some measure of transparency in policy-decision making. But in practice, NYU had long ago crossed that threshold, and in the larger world of higher education, the distinction between onshore and offshore education—like that between private and public, or nonprofit and for-profit—has become very blurry, indeed.

The distinction matters even less when viewed from the perspective of how the export trade in educational services is defined. The WTO, for example, recognizes four categories under this heading. Mode 1 involves arms-length or cross-border supply such as distance learning. Mode 2 is consumption abroad, which is primarily covered by international students' studying overseas. Mode 3 is commercial presence, or, basically, foreign direct investment in the form of satellite branches of institutions. And Mode 4 is movement of natural persons, such as academics teaching abroad.[5] Most of the current and foreseeable growth is in Mode 1 and Mode 3, and much of this is assumed to be linked to a perceived decline in Mode 2 growth. Statisticians justify their own trade as well the core principles of free trade by showing how these patterns of ebb and flow are interconnected. In response, and as a general fiscal principle, organizations will try to balance their budgets by pushing expansion in one area to compensate for shortfalls in another. This is how global firms have learned to operate, by assessing and equalizing the relative return on their investments in various parts of the world, both in the world of real revenue and in the more speculative realm of brand building for the future. University accounting departments have begun to juggle their budgets in a similar way. A deep revenue stream from a facility in the Middle East will be viewed as a way to subsidize unprofitable humanities programs at home (as is the case at one Midwestern institution where I inquired) just as an onshore science center capable of capturing U.S. federal grant money may be incubated to help fund an Asian venture considered crucial to brand building in the region.

A Balance of Trade

In the interviews I conducted with faculty and administrators at NYU and elsewhere, a clear pattern of talk about this kind of fiscal juggling emerged (though no hard numbers could be accessed with which to match the rhetoric). NYU's own global programs are an eclectic mix of ventures, spread across several schools and divisions, each of which has its own fiscal boat to float. When viewed in their entirety, the programs clearly do not hold to any overall rule about the demarcation of onshore from offshore education, let alone any systematic educational philosophy. Though they lack a coherent profile, they show a clear pattern of exponential growth and expansion onto every continent—beginning, historically, with the Madrid and Paris study-abroad programs in "Old" Europe—and into each regional market as it was declared open to foreign direct investment.

While its eight study-abroad sites are primarily for NYU students to spend a semester abroad, places are offered to non–NYU students as and when vacancies open up. In addition, as many as sixty summer study-abroad programs are currently offered to non–NYU students in Brazil, Canada, China, Cuba, the Czech Republic, England, France, Germany, Ghana, Greece, Ireland, Italy, Mexico, the Netherlands, Russia, South Africa, Spain, Sweden, and Switzerland. The absence from New York, during the fall and spring semesters, of between a quarter and half of its students allows NYU the option of increasing enrollment at home or reducing the costly expense of providing leased dorm space in downtown Manhattan. Either option has a huge impact on revenue and seems to be a primary motivation not only for university policy in this area, but also for other colleges to emulate NYU's successful fiscal example. By 1998, less than a decade after then President Jay Oliva pledged to shape a global university to match Ed Koch's global-city aspirations for New York itself, NYU had outstripped all other American universities in the volume of students it sent overseas. It also enrolled the highest number of international students. Oliva was known internationally as the founder and host of the League of World Universities, whose rectors met regularly in New York to discuss how to respond to the challenge of globalization, and his successor John Sexton had made his name by pioneering a Global Law program as dean of the NYU Law School.[6]

In the years since then, NYU has found itself in the forefront of online efforts to offer distance learning abroad (one of which, NYU Online, was a notorious $20 million casualty of the dot.com bust, though its successor has thrived) while each of its schools has been encouraged to make global connections. The Stern business school entered into partnership with the London School of Economics and the Ecole des hautes études commerciales to offer an Executive MBA on a global basis, and the law school set up a Master of Laws (LLM) program in Singapore for Asian students. The scale of the university's proposed joint venture with the American University in Paris has upped the ante. While it is not likely to involve more than a small minority of NYU students, its growth potential is tied to recruiting well beyond the one thousand international students currently enrolled by the American University.

Most conspicuously, NYU's School of Continuing and Professional Studies (SCPS), which educates more than fifty thousand adult learners annually in more than one hundred twenty-five fields, has become widely known for its provision of services abroad. This has even extended to graduate programs, which it has offered online since 1994, first through the Virtual College and now through NYU Online. The SCPS was one of the first university institutions in the United

States to register with the Department of Commerce's BuyUSA program, described as "an electronic marketplace that connects U.S. exporters with qualified agents, buyers, and partners overseas." In the words of one of the school's assistant deans, this program has helped SCPS to locate agents and partners in countries that they "never would have considered otherwise."[7] Examples of the school's penetration in the China market include instructional seminars offered to executives in that country's publishing industry and a program in real-estate finance designed for brokers and developers active in the People's Republic of China's vast construction boom. The SCPS is a hugely profitable arm of NYU, and its instruction is carried by an almost wholly adjunct workforce whose compensation in no way reflects the lucrative revenue harvested by course offerings in such non-orthodox disciplines as Philanthropy and Fundraising, Life Planning, Food and Wine, and Real Estate.

Not surprisingly, the SCPS was one of the first educational institutions in the nation to receive the President's Export Award for its work in promoting U.S. educational services overseas. In the U.S. trade balance, education is the fifth-largest export service, bringing in $12 billion in 2004, and arguably the one with the biggest growth potential. In New Zealand and Australia, among the other leaders in this field of trade, education is the third- and fourth-largest export services. Given the intensification of the global competition for high-skill jobs, educational services are increasingly a number-one commodity in fast-developing countries.[8] The Department of Commerce will help any U.S. university to develop this trade, here or abroad, in much the same way as it helps corporations. For relatively small fees, its Commercial Service will organize booths at international education fairs, find an international partner for one of your university's ventures, help it with brand recognition in a new market, perform market research, and, through use of the premium Platinum Key Service, offer six months of expertise in setting up an overseas campus and marketing that campus in one of more than eighty countries.

The Race to Deregulate

The U.S. Commerce Department's activities are fully aligned with the trade-liberalization agenda of the WTO, where higher education falls under the General Agreement on Trade and Services (GATS). Dedicated, like all WTO agencies, to the principle that free trade is the best guarantee of best quality at lowest cost, GATS was formed in 1995, and higher-education services were added to its jurisdiction largely as a result of pressure in 2000 from the U.S. representative to the WTO, backed by representatives from Australia, New Zealand, and Japan. This inclusion has been fiercely opposed by most higher-education leaders in WTO member nations, most prominently by a 2001 Joint Declaration of four large academic organizations in North America and Europe (see http://www.eua.be/eua) and the 2002 Porto Alegre Declaration, signed by Iberian and Latin American associations (see www.gatswatch.org/educationoutofgats/PortoAlegre.doc).

The signatories of these two declarations agree that trade liberalization risks weakening governments' commitment to and investment in public higher education, that education is not a commodity but a basic human right, and that its reliance on public mandates should make it distinct from other services. Yet the concerted opposition of these professional bodies has made little difference to the forty-five countries (the European Union counts as one) that had already made commitments to the education sector by January 2006.[9] Indeed, if the Doha Round of WTO negotiations had not been log-jammed by acrimonious disagreements over agricultural trade, GATS would have concluded its work some time ago, imposing severe constraints on individual government's rights to regulate education within their borders.

Such constraints are particularly debilitating to developing countries that will lose valuable domestic regulatory protection from the predatory advances of service providers from rich nations. Indeed, a new ministerial mandate at GATS allows demandeurs such as the United States, New Zealand, and Australia to band together to put plurilateral pressure on the poorer target countries to accept their education exports (demandeur governments are those doing the asking under the WTO's request–offer process).[10] Officially, GATS is supposed to exclude services "supplied in the exercise of governmental authority"—that is, by nonprofit educational organizations—but most nations that are committed have chosen not to clarify the distinction between nonprofit and for-profit. With good reason we can expect creeping, if not galloping, liberalization in all sectors if the GATS trade regime proceeds. After all, the free-trade culture of the WTO is one in which public services are automatically seen as unfair government monopolies and should be turned over to private for-profit providers whenever possible, all in the name of "full market access." From the standpoint of teaching labor, this tendency points in the direction of increasing precarity, an interim environment of job insecurity, deprofessionalization, and ever eroding faculty governance in institutions stripped of their public-service obligations and respect for academic freedom.

Even in the absence of any such formal trade regime, we have seen the clear impact of market liberalization at all levels of higher education; the voluntary introduction of revenue-center management models in which every departmental unit has to prove itself as a profit center; the centralization of power upward into managerial bureaucracies; the near-abdication of peer-review assessment in research units that are in bed with industry; the casualization of the majority of the academic workforce, for whom basic professional tenets such as academic freedom are little more than a mirage in a desert; and a widening gap between the salaries of presidents and the pittance paid to contingent teachers, which is more and more in line with the spectrum of compensation observed in publicly listed corporations. None of this has occurred as a result of an imposition of formal requirements. Imagine, then, the consequences of a WTO trade regime that legally insists that regulatory standards affecting procedures of accreditation, licensing, and qualification might pose barriers to free trade in services.

By the time that GATS negotiations over education were initiated in 2000, the range of educational organizations that had established themselves overseas was already voluminous. These organizations included (1) corporate spin-offs that do employee training and offer degrees such as Motorola University, McDonald's Hamburger University, Microsoft's Certified Technical Education Centers, General Electric's Crotonville Colleges, Fordstar's programs, and Sun Microsystems' Educational Centers; (2) private for-profit education providers such as the mammoth Laureate Education group (which now owns higher-education institutions all over South America and Europe, operates in more than twenty countries, and teaches a quarter-million students), the Apollo Group, Kaplan Inc., and DeVry; (3) virtual universities such as Walden University and Western Governors Virtual University in the United States, the Learning Agency of Australia, India's Indira Gandhi National Open University, and the United Kingdom's Open University; (4) traditional universities that offer distance learning, especially in countries such as Australia and New Zealand, where governments mandated the marketization of higher-education services; and (5) for-profit arms of traditional universities such as NYU's SCPS, the University of Maryland's University College, and eCornell.[11]

In the years since then, the volume and scope of overseas ventures has expanded to almost every institution that has found itself in a revenue squeeze, whether from reduced state and federal support or from skyrocketing expenses. As a result of market-oriented reforms in higher education, every one of Australia's public universities is aggressively involved in offshore education in Asia, creating a whole class of educational entrepreneurs, onshore and offshore, whose pursuit of monetary gain has inspired repeated calls for audits. Since many of these programs carry large fiscal risks, the tendency increasingly is to favor conservative models such as franchising or producing syllabi in Australia to be taught entirely by local instructors offshore.[12] There is not even a pretense of academic exchange involved in this arrangement, in which education is little different from a manufacturing product designed at home, produced and assembled by cheaper labor abroad, and sold to consumers in emerging markets. In the U.S. for-profit sector, entrepreneurs scrambling to meet overseas demand for degrees ("with no frills") that have an unambiguous market value are taking advantage of notoriously loose accrediting procedures to set up shop and pitch their products. Lax regulation in some Southern and Western states and in offshore diploma-mill havens such as St. Kitts, Liberia, and the infamous Sebroga, a small self-proclaimed principality in Italy that has granted accreditation to dozens of dubious degree-granting entities, make it easy to license operators who open and close programs overnight to suit market demand.

Most recently, the widespread practice of outsourcing study-abroad education to for-profit intermediaries has attracted investigative scrutiny. In August 2007, New York Attorney General Andrew Cuomo's probe into the student loan kickback scandal was expanded to assess evidence that universities had received perks from companies that operated their study-abroad programs. These included "free and subsidized travel overseas for officials, back-office services to defray operating expenses, stipends to market the programs to students, unpaid membership on advisory councils and boards, and even cash bonuses and commissions on student-paid fees."[13] The investigations began to uncover patterns of corruption endemic to the economy of subcontracting and offshore outsourcing.

With China's economy leapfrogging up the technology curve, the jumbo demand for high-value, professional–managerial talent there has sparked a gold rush, with foreign universities scrambling to meet a need that the state (whose professed priority is to fund basic rural education) cannot. There are few U.S. colleges that have not sent prospecting missions to China to scout out offshore opportunities in the past few years. As for their return on investment, many administrators come back from these trips pondering the lesson that foreign companies learned: It is not at all easy to make money in China, let alone break even, and least of all from a joint venture with a Chinese partner, which is the obligatory arrangement for most colleges.[14] Even in the absence of guaranteed revenue, many will set up shop for the same reason that corporations have per-severed there: to build their brand in the China market or establish their name in the region in anticipation of a future windfall.

Corporate Universities?

If universities were to closely follow the corporate offshoring model, what would we expect to see next? In a labor-intensive industry (a characteristic that educa-tion shares with the garment industry; 75 percent of education costs go to teach-ing labor), the instructional budget is where your employer will seek to minimize costs first, usually by introducing distance learning or by hiring local, offshore instructors at large salary discounts. Expatriate employees, employed to set up an offshore facility and train locals, will be a fiscal liability to be offloaded at the first opportunity. If your satellite campus is located in the same industrial park as Fortune 500 firms, then it will almost certainly be invited to produce custom-ized research for these companies, again at discount prices. It will only be a mat-ter of time before an administrator decides it will be cost-effective to move some domestic research operations to the overseas branch to save money. And once the local instructors have proved themselves over there, they may be the ones asked to produce the syllabi for and, ultimately, teach remote programs for onshore students in the United States. Inevitably, in a university with global operations, administrators who have to make decisions about where to allocate budgets will favor locations where the return on investment is relatively higher. Why build expensive additions at home when a foreign government or free-trade–zone authority is offering you free land and infrastructure? Why bother recruiting overseas students when they can be taught more profitably in their countries of origin? If a costly program can only be saved by outsourcing its teaching, then surely that is the decision that will be made. And so on.

But is this the way it has to be? For all the zealous efforts to steer higher education into the rapids of enterprise culture, it would not be hard to demonstrate that, with the exception of the burgeoning for-profit sector, most universities for the most part do not and cannot function fiscally like a traditional marketplace and that the principles of collaboration and sharing that sustain teaching, learning, and research are inimical or irreducible in the long run to financialization after the model of the global corporation. Yet one could say much the same about the organizational culture of the knowledge industries. High-tech firms depend increasingly on internationally available knowledge in specialized fields; they collaborate with one another on research that is either too expensive or too multisided to undertake individually, and they depend, through high turnover, on a pool of top engineers to circulate brainpower throughout the industry. So, too, the management of knowledge workers has diverged appreciably from the traditions of Taylorism and is increasingly modeled after the work mentality of the modern academic, whose job is not bounded by the physical workplace or by a set period of hours clocked there. Modern knowledge workers no longer know when they are on or off the job, and their ideas—the stock-in-trade of their industrial livelihoods—come to them at any waking moment of their day, often in their most surveillance-free moments. From this perspective, talk about the "corporate university" is lazy shorthand. The migration of our own academic customs and work mentalities onto corporate campuses and into knowledge industry workplaces is just as important a part of the story of the rise of knowledge capitalism as the importation of business rationality into the academy, but the traffic in the other direction is all too often neglected because of our own siege mentality.

In all likelihood, we are living through the formative stages of a mode of production marked by a quasi-convergence of the academy and the knowledge corporation. Neither is what it used to be; both are mutating into new species that share and trade many characteristics. These changes are part and parcel of the economic environment in which they function, where, on one side, a public commons unobtrusively segues into a marketplace of ideas, and a career secured by stable professional norms morphs into a contract-driven livelihood hedged by entrepreneurial risks, and on the other side, the busy hustle for a lucrative patent or a copyright gets dressed up as a protection for creative workers, and the restless hunt for emerging markets masquerades as a quest for further international exchange or democratization.

It may be all too easy for us to conclude that the global university, as it takes shape, will emulate some of the conduct of multinational corporations. It is much more of a challenge to grasp the consequences of the *co-evolution* of knowledge-based firms and academic institutions. Yet understanding the latter may be more important if we are to imagine and build practical educational alternatives in a civilization that feeds on mental labor to enrich its economic lifeblood.

Notes

1. Organization for Economic Cooperation and Development (OECD) figures, which covered only students studying abroad, were $30 billion for 1999. Quoted in Thomas Fuller, "Education Exporters Take Case to WTO," *International Herald Tribune*, February 18, 2003, 15. Estimates of the global market for educational services vary wildly. For example, Richard T. Hezel, president of Hezel Associates, a research company focused on e-learning, values the market at about $2.5 trillion in 2005: Elizabeth Redden, "No Risk, No Reward," *Inside Higher Ed*, December 7, 2006, available online at http://insidehighered.com/news/2006/12/07/for_profit (accessed December 27, 2006).

2. The Guggenheim and the Louvre have been named as initial players in a plan for a 670 acre cultural district on Abu Dhabi's Saadiyat Island: Nicolai Ourossoff, "A Vision in the Desert," *New York Times*, February 1, 2007.

3. Knowledge Village's official website is available at http://www.kv.ae/en. For the Qatar Foundation, see http://www.qf.edu.qa.

4. Elizabeth Redden, "A Mini-NYU," *Inside Higher Ed*, August 31, 2007, available online at http://insidehighered.com/news/2007/08/31/nyu (accessed October 13, 2007).

5. These basic GATS definitions can be found at http://www.wto.int/english/tratop_e/serv_e/cbt_course_e/c1s3p1_e.htm. Mode 3, in particular, has seen intense plurilateral pressure on developing countries from OECD states to open up their service sectors.

6. The philosophical drive beyond NYU's global aspirations in the Oliva years is summarized in "NYU: The Global Vision" (New York University, 1995). In that document, Duncan C. Rice, vice-chancellor at the time, argued that NYU had a "unique obligation among colleges to become internationalized" because "it serves the greatest international entrepôt in the world." The university's history of fulfilling the educational aspirations of the "sons and daughters of working Americans and waves of succeeding immigrants," he observed, made this an especially appropriate mission to undertake.

7. See Jennifer Moll, "Trade in Education and Training Services: Excellent Opportunities for U.S. Providers," in *Export America: The Federal Source for Your Global Business Needs*, U.S. Department of Commerce, International Trade Administration, available online at http://www.ita.doc.gov/exportamerica/NewOpportunities/no_edu_0902 (accessed September 12, 2007).

8. For an ultimately enthusiastic, though broad-ranging, summary of some of the salient issues in the GATS debate over educational services, see Pierre Sauve, OECD Trade Directorate, "Trade, Education and the GATS: What's In, What's Out, What's All the Fuss about?" available online at http://64.233.167.104/search?q=cache:b88rD1wCi5MJ:www.oecd.org/dataoecd/50/50/2088515.pdf+GATS+education+services&hl=en&gl=us&ct=clnk&cd=26 (accessed September 12, 2007).

9. Jane Knight, "GATS: The Way Forward after Hong Kong," *International Higher Education* 43 (Spring 2006), available online at http://www.bc.edu/bc_org/avp/soe/cihe/newsletter/Number43/p12_Knight.htm (accessed September 12, 2007).

10. David Robinson, "GATS and Education Services: The Fallout from Hong Kong," *International Higher Education* 43 (Spring 2006), available online at http://www.bc.edu/bc_org/avp/soe/cihe/newsletter/Number43/p14_Robinson.htm (accessed September 12, 2007).

11. See Sauve, "Trade, Education and the GATS."

12. Fazal Rizvi, "Offshore Australian Higher Education," *International Higher Education* 37 (Fall 2004), available online at http://www.bc.edu/bc_org/avp/soe/cihe/newsletter/News37/text004.htm (accessed September 12, 2007).

13. Diana Jean Schemo, "In Study Abroad, Gifts and Money for Universities," *New York Times,* August 13, 2007. See also Elizabeth Redden, "Study Abroad under Scrutiny," *Inside Higher Ed,* August 14, 2007, available online at http://insidehighered.com/layout/set/print/news/2007/08/14/abroad (accessed October 13, 2007); idem, "The Middlemen of Study Abroad" *Inside Higher Ed,* August 20, 2007, available online at http://insidehighered.com/layout/set/print/news/2007/08/20/abroad (accessed October 13, 2007).

14. Paul Mooney, "The Wild, Wild East," *Chronicle of Higher Education,* February 17, 2006, A46–49.

Activists into Organizers!

How to Work with Your Colleagues and
Build Power in Graduate School

MONIKA KRAUSE AND MICHAEL PALM

L abor organizers can recite a number of reasons why working with
graduate students is different and why it is difficult. Many of these
organizing challenges have been described in print before, during, and
after union drives by graduate-student organizers themselves.[1] Any bargaining unit of graduate students will experience high turnover in membership
and leadership, which hinders the development of organizational memory
and collective learning about the employer and the benefits of prior organizing and collective action. Turnover also makes it harder to develop relationships and trust, as does the fact that graduate students are divided by disciplines and into departments; many pursue their degrees part-time while
working other jobs or honoring other commitments. Graduate students have
at times been hesitant to identify as workers even while working long hours
teaching or researching for others. Graduate students can be tempted to
endure exploitation, insecurity, and relative poverty in exchange for promises
of future status.

The fundamental challenges of organizing, however, are the same across
sectors and communities: How do you explore shared interests? How do
you challenge domination collectively? How do you coordinate collective
action in the common interest? How do you build power as students and
as workers?

Rather than dwell on what makes graduate students different—or what
makes graduate students at NYU different—we start from the assumption
that graduate students do organize and that they benefit from organizing.
We ask how it is done well.

In what follows, we draw some lessons from the experience of organizing with GSOC during the strike and, more importantly, since the strike. Hardly any of the organizers in 2006–2007 were at NYU when GSOC became the first union to negotiate a contract with a private university in the United States. For five years, graduate assistants at NYU worked with the protection of a contract that raised our wages by an average 40 percent and guaranteed health-care coverage for the first time. That contract gave us what in hindsight must read as a false sense of security. We operated a steward system and addressed a number of grievances. But attempts to keep the members at large active in their union were largely abandoned. What we thought GSOC had taught us about union life has been put to a dramatic test by a determined employer ready to play every card in the union-busting deck and willing to inflict huge costs on the university and its constituents.

GSOC began the 2006–2007 academic year without a contract and back at work after a prolonged strike. No graduate union has conducted a seven-month strike, and no graduate union has tried to rebuild after such a strike. But fall 2006 was also, in many ways, no different from any recent year for this union, and, we suspect, for many others. The bargaining unit had turned over by at least one-third, as it does every year, and many members were new, as they are every year, not only to working at NYU, but also often to graduate school, to New York City, to the United States, and to union membership. GSOC's most fundamental tasks were to reach out to each member, help orient him or her to NYU's political economy and labor politics, and introduce the union as a way to advocate for fair pay, benefits, and working conditions, as well as for social and economic justice on campus and beyond.

The year after the strike GSOC turned inward, did not seek any publicity, and dropped nearly all coalitional work in favor of rebuilding its membership and leadership. Labor-movement veterans familiar with the impact of a drawn-out strike were amazed when GSOC reestablished majority support among its members in fewer than two months, deep into the second semester on strike and after a majority of members had returned to work. No less significant, given the high turnover in the bargaining unit, GSOC more than doubled the number of members actively organizing in their own or other departments on campus in the first semester after the strike, and during the following spring a majority of members again signed union cards, for the third year in a row, the academic years before, during and after the strike.

Looking forward as well as back, GSOC members have a lot in common with graduate workers across the United States and Canada. We are working, again, without a union contract, and we share this predicament with graduate students in every private university in the United States. At public schools also, administrators have been emboldened by the *Brown* decision to undermine workers' rights, turning contract negotiations required by law into farcical stalemates.[2] Lacking legal protection, we are no longer the exception among workers in the United States more generally: More and more workers are losing the right to union representation, as a recent federal ruling reclassifying nurses as supervisors highlights.

We hope the lessons that follow might be of value to graduate students who are interested in working with their colleagues to address the conditions of their working lives. What we have to say may be valuable to members in unions, especially academic unions, more broadly, where organizing is not emphasized as strongly as it could be.

Progressive elements of the labor movement have always been critical of a reliance on bureaucratic procedure to administer past gains and service existing membership. In the current legal context and given the decline in union membership, this strategy today seems suicidal for individual unions and the labor movement as a whole.

The Law Is Overrated

The law should protect workers, and it can have an important role in addressing some of the structural disadvantages workers face when confronting their employer. The National Labor Relations Act (NLRA) offered some of that protection, but subsequent legislation and, most recently, the courts have been undermining that potential of the law. For better or worse, we have to think beyond the law and treat it like a resource and a context among many rather than the ultimate arbiter.

It is important to remember that the law has always had limits as a tool for unions. Legal protection is weak even for those workers who are recognized by the National Labor Relations Board. The NLRA provides no substantive penalties for an employer's violations of workers' collective rights. Unless individuals are hurt in wages, the ultimate legal remedy is to obtain a "cease and desist order." If found guilty, employers are required only to post a sign indicating that the law was broken, usually years after the violation occurred.[3]

It proved a significant turn in GSOC's campaign when the NLRB ruled in 2000 that NYU was legally obligated to recognize the union and negotiate. But it is important to remember that the NLRB decision did not simply bestow a contract on graduate students at NYU. It was just one step in a long campaign. Graduate students had started to organize in the fall of 1996 and had demonstrated majority support for the first time in 1998. After the decision, NYU dragged its feet for months, threatening to appeal in federal court, and GSOC had to call its first strike vote before NYU's lawyers and head of labor relations would finally sit across the table from graduate students and negotiate with them. GSOC won a contract not per legal fiat but because its members were organized and able to mobilize pressure against their employer. When NYU's administration decided to oust the union five years later, it succeeded not only because the law had changed, but also because it was prepared to incur a great deal of damage to the university community, and we were not prepared to outlast the administration.

Some GSOC members and supporters consider our situation hopeless until a future NLRB recognizes graduate students' right to a union, but waiting for the law to change is not an option if for no other reason than that workers have interests and concerns now. The security of a good contract can tempt leadership to take members for granted and foster complacency among union members. Since our contract expired, we have also learned that there is much work to be done defending workers without legal protection, and without a contract. Graduate students at Yale have been organizing without a contract for years and have used their power to successfully address discrimination against non-citizen graduate employees.[4]

After the strike, GSOC had to learn to exist as a union without the protection of a contract while continuing to fight for a second one. GSOC had lacked a strong presence in the sciences going into the strike, yet scientists became the first group to stand up for their rights in the new academic year. Graduate assistants in chemistry had begun to organize during the strike's second semester, when during March and April 2006 GSOC organizers and supporters in chemistry circulated a petition for union rights. A majority of eligible chemistry graduate students signed the petition, and other GSOC members began to learn more about exploitation and discrimination in the Chemistry Department and in other science departments.

In chemistry, many graduate assistants work throughout the summer yet are only paid on a nine-month schedule. When the fall semester began, they learned that their pay schedule had been changed without prior notice, leaving them without their first check while needing to catch up on bills incurred over the summer. A majority of graduate employees in the department signed a petition to protest and delivered the letter en masse to the dean of the Graduate School. The former system was reinstated, and more than one hundred graduate assistants received retroactive payment. Yeliz Utku, president of the chemistry graduate student organization said, "Our success shows that by acting collectively, we can make NYU a better and fairer place to work. We can only hope that everything goes smoothly. But if not, we at least know that we can get together and make a change."[5]

The action and advocacy organized by graduate assistants in the Chemistry Department was significant for several reasons. It demonstrated that GSOC members could still work together to effectively improve our collective situations, even without a contract and even after a year on strike, in this case maybe even because of the strike. GSOC members are taking collective action in new ways and new places—namely, in a department with a higher percentage of international students than most, where gender discrimination is rampant, and where every student is vulnerable to faculty pressure and coercion. The chemistry graduate assistants were not fighting directly for a contract, but they were continuing to fight for the very things a contract provides.

Waiting for the law to change is also not an option because it relies on a misleading conception of the political process. Given the weakness of political parties, there are few effective mechanisms to hold elected politicians account-able to workers' interests as laws get made. Labor leaders have long repeated the maxim that organizing does not follow the law—the law follows organizing. If workers do not build power on the ground, the law will not change.

How Do Hundreds of People Have a Conversation?

The first step is to accept the challenge. It is not good enough to speculate about what members think, want, or are prepared to do. It is our job to find out. A conversation among hundreds of members of a bargaining unit is not a conversa-tion easily had in meetings or by e-mail—or, rather, such conversations will not happen solely (or even primarily) in meetings and not only by e-mail.

Even the best-attended meetings bring together only a fraction of self-selected members. Among those who attend, only few people speak at meetings, and there is no way to know what those who are silent think and care about. A public meet-ing is often not a good space to talk about personal fears or raise criticisms, including what may be justified personal criticism. Electronic media do not nec-essarily solve the problem of mass conversation: An open e-mail list can turn into a round-the-clock meeting to the point where only the most passionate on both sides of the debate stay tuned in.

Meetings have an important place. Meetings bring people together and allow for an exchange of energy as well as ideas. They are important to provide a formal control mechanism for and give authority to decisions emerging out of a broader set of conversations. Meeting can be an efficient way to share information and provide training, and well-run meetings create a sense of togetherness and dem-onstrate collective strength to one another. Good union meetings are a space to address weaknesses, as well.

Even well-run meetings, however, cannot take the place of the hard work of organizing conversations and building personal relationships between members. Good meetings, ultimately, are the result of these conversations and a product of these relationships.

Because we had not built organizing structures strong enough to withstand the pressures of a long strike, a lack of actual representation of members in both membership and organizing committee meetings began to show. By the end of the first semester of the strike, organizing committee meetings were informed not primarily by conversations with individual colleagues but by a series of descriptions about what one or another group of members think or thought or wanted and by speculation or conjecture about what might appeal to members in whichever new moment of crisis.

In the absence of strong relationships and collective power, the temptation grew to turn the meeting room into a seminar. Some GSOC members were very knowledgeable about the problematic history of trade unions. Others provided incisive analyses of relationships structured by race and citizenship. These cri-

GSOC is here to stay. The union regrouped after the strike and pursued new strategies in the course of the following year. *(Padraig O'Donoghue)*

tiques were often valid, but they could not stand in for the actual representation of GSOC's diverse membership through organizing.

We have learned how important it is to build a structure of relationships in which to coordinate the organizing conversation. It can work with a few dedicated people taking on the bulk of this work, but during GSOC's rebuilding after the strike one mantra among organizers was "more doing less." We are building a more decentralized structure, in which conversations are coordinated among members of an organizing committee in each department.

Each departmental organizing committee develops its own patterns of communication, which strive to facilitate members' participation beyond the provision of feedback to leadership. Organizers set out to discuss with every interested colleague the past, present, and future of our union. These smaller groups meet more often and try to be more responsive to individual problems and to collective issues at the departmental level. The entire organizing committee meets less often than before or during the strike, while a half-dozen GSOC members remain on staff, employed half-time by the UAW, and meet weekly. In this model, every organizer is responsible to a handful of members, and the staff organizers are responsible to a handful of volunteer organizers. The one-on-one conversations provide the basis for exploring common ground in an open environment across the bargaining unit.

Mobilizing Is Not Organizing

Organizing engages existing support and generates new support. Mobilizing produces turnout to a rally, demonstration, protest, or some other action performed by people who already support the cause. Organizing happens independently of mobilization and is its foundation. Organizing is an ongoing conversation that changes not only what people think and do but how they relate to one another, and thereby who they are. Organizing changes both parties. Mobilizing is letting people know about an event and why it is happening and encouraging them to participate. Organizing is an end in itself; mobilizing is instrumental. Mobilizing turns organized support into collective action (or, at least, into collective statement).

There is a place for both organizing and mobilizing in any campaign, but mobilizing can never be a substitute for organizing. Organizing makes mobilizing easier, and any mobilization will take place amid incomplete, unfinished, ongoing, and imperfect organizing.

GSOC mobilized many times to win its first contract, and leading up to the strike we underwent at least three mass mobilizations to pressure NYU administrators: a petition drive and demonstration during April 2005; turnout for a Town Hall meeting in June called by NYU administrators; and a larger demonstration and civil disobedience on August 31, 2005, the day our contract expired. All three of these mobilizations were considered successful by organizers, and they gave GSOC leadership confidence—perhaps false confidence—about the prospects of a strike. Much support for the union among GSOC members was the result of anger at the administration and its treatment of graduate students. The general discontent and disaffection at NYU made mobilizing easier for rallies, petitions, and so on, but it did not substitute for organizing and it did not necessarily prepare us for the strike. The higher stakes of the strike also directed members' scrutiny toward the union, often for the first time, and in the spotlight GSOC turned away as many potential organizers as it attracted. We knew how to mobilize, but we had not organized well enough to prepare for or endure the challenges of a long strike.

Activists and Organizers

Unions attract activists who already identify as "pro-union" for reasons of personal biography or political persuasion. Union activists take the initiative, volunteer their time, and are essential to any campaign, but activists are not necessarily organizers, and the most active activists are not automatically the best organizers.

Organizers must be oriented toward representing the membership as a whole. They must commit to talk to their colleagues about their concerns and be responsible to them as concrete and complete others, over and beyond their own political ideas.

Activists may already have a strong opinion about why to fight, what to fight for, and how to fight. An organizer learns these things and decides which problems matter and how to address them from the members he or she speaks to.

Union activists who have an investment in being politically or morally superior to their colleagues might find it more difficult to engage in common projects with the majority of them. Activists of competing visions for the union may fight over the union's priorities, goals, strategies, and tactics. Some activists grow comfortable remaining disappointed in colleagues for what they will not think, say, do, or risk, and they lose the will to engage their colleagues in dialogue. At the same time, members who do not identify as political radicals might be reluctant to become involved when the union is presented to them as a chance for self-improvement through activism.

The distinction between activist and organizer as we discuss it here is not one between radical and reformist or between someone interested in broader political change and someone interested in the workplace only. In each area of struggle and on each scale of struggle, it is possible to distinguish between an orientation toward the distinction that radical ideas offer and an orientation toward building institutions together.

How do we connect our struggle to broader struggles? It is tempting to draw on our scholarly training and answer this question as intellectuals by relying on the abstractions of political ideology. But in doing so, we risk building a parallel world of discourse where we can be radical without ever threatening those in power.[6]

Organizing offers a different vision. Social transformation begins with building power through building relationships; collective institutions produce new experience and insight into contexts of domination and possibilities of practical action; the experience of successful collective action has its own way of radicalizing those who are a part of it.

The burden of transformation is on the organization as much as the individual. It is tempting for a collection of union activists to blame the broader membership for its lack of commitment, vision, or courage. Activists are often less threatening to leadership than organizers, but activists may be self-motivated and eager to learn "the way things are done" in a union. Even when activists are critical of leadership, they seldom build the collective power necessary to push for change within a union. Organizers are more likely to foment change because they do more than insist on it. Organizers who build power can implement democratic decision making with their colleagues and insist on it in the broader organization.

It is important to consider how our framework can attract and best support and train organizers as well as activists. Organizing involves personal relationships and emotional reactions. Do we have structures to support organizers as we reach out to our colleagues? Do we help each other prepare for organizing conversations? Reflexive conversations about organizing can help us understand our own reactions to conversations with members and decide how to act on them.

Power—Means and End

Hannah Arendt defines power as "the human ability not just to act but to act in concert. Power is never the property of an individual: it belongs to a group and remains in existence only so long as the group keeps together."[7] In her view, power is an end in itself. If you use it and turn it into an instrument, it turns into violence, and you destroy it.

Arendt was no friend of the labor movement. Idealizing politics as an end in itself, she thought it reduced politics to a question of interests. There is an element of elitism in her failure to appreciate that people sometimes have good reasons to fight for something. But it is worthwhile to think about power at least to some extent as an end in itself and, when considering actions, to distinguish ways to use power that enhance it and ways to use power that risk spending it.

Organizers generate power by building links between people. Power is to some extent an end in itself: If we keep building it, it will constrain the employer whether it is formally recognized or not and it enables us to act and react collectively.

Some actions can be a drain on resources and power. Other actions are an expense in time and energy yet leave you with more resources after than you had before. The single campuswide organizers' meeting held during the fall semester after the strike cost GSOC a lot of time and resources, and graduate students are as reluctant as anybody to spend another evening in another meeting. Dozens of organizers had dozens of conversations with members. Organizers talked to one another to plan the meeting. At the meeting, organizers were able to see one another and spend time together as a group. Organizers had an occasion to reflect on past conversations and plan for the rest of the semester. We left with more than we had before we started, learning much from one another. The power "spent" for this particular meeting resulted in more members talking to more members and building more power.

Prepare for Pressure

Standing up for one's rights is different from a commitment to the causes of other people. It leaves less space for selective engagement or neutrality than other forms of activism.

In hindsight, it may seem obvious that we could not expect to win against a determined employer without having adequately prepared to absorb a great deal of pressure in large numbers and deflect it back onto the university's administration.

Such preparation includes facing the material challenges of threats and firings and considering how different workers are affected differently by them. GSOC had the UAW's strike fund to fall back on as long as the strike lasted, and Local 2110 collected thousands more dollars in donations. But few could expect to be able to pay rent in New York City solely by relying on strike benefits. All graduate students here on student visas are barred from accepting employment outside the university and had no hope of supplementing strike benefits with other sources of income; many international students were unsure whether strike benefits would count as income for the immigration authorities. Students from non–European Union countries were particularly vulnerable in their status vis-à-vis the immigration authorities

Most important, preparing for pressure means building the relational ground for solidarity across campus so that workers have a substantive reason to resist the employer's attempt to divide the workforce in their commitment to one another and a shared plan to win.

Organize without Crutches

Flyers, posters, books—imagine what it would be like to run an entire campaign without a piece of paper. Flyers can disseminate information if they are read and remembered. They cannot create serious engagement, which is why some of the best organizers in the labor movement consider them crutches, distractions from the proper task of building relationships.

Flyers and information can lead one to forget that reaching out to other members is an end in itself and the main task—not a means for delivering a ready-made message most efficiently. Every flyer handed out, every e-mail sent, is a missed opportunity to hear what the other person thinks and to engage her or him.

Providing information is not organizing. Organizers often have news to share, but they must also listen to members. Organizers are sometimes advised to consider a ratio of 20 percent talking to 80 percent listening as ideal for a typical conversation with a union member. Building relationships implies mutual support in excess of any exchange of information.

During the strike, members often asked for more information on paper—a symptom that we had not built the necessary trust.

Some organizers have taken prioritizing relationships to the very extreme and even consider automatic dues collection a crutch. A contract that forces the employer to automatically deduct dues from members' wages is a huge logistical and organizational advantage for any union. But the Wobblies see automatic dues deduction as an excuse for not organizing properly. Stewards in the Industrial Workers of the World are expected to collect dues every week from each member; these encounters are the foundation of their union.

Organize as Students and Workers

Graduate students' entire lives are organized around the university: We learn when we work, but we also work while we study. We may take from the university as students, but we also give a lot in return. Most of us work very long hours. We present at conferences, we publish, we run seminars and contribute both intellectual and logistical labor to our departments, organizing events and forming the audience for others. Graduate students also routinely participate in student as well as faculty recruitment.[8]

Labor law encourages us to foreground our work as teachers and research assistants, but it is worth keeping in mind the broadest contexts in which collective action can help us influence the conditions of our lives. The contract has given us a basis on which to construct a supportive environment for our studies. Active citizenship through the union without a contract can foster supportive collegial relationships.

Being a student at the same time as being a worker has been used against graduate students by the administration, by faculty, and by the NLRB. It is often constructed as signifying a "not yet"—not yet a full member of the profession, not yet deserving of a living wage, not yet deserving of respect. But being students as well as workers need not just be a source of embarrassment; it can also be a source of power. A graduate student is valuable to the university as more than cheap labor. The institution also invests in graduate students as future scholars. Schools train graduate students and then exchange them with other universities on the academic job market. The power produced here is constructed as a market power inherent in individuals. We might think more actively about how we can use that power for collective ends—if need be, against the university.

Use Whatever They Throw at You

At the height of the strike, a previously little-known student committee proposed an alternative body for the representation of student's interests as workers, the House of Delegates. The Graduate School of Arts and Sciences, where most graduate students who work are employed and GSOC is strong, is massively underrepresented. Its constituents go beyond the bargaining unit and include all funded graduate students, whether that funding includes employment or consists entirely of fellowship money, such as M.D. and Ph.D. students whose graduate degrees at NYU do not include employment. Graduate students at NYU did not ask for, let alone demand, a new "dummy parliament," and most elected delegates recognize it as a façade, a stand-in for a real union.[9]

When elections came up, GSOC could have boycotted them—and very few people would have voted. Some organizers were worried that our participation might legitimize the new body. But organizing means worrying less about countering their statements with ours than on focusing on building strength through organizing. The core strength of any union is the power generated among its members. Consequently, we decided not to ignore the House of Delegates but to integrate it into our organizing. Candidates were recruited in ten different departments, and our campaign for votes was our first campuswide mobilization since the strike.

GSOC candidates garnered the support of about five hundred voters, fewer than voted to authorize the strike, but not by much. The campaign for voter turnout sparked literally hundreds of organizing conversation about working conditions and members' concerns about both the union and the university. As we move forward, we are learning how to be a union again—not a union on strike, but a union trying to improve the working lives of its members. The landslide victory for the "GSOC slate" of delegates demonstrates that the union is still the only organization on campus with the ability to mobilize hundreds of graduate students. It remains to be seen whether effective representation for graduate employees can be wrought from this new student group.

Notes

1. Corey Robin and Michelle Stephens, "Against the Grain: Organizing T.A.s at Yale," in *Will Teach for Food: Academic Labor in Crisis,* ed. Cary Nelson (Minneapolis: University of Minnesota Press, 1997); Eric Dirnbach and Susan Chimonas, "Shutting down the Academic Factory: Developing Worker Identity in Graduate Unions," in *Cogs in the Classroom Factory: The Changing Identity of Academic Labor,* ed. Danielle Herman and Juliet Schmid (Greenwood Publishing, 2002); Benjamin Johnson, Patrick Kavanagh, and Kevin Mattson, eds., *Steal This University: The Rise of the Corporate University and the Academic Labor Movement* (New York: Routledge, 2003); William Vaughn, "Learning to Be Labor," *Workplace* 6, no. 2 (2005).

2. See coverage of negotiations at the University of Illinois, Urbana-Champaign, available online at http://www.shout.net/~geo/mt-archive/000342.htmland (accessed September 16, 2007).

3. Human Rights Watch, *Unfair Advantage: Workers' Freedom of Association under International Human Rights Standards* (New York: Human Rights Watch, 2000); Brent Garren, "When the Solution Is the Problem: NLRB Remedies and Organizing Drives," *Labor Law Journal* 51, no. 2 (2000): 76–78

4. Available online at http://www.yaleunions.org/geso/is_griev.htm (accessed September 16, 2007).

5. Quoted in *GSOC Journal,* October 31, 2006, e-mail newsletter in possession of the authors.

6. Oskar Negt and Alexander Kluge, *Public Sphere and Experience* (Minneapolis: University of Minnesota Press, 1993).

7. Hannah Arendt, *On Violence* (London: Allen Lane, 1970), 44.

8. See Michael Gallope, "The Professionalizing of Graduate 'Students,'" *Workplace* 9, no 1 (2007): 31–39, available online at http://www.cust.educ.ubc.ca/workplace/issue7p2/index.html (accessed September 16, 2006).

9. Sergio Hernandez, "New Graduate Delegation Dominated by GSOC," *Washington Square News,* January 16, 2007, available online at http://www.nyunews.com/archive (accessed January 10, 2008).

Sorely Needed

A Corporate Campaign for the Corporate University

GORDON LAFER

For at least fifteen years, academics on the left have talked about the "corporatization" of universities. One after another, smart critics have spelled out searing indictments of how the "corporate university" has abandoned the core values of higher education. Some of the harshest critics of this trend have come from the labor movement, who note how the exploitation of campus employees flies in the face of university claims to constitute a community devoted to collegiality and the noble pursuit of truth. In all these years, however, the campaign strategies of campus unions have remained unchanged.

Even while voicing increasingly harsh and incisive attacks on the corporate ethos of university administrators, unions have continued to run campaigns based on strategies appropriate to the pre-corporate university. Specifically, the vast majority of campus union campaigns rely on strikes, public shaming of administrators, or, in the case of state schools, an appeal to legislators to exert influence on university governors. Unfortunately, none of these strategies provides enough power to really change the policies of university administrators. Strikes have always been a weak weapon in higher education for one simple reason: They do not cut off the cash flow. A strike by auto workers in a car-parts plant may cost the parent company tens of millions of dollars a day, as related assembly lines are forced to shut down. But in a university, the main sources of revenue—tuition, government contracts, endowment investments, alumni contributions—are already in the bank at the start of the school year. Interrupting the day-to-day operations of a school does not have much of an impact on any of these. Similarly, political strategies have grown dramatically less useful as public funding for higher education has been repeatedly cut over the past two decades. Obviously, as the government's share of school budgets is diminished, so, too, is legislators' influence over administrators. Finally, the ability of unions to win campaigns by calling out their bosses on the contradiction between their lofty rhetoric and sleazy practices has almost entirely evaporated. Such critiques are, of course, completely right. However, like managers in other industries, university leaders are willing to be morally embarrassed without changing their employment practices—particularly given the constant turnover and short memories of student-led movements.

Despite these readily apparent facts, higher-education unions continue to run virtually the same type of campaigns they ran in the 1970s. For instance, at the University of Oregon—where I teach—state funding constitutes about 23 percent of the university's budget.[1] But union strategies remain the same as if the state provided 100 percent of the budget, generally focusing on a combination of strike threats and legislative lobbying.

To be sure, we continue to see cases where all three of the strategies I have declared discredited have proved effective in winning good contracts. And all of us are indebted to the men and women who bravely put their careers on the line in strikes aimed at improving campus labor relations. But such victories are fewer and fewer. And they are largely confined to winning marginal improvements for already unionized employees. When we look at the track record of winning recognition for new unions—particularly for private-sector faculty and graduate students, where there is no legal requirement for universities to recognize employee unions—it becomes clear that the current range of union strategies is insufficient. If we dare to think about what it might take to roll back some of the most devastating aspects of "corporatization"—for instance, restoring the intellectual-property rights of researchers, requiring that a majority of classes be capped at thirty students and taught by tenure-track faculty, or mandating that support services be provided through the hiring of local community members as regular university employees rather than through a low-bidding process designed to reward contractors who go the furthest in cutting employees' wages and benefits— it becomes even more painfully clear that unions currently have no source of leverage that could enable us to make meaningful progress on these fronts.

What is needed, then, is a corporate campaign for the corporate university.

What Does It Mean to Talk about the "Corporate University"?

The idea of the "corporate university" refers to a specific set of concrete practices that have increasingly come to characterize university administration. They are not a function of individual administrators' personal morality; indeed, identical policies have been carried out by university presidents whose personal politics otherwise have little in common.

Among the most salient traits of the emerging model of higher education are dramatic cuts in public support for universities; similar cuts in student financial aid; tuition "deregulation," freeing state schools from the burden of providing affordable education to in-state students; intellectual-property laws that encourage corporate-backed research and allow universities to profit from publicly funded lab research; the casualization of teaching; technological innovations that facilitate large-scale and long-distance learning; and the standardization of curricula to control teaching costs. What all of these features share is an overarching mindset among administrators that looks at every activity of the university first and foremost in terms of how much money it can bring in. This has two broad implications. The first is a change in how traditional activities are valued. In the old days, it was assumed that the core functions of the university—classrooms, libraries, labs, dorms, and dining halls—were not moneymakers; the revenue to support them would come from the government, the endowment, or the alumni. In the new model, virtually everything—the English Department, the dining room, the gym—is supposed to function as an independent "profit center." New accounting practices require administrators to evaluate any given activity in terms of the extent to which it is a net cost or revenue producer. Obviously, the money losers are also steadily losing institutional support—hence, the underfunding of things like philosophy and classics. The second implication of this change in internal mindset is that administrators have focused much greater attention and resources on developing activities that bring in revenue. Thus, at the same time that administrators are giving short shrift to much of the traditional liberal arts, they are expanding investments in new research areas that promise an influx of federal or corporate funds. If one wants to know which departments will be given slots for tenure-track hires and which will be cut back, all one need do is to track who generates tuition dollars and outside grants. Whatever moral or intellectual principle used to guide the size of departmental faculty has been largely replaced by a financial calculation.

What do administrators now look to as major profit centers? To some extent, the answer varies from school to school. Community colleges do different things from research universities to make money. Rich schools are different from poor ones; urban schools are different from rural. Even within the same market niche (what administrators like to term their "peer institutions"), individual universities may pursue distinct business plans. However, there is a short list of activities that, in various combinations, encompass the revenue strategies of most large schools.

Real Estate

In many cities, the local university is the biggest employer and largest landowner in town. This is true of Johns Hopkins and Baltimore, Yale and New Haven, Tulane and New Orleans, Vanderbilt and Nashville, and many others. This is particularly the case for universities in towns that have undergone deindustrialization, leaving the school by far the dominant player in local real-estate markets. These schools may invest heavily in large-scale real-estate projects, and the profits that accrue from such ventures may be significant.

Medical Services

For schools that have hospitals, medical services can be an important source of revenue. NYU, for instance, realized nearly $350 million in medical and hospital revenue in the last year for which data are available. While these institutions may be called "teaching hospitals," their operations are dictated not by what would be most educational for the interns but by what is best for the bottom line. Like any hospital, university medical centers develop high-profit niche specialties; forge partnerships with physician groups; negotiate reimbursement rates with insurers; and send pit-bull collection agencies after the poor and uninsured.

Corporate-Sponsored Research and Earnings from Intellectual Property

Over the past twenty years, universities have turned to corporations to make up for the cutbacks in federal funding. The advent of corporate-sponsored science has had a number of nefarious results for the science community, including corporate direction on what is to be studied; a falloff in support for basic science research; restrictions on the publication and dissemination of findings; and the reconfiguring of lab research around a corporate model of one principal investigator backed by a horde of post-docs and graduate students—thus dramatically limiting the chances of current Ph.D. students and post-docs to ever run labs of their own. In some cases, the new business model is particularly odious, as when Stanford University launched a $225 million Center on Energy and Climate Change in partnership with ExxonMobil, which explained its goals for the project by noting that "we . . . continue to . . . doubt . . . the attribution of climate change to human activities."[2] In other cases, the requirements of business have directly reversed the centuries-long ethic of disseminating findings to the broader scientific community. Thus, for instance, Harvard and DuPont have jointly patented mice that are genetically modified to be susceptible to cancer. These are ideal creatures for experimentation with a wide range of cancers, but scientists across the country have complained that they cannot afford to undertake such research because DuPont now charges exorbitant licensing fees for others to use their mice.[3]

For university managers, business-backed research offers not only lab funding but also the promise of lucrative intellectual-property rights that result from patenting lab discoveries. Until twenty-five years ago, federal regulations held that any inventions that resulted from publicly funded research were the property of the public. In the early 1980s, however, Congress reversed this policy, allowing universities to patent the results of government-funded research. Since that time, administrators have increasingly sought to capitalize on commercially viable research. From 1965 through the year 2000, the number of patents annually awarded to American universities grew from 95 to 3,200.[4] NYU President John Sexton has himself noted that patents and royalties have become an increasingly important revenue source for research universities, with several schools now earning more than $200 million per year from this work.[5]

Federal Grants and Contracts

While general public support for universities has been dramatically decreased over the past twenty years, there has been an increase in funding for specific projects at the federal level. At NYU, federal funding totaled $260 million in the most recent year reported. Tens of millions of dollars are granted directly to specific schools through earmarks attached to congressional appropriations. In addition, every major research university earns a significant amount of money through overhead charged on federal grants. When the government pays a biologist $1 million to fund lab research, that researcher's institution gets an additional sum—often equal to nearly 50 percent of the original grant—as a contribution to its general funds, to be used in any way it deems fit. In theory, this payment goes to support the infrastructure—libraries, cafeterias, dorms—that makes the lab research possible. Since richer universities have larger and pricier academic infrastructures, they report higher "overhead" costs and get higher percentage payments from the federal government for every dollar of direct research funding. Thus, the system guarantees both that the rich get richer and that every administration has a powerful incentive to report the highest possible overhead costs.

Alumni

The extent of alumni giving varies tremendously from school to school, but in many cases alumni contributions form a significant part of the operating budget. At elite schools such as Harvard and Yale, alumni donations amount to more than $200 million per year. NYU, by contrast, has a relatively small alumni giving program: Only 11 percent of NYU graduates donate to their alma mater, compared with 34 percent at Columbia.[6] The drive to improve this number is one of the university's key business strategies going into the future. Indeed, NYU President Sexton achieved his position largely on the basis of his successful expansion of alumni giving to the NYU Law School.

Endowment Earnings

Nonprofit accounting rules allow universities to keep a separate set of books for their endowment, which does not appear in the operating budget.[7] In state schools, the endowment is often kept in a separately incorporated university "foundation" that is less susceptible to university governance. For schools that are lucky enough to have sizable endowments, this is a critical source of revenue, and generally a highly secretive one. Universities use their nonprofit status and, in some cases, the connections and inside leads of powerful alumni to realize investment profits that have often been significantly ahead of the stock market. In the course of doing so, universities have a long history of engaging in ethically questionable investments.[8]

Tuition and Teaching

For all those who wonder why schools keep raising their tuition faster than the rate of inflation—and certainly faster than campus salaries—the answer is simple: because they can. In an economy plagued by permanent insecurity, the demand for college credentials only becomes more intense. For administrators, tuition is a strategic revenue stream to be maximized. Thus, the past decade has seen tuition increases coupled, in the public sector, with the "deregulation" of tuition. Public schools have sought waivers from requirements that they serve low-income students from their home state, concentrating instead on out-of-state students who pay higher fees. Schools have also sought and won legislation allowing individual campuses to retain tuition payments rather than turn them over to a central state fund, thus freeing flagship schools from the burden of subsidizing poorer campuses. The result has been a disintegration of the state "system," with elite public schools operating more and more like private universities. Indeed, there is now an active debate as to whether the University of Michigan should be privatized, partly to raise tuition above the level allowed by the state.[9]

The flip side of maximizing tuition revenue is minimizing the costs of instruction. Universities have dramatically cut back the number of tenure-track positions, replacing these positions with graduate students, adjuncts, part-timers, and a whole slew of new job titles. At NYU, for instance, President Sexton advocated the creation of a new position termed "university teacher," which would designate a full-time, non–tenure-eligible professor with higher teaching loads and no compensation for research time.[10] Along with degrading the professoriate, administrators have adopted strategies to encourage large-scale, low-cost education. At my own University of Oregon, the administration adopted a budget model in which 50 percent of each department's budget is determined by the number of student tuition credit hours they bring in. Inevitably, the incentive under such a system is to offer large, popular lecture classes and to avoid small, writing-intensive seminars. The extreme version of big lectures and machine-graded exams is distance learning, which offers the promise of a completely online pedagogy, thus vastly cutting labor and infrastructure costs per credit hour. The future of online learning got a major boost in 2006 when Congress abolished its longstanding requirement that students spend 50 percent of their credit hours in a traditional classroom to qualify for federal financial aid. With this major barrier removed, we should expect to see more traditional universities expand into this market.

Mapping the University

If faculty were asked to draw a schematic map of their university, they might produce a diagram of all the departments, grouped together according to college, reporting in turn to the provost and president. If we ask top administrators to map out the major categories of university activity, they would not draw the Philosophy Department or the football fraternity. They would, instead, produce something that drew on the categories described above. This is what a university looks like from the top looking down. And it is this map that we need to use when understanding how a corporate university works and when creating a strategy to exercise countervailing power against those at the top.

What Is a Corporate Campaign?

The term "corporate campaign" gains its name from the fact that it aims at exerting financial pressure on all parts of a corporation's business, not just in the workplace.

Such campaigns developed in the late 1970s and early 1980s, as it became harder for workers to win fair contracts simply by striking. The first campaign widely termed "corporate" was that of textile workers at J. P. Stevens mills, memorialized in the film *Norma Rae*. Stevens's employees confronted an employer that seemed all-powerful in the communities where it operated, and that was willing to break the law to deny its employees the right to represent themselves through a union. Stevens's production was dispersed in multiple factories across the Southeast. To win by striking, the workers would have needed to strike simultaneously at multiple locations and to prevent the company from replacing them. Since this seemed too much to count on, the workers were forced to develop new strategies. The union researched its employer and discovered that Stevens's primary source of financing came from the Metropolitan Life Insurance Company. Over a period of years, the workers sent picket lines up to MetLife headquarters in New York, urged other unions to withdraw pension funds from accounts managed by MetLife, and supported an alternative slate of candidates for election to the MetLife board of directors. Over the course of a long struggle, workers succeeded in winning through these "corporate" strategies what seemed impossible to gain through striking alone.

In the years since the Stevens campaign, workers in a variety of industries have confronted the same problem of being unable to win justice simply by striking and have adopted a similar approach. Unsurprisingly, employers tend to hate this strategy and often suggest that it should be illegal. As a rule, employers want workers to believe that their only option for fighting back against unethical management is to strike. While strikes can be powerful, they are also the tactic that takes the single heaviest toll on workers themselves; thus, management's message is "Do as I say, or watch your family suffer with no income, no health insurance, and the specter of permanent unemployment." Workers who develop corporate campaigns refuse this deal, insisting instead that if the boss is going to attack their ability to make a living, they are going to hit back not only on a picket line but at every part of the employer's business. Sometimes the critical leverage that makes a boss do the right thing may be a lawsuit; in other cases, it may be a consumer boycott or appealing to elected officials to deny economic-development benefits to those who mistreat their employees.

In this sense, a "corporate campaign" is simply workers' ways of engaging the same type of tactics that companies use in competition with each other—but that they would prefer their employees not know about. The ultimate goal of a corporate campaign, as of a strike, is to convince employers that it will cost more in the long run to fight their employees than to treat them with dignity. Critically, corporate campaigns aim to win fair agreements not by appealing to the hearts and minds of top administrators, but by making it a rational business calculation to agree to a fair contract. Thus, this approach takes seriously the understanding of university leaders as corporate executives and eschews the temptation to romantic obsession with divining the character of individual provosts or presidents.

To some extent, corporate campaign tactics may be standardized across industries. For instance, many groups of workers have sought to influence their employers by advocating shareholder resolutions. The steps for doing this are the same in any industry. Largely, however, the most powerful pressure points are specific to individual industries. And the more serious one is about developing the power to change unethical behavior, the more critical it is to dig deeply into the specifics of industry practice. It does not take specialized knowledge to appeal to politicians to speak out in support of strikers. But figuring out how to appeal the tax assessment on a stand of timber; or how to withhold export-assistance benefits to companies that exploit immigrant workers; or how to deny expansion rights to a hospital that has cut staffing levels to the point of endangering patient safety; or how to revise a hotel-industry tax to make unscrupulous wholesalers pay their fair share—all of these things require a serious investment of time, money and staff. Furthermore, the nature of this research process is that, for every example of a successful strategy, staff researchers have probably looked at ten other issues that turned out to be irrelevant. Thus, it is not possible for a union to decide to adopt a corporate campaign strategy on the spur of the moment if it has not committed to such an effort for the industry as a whole. The level of staff commitment and financial resources necessary for a serious campaign is simply too great to be justifiable by a single employer. Every union that has developed a serious campaign capacity has done so through a process of trial and error, slowly learning from mistakes and improving strategies from one campaign to another, over a period of many years. Such campaigns get easier to run over time because one starts each new round knowing more than the time before and having already developed relationships with key industry, media, and regulatory actors. If we are serious about developing corporate-campaign capacity in higher education, one or more unions will need to make a significant, long-term commitment to developing the knowledge and techniques of how to fight for justice in this industry.

What Might a Corporate Campaign Look Like in Higher Education?

If campus unions are to safeguard the quality of education and the dignity of working conditions, they must be able to speak to university managers in the language they understand. This means that they must learn to understand, and intervene in, the key profit centers of higher education. The specifics of a campaign will vary from school to school and cannot be planned in a cookie-cutter manner. But some examples of potential strategies are clear. It is likely that, in each of the major revenue sources of universities, there are questionable practices and possibilities for campus employees to guarantee that unethical employers do not receive undue financial advantage. For instance, at both the state and federal level, universities are competing for large research funds targeted to special projects such as AIDS or stem-cell research. So, too, many schools receive targeted funds through the congressional earmark process. In all of these cases, unions should be arguing that federal favors should be reserved for ethical employers. Similarly, it is long past time that the labor movement held administrators to account to make sure they are not defrauding the public and the federal government in padding "overhead" expenses and not defrauding students in the operation of student-financial aid programs.[11]

Many of the key profit centers in higher education are dependent on the goodwill of the general public. It is thus important that unions broaden the struggle over higher education to mobilize appropriate allies. If a city council conditioned zoning variances for university expansion on the school's acting as an ethical employer, this might create significant financial incentive for administrators to do the right thing. So, too, if administrators came to believe that preferential Medicaid treatment might be held up as a result of campus unrest, or that ethically questionable but lucrative endowment investments might be exposed and undone, or that entrepreneurial teaching ventures (involving new technologies or foreign markets) might be derailed, the logic of adopting more ethical policies might suddenly become more apparent. All of these possibilities have two things in common. First, they require further research, and learning through the trial and error of campaigns, before academic unions can figure out a regular approach to exerting influence in these areas. Second, if such strategies were figured out, it is likely that any of them would prove more powerful than a strike.

Ultimately, I believe that undoing the "corporatization" process and restoring a more humane education system will require a movement that stretches beyond campus employees themselves to embrace students, parents, and taxpayers. When

Picketing and rallies during the strike were often motivated by the perception that the GSOC struggle was a front-line cause for the future of the academic labor movement.
(*Joshua Evans*)

the working conditions of campus employees are degraded, the education of students almost always suffers. Certainly, the broad transformations that mark the "corporate university" have generally resulted in poorer quality and more expensive education. For many academics, it is this abandonment of traditional educational ideals that motivates their union activism, even more than economic concerns. The interests of these groups overlaps with that of academic unions, and the scale of change we need to effect requires an alliance much broader than can be constructed out of campus employees alone. In ballot-initiative states, unions should be thinking about proposals to cap class size, guarantee adequate numbers of tenure-track faculty, or commit to educating in-state working-class students through public initiative campaigns. An alliance based on the shared interests of academics, students, and taxpayers holds tremendous potential power; but it will require strategic planning and a commitment of resources from the labor movement to make this happen.

Figuring out exactly which strategies will prove effective is an intensive effort. Each of the unions that has developed campaign competence in its industry has done so by dedicating significant staff to the effort, over a period of years. If we are going to make real progress in higher education, campus unions must dedicate themselves to a similar effort. Currently, the union at NYU is working hard to win justice for university employees, but in terms of exercising financial pressure to convince administrators to do the right thing, the union is in the position of creating new strategies from scratch.

The UAW has taken an admirable approach in this campaign, but it is handicapped by the fact that there is no history of university corporate campaigns to learn from. The union has an admirable track record of bold campaigns and creative strategies in a number of industries, including higher education. In the 1990s, the UAW combined strategic political action with a credible strike threat to win something that many had dismissed as impossible: a graduate teachers' union in all eight campuses of the University of California. More recently, it has led the successful organizing of adjunct faculty at both NYU and the New School for Social Research. But in the struggle of NYU graduate employees—confronting an aggressively anti-union administration that has no legal requirement to bargain in good faith—the UAW is up against something that requires new strategies. And while the union has an laudable track record in organizing academic employees, higher education is not the core of its membership, and therefore it cannot be expected to take the lead role in developing corporate campaign strategies for this industry.

Ultimately, it rests above all with the American Federation of Teachers (AFT) to establish such an effort. The AFT is the largest academic union in the country and the logical actor to take the lead in exploring new strategies for the changed university. Since corporate campaigns apply equally well to classified employees as to academics, it would be logical for the AFT to join in this effort not only with the UAW and other academic unions but also with the Service Employees International Union (SEIU), American Federation of State County and Municipal Employees (AFSCME), Union of Needletrade, Industrial and Textile Employees–Hotel Employees and Restaurant Employees (UNITE-HERE), and other unions representing the secretaries, custodians, and dining-hall workers who make our campuses work. The NYU campaign is a good opportunity to learn more about how to deal effectively with "corporate" universities. But it will be an opportunity squandered if the major campus unions do not use the lessons of the NYU fight as a starting-off point for developing an ongoing, in-depth, long-term process of crafting effective corporate campaigns for this industry.

Notes

1. For similar examples, state funding constitutes 25 percent of the University of Illinois budget, 18 percent at the University of Michigan, and 8 percent at the University of Virginia: Nicholas Von Hoffman, "The Increasingly Private Public School," *Nation*, October 25, 2005, available online at http://www.thenation.com/doc/20051107/vonhoffman (accessed August 31, 2007).

2. Martin Van Der Werf, "Stanford U. Receives $225-Million in Corporate Backing for Research Center on Energy and Climate Change," *Chronicle of Higher Education*, November 21, 2002.

3. Paul Elias, "Dilemma Has Researchers By the Tail: Scientists Criticize a Company's Hold on Genetically Engineered Mice," *Eugene Register-Guard,* November 4, 2003, B3.

4. Melody Petersen, "Uncoupling Campus and Company," *New York Times,* September 23, 2003.

5. John Sexton, "The Research University in a Global Context," address delivered September 5, 2004, available online at http://www.nyu.edu/about/sexton-globalization.html (accessed August 31, 2007).

6. NYU Alumni Office, "The Fund for NYU," available online at http://alumni.nyu .edu/giving/thefund.shtml (accessed January 14, 2007).

7. A small percentage of the endowment's annual earnings is normally donated to the operating budget, but this should not be confused with either the total size of the endowment or the total annual earnings it generates.

8. I don't mean that most university investments are morally questionable, but simply that endowments generally operate simply to generate the highest possible return, with little or no additional ethical guidelines.

9. "Privatize the University of Michigan," Mackinac Center for Public Policy, March 1, 2004, available online at http://www.mackinac.org/article.aspx?ID=6313 (accessed August 31, 2007). In 2003, South Carolina gave all thirteen of its universities authorization to become private schools if they so chose.

10. John Sexton, "The Common Enterprise University and the Teaching Mission," November 2004, available online at http://www.nyu.edu/about/sexton-teachingmission04 .html (accessed August 31, 2007).

11. For the most recent chapter on unethical profiteering from student-loan programs, see Jonathan Glater, "Senator Calls for Student Loan Inquiry," *New York Times,* November 1, 2006.

Graduate-Employee Unionization and the Future of Academic Labor

Cary Nelson

The graduate-employee unionization movement is the single most promising development in higher education over the past twenty years. It arrives at a time when much of the news about the industry is not good—the massive casualization of academic labor over two generations, the rampant corporatization of many elements of the academy, the revitalization and adaptability of the culture wars and their increasing focus on higher education, the grotesque inflation of upper-administration salaries, the decline of shared governance at many institutions, the predominance of careerism and lack of community responsibility among many of the full-time, tenurable faculty. As good a statistical indication of several of these destructive trends as any is the more than 50 percent decline in American Association of University Professors membership from the 1970s to the 1990s. Faculty who see themselves as exclusively devoted to their careers and their disciplines—who are unconcerned with the principles and goals that unite the professoriate—are less likely to join in the defense of academic freedom and its application to new technologies and new institutional structures.

One key thing about graduate-employee unionization is how it responds to and helps us reverse several of these developments. Of first importance, of course, is the potential for unionization to raise the wages, benefits, and working conditions of all contingent workers in the academy and its proven capacity to spread workplace justice to other industries in a given area. But equally critical is its other clear legacy: its capacity to create new, socially responsible identities for both graduate students and faculty. The graduate-employee unionization movement is the best source of faculty members devoted to both their personal academic work and their community responsibilities. Graduate-employee activists learn to work collectively for the common good, meanwhile learning advocacy and organizing skills. They are at the core of a generation that has the potential to reverse the dominance of identities based, ironically, on disempowered self-interest among the faculty.

Faculty unions also need the new blood that graduate activists bring when they graduate to faculty status. A disturbingly large number of faculty unions formed in the 1970s or later have not grown a sufficient cadre of new, younger leaders. Some have also let the practice of recruiting new members slide and thus seen their percentage of membership drop to the point where decertification at the hands of administrators is a real risk. There is nothing quite like a leader who has been through a founding organizing drive. By far the largest pool of such people is graduate-student union activists. Those activists should be cultivated as the faculty leaders of the future.

Graduate-employee activists also gain personally by acquiring skills in self-presentation that play extremely well in job interviews, for they have learned to present arguments convincingly to strangers, learned to listen carefully, and learned the psychological complexities of negotiating advocacy as part of inter-personal relations. At the same time, they learn to juggle competing demands on their time, moving back and forth between organizing their colleagues and taking courses or writing their dissertations. They live with demands on their time that can be all-consuming while also realizing that such responsibilities reach a point when they must be passed on to others. When union activity is combined with AAUP membership, graduate employees can add to this mix a deep knowledge of the principles that sustain and link academic freedom and job security.

Based on the long-term experience of faculty unions in Canada and the United States—and on decades of graduate-employee unionization at the University of Wisconsin and the University of Michigan—a clear pattern emerges about the practical benefits union members can expect. Improvements in health benefits are often the most immediate gain, supplemented by gradual progress on compensation. But the more fundamental difference unions make, I believe, is in grieving unfair or unsafe working conditions. Unions have the authority to establish workplace justice. Whole classes of employees for the first time have the advantage of dispassionate, well-informed third-party negotiation of exploitive practices—negotiations, moreover, that guard against retaliation against the victims.

Of course, even the strongest faculty union cannot establish workplace justice by looking solely after its own economic interests when contingent faculty are being exploited on the same campus. It should be a fundamental ethical and professional principle for existing faculty unions to help organize graduate employees, part-time faculty, and full-time faculty off the tenure track. The AAUP has been encouraging its full-time–faculty unions to do just that, and some have answered the call and succeeded. Not long ago, the AAUP's full-time–faculty collective-bargaining unit at the University of Rhode Island took responsibility for the successful drive to organize graduate employees and then integrated servicing of the new bargaining unit into existing chapter activities. They are now seeking to do the same for part-timers. Our Rutgers chapter, of course, has long had units for full-time faculty, graduate employees, and part-timers, and it now has a Service Bureau that handles needs on an integrated basis.

But not all AAUP locals have been sympathetic. During the 1995–1996 graduate-employee grade strike, the Yale AAUP chapter was largely hostile toward GESO. My own AAUP local declined to endorse the national policy in support of graduate employees' collective-bargaining rights, despite the fact that I had written the policy and had given sworn testimony before the Illinois Labor Relations Board. The NYU AAUP chapter opted to devote its energies and resources to a more spontaneous and effective formation called Faculty Democracy. Now that graduate students have full membership and voting rights in the AAUP, the opportunity exists to revitalize rather dormant AAUP chapters such as Yale's with local membership drives that concentrate in part on graduate-student membership.

However, some non–AAUP faculty unions behave as if every dollar won by contingent teachers is a dollar taken from their own pockets. Yet denying contingent faculty a living wage and salary parity actually helps keep salaries for tenure-track faculty low in a number of disciplines. A faculty union that either passively or actively collaborates in the exploitation of its brothers and sisters has simply lost its soul. At some level, it has become an arm of administrators devoted to extracting labor at its lowest possible cost. Worse still are those faculty unions that grieve their own workplace inequities while tolerating the mistreatment of contingent faculty or graduate employees down the hall.

Interestingly, one of the major groups of graduate employees who benefit from this kind of arbitration are those who work in engineering or science laboratories. Work weeks of a hundred or more hours can be reduced to a humane level when a union intervenes. Paradoxically, these are among the most difficult graduate employees to organize, not only because they are often relatively well compensated financially, but also because they feel exceptionally vulnerable. Labs are often constructed around a core of foreign students who are anxious about visa renewal. If their families have remained in the home country, they may be less stressed by long working hours. For all of these reasons, they are more readily influenced by false propaganda from administration spokespeople, propaganda that is often enough grounded in a mix of antagonism and ignorance. I believe unions should work together on a national educational campaign aimed at these employees and their supervisors. Meanwhile, emerging unions often agree to leave them out of the bargaining unit, a strategy administrators are sometimes willing to accept.

Faculty attitudes toward collective bargaining have always varied, especially at institutions where there are wide differentials in compensation by discipline. Tenurable faculty also show disciplinary differences in their approach to graduate-employee unionization campaigns. Few humanities faculty see themselves as employers. Even if graduate employees are assisting in large lecture courses, faculty are generally happy to see them better compensated. Running a lab staffed with graduate employees is another matter. There faculty can be corrupted by the temptation to extract the maximum labor at the lowest possible cost, for they supervise their workers directly and benefit professionally and financially by the work they do. Most laboratory faculty obtain funds for graduate employees' salaries through the grant-application process, and they worry that a union contract will increase compensation before a new grant cycle will enable them to obtain additional funds. A responsible administration would begin to set aside enough indirect-cost revenue to deal with this possibility as soon as a unionization drive gained strength. Instead, most administrations prefer to exploit faculty anxiety.

One of the most unethical faculty practices in both science and engineering labs is that of deliberately delaying Ph.D. completion to retain experienced graduate employees as long as possible. It is a widely recognized national phenomenon, but neither department heads nor graduate-school deans, in my experience, do a very good job of policing the problem. This is another area where a union can step in and make a difference and another reason why training in workplace ethics needs to be built into faculty culture.

The past thirty-five years have seen successful graduate-employee unionization drives at public universities in the East, the Midwest, and the West. Both experience and careful studies have shown that campus relations are improved, not damaged, by unionization—even in more volatile lab environments—though administrators often claim otherwise. The movement picked up speed in the 1990s and was supported by sometimes eloquent and witty state court opinions in such venues as Kansas and California. When the National Labor Relations Board (NLRB) first ruled in favor of New York University graduate employees, it thus had no formal federal precedent but substantial state arguments defending the notion that graduate students could be both students and employees according to the roles they played at different times during the day.

The NLRB, of course, has jurisdiction over private universities, and the story of graduate-employee unionization has been more troubled. Generation after generation of graduate-employee activism has been sustained at Yale University, but the Yale Corporation's hostility to all forms of unionization, now moving toward a century-long history, has successfully wielded administrative and legal power to prevent these employees from realizing this right recognized by the United Nations. The activists I worked with at Yale in the days during and after the historic grade strike are now long gone; many are tenured faculty elsewhere or union organizers in other industries. The struggle for unionization at NYU has its own long, unique story. Recognized by the NYU administration after a positive NLRB ruling, the union negotiated a strong contract and then was effectively decertified when the NYU president took advantage of an NLRB reversal to stop bargaining a new contract. He was not required to do so; he chose to disenfranchise his employees.

Neither at Yale nor at NYU were strikes successful at winning or restoring union recognition. There are lessons to be learned from these and other struggles, however, that can help prepare the ground for future job actions. The most obvious lesson appears to be the most difficult for those of us within the campus bubble to internalize: The withdrawal of teaching labor never wields sufficient force to bring an administration to the bargaining table. It is easy to succumb to the expectation that a classroom strike will matter. The classroom is at the center of our lives and many of our social relations, but a forced vacation does not communicate imminent peril to students who assume they will end up graduating anyway. Parental protests do not wield decisive power, either. It is a storm most administrators assume they can weather. The major economic pressures fall on the strikers themselves—unless they plan carefully to assure the reverse.

A strike is a major emotional event; for some academics, it will be the first powerful collective action they have ever taken, and the experience may prove life-transforming. The eloquence, passion, and dedication of long-term graduate-employee activists is never less than inspiring. At NYU, a major local and national mobilization took place, drawing in graduate assistants, undergraduates, faculty, and external allies. Like the multigenerational struggle at Yale, it included events that embodied unforgettable solidarity. It is thus surely forgivable to romanticize the experience. But it is best to avoid romanticizing the projected outcome. A cold calculation of likely results and strategies is in order.

I recently told a large faculty union planning to reduce its dues that it ought instead to use the excess money to build a substantial strike fund; even if it never had to use it, the fund's existence would limit administrators' confidence in their ability to break a strike. That particular union had the power to build a $1 million strike fund in three years—hardly enough to cover salaries for a long strike, but enough to cover health-insurance costs, and that alone would make a considerable difference. Graduate-employee unions cannot build comparable financial reserves, but the focus on economic issues helps members recognize the centrality of fiscal power. Political power can also be effective—if it is real, not merely symbolic—but it is generally economic power that is truly decisive. The NYU strikers eventually received their most dramatic political support in the form of a letter jointly signed by New York's two U.S. senators, Hillary Clinton and Chuck Schumer, but, despite many assurances, there was little evidence of any politicians applying effective behind-the-scenes pressure—quietly delaying building permits and contracts, complicating inspections, refusing multiple forms of cooperation, orchestrating public embarrassments for administrators, and so on.

The first and most necessary form of economic pressure is cooperation from other unions in blocking all deliveries to campus. It is certainly easiest to prevent deliveries to a self-contained campus with its own clearly defined boundaries and with a limited number of entrances. An urban campus such as NYU, with buildings owned by multiple businesses in the same area, presents much greater difficulties, but it is still possible to map major delivery sites, loading docks, and other points where pickets can inhibit deliveries. Few drivers will pass a Teamster picket, although it was several months into the GSOC strike before some Teamsters refused to do some garbage pick-ups. Construction sites can also be shut down with union cooperation. A campus administration may be able to hire non-union day laborers to keep some projects going, but somewhere in the supply chain a union is likely to be in place. During a 2006 strike by an AAUP-affiliated faculty union at Eastern Michigan University, the people who drove concrete trucks were non-union and willing to pass picket lines, but the workers who loaded the concrete were unionized and honored a strike. Decades ago, a strike at the University of Wisconsin was won in part because conservative faculty pressured the administration to settle when food deliveries to animal labs were prevented and long-term experiments were on the verge of collapsing. GSOC was unable to organize effective cessation of campus deliveries, and that was an early sign that its strike was in trouble.

The United Auto Workers might have done more to help the NYU students at that point, but my own view is that it is unwise to rely on even a strong national union to win full local cooperation from other unions in blocking deliveries. A history of campus support for other unions can be a critical component. Join the picket lines of other striking unions. Attend their rallies with signs identifying your own local. Honor and publicize their boycotts. Meet with their leaders to offer assistance and build relationships. Build local solidarity, both because you believe in it and because you know you will need it yourselves in time. Then add the component of advocacy from a national.

AAUP leaders typically support all graduate-employee unionization drives, no matter which international is backing the effort. Indeed, graduate employee activists typically see themselves as part of one large national movement. At NYU, critical support came from Yale graduate employees. They filled key roles at NYU and participated in large numbers in all job actions, thereby supplementing the terrific job NYU activists did at department-level organizing. The Yale graduate employees, notably, are affiliated with UNITE-HERE, a union committed to wall-to-wall organizing in New Haven but not competing to represent graduate employees elsewhere. A victory against a private university administration for the UAW in New York would thus also be a clear victory for UNITE-HERE in New Haven. Idealism and practical politics were perfectly fused.

Any disruptive job action should also be timed to begin immediately after paychecks are distributed, so that participants have some waiting power. Strikers and their allies should also consider boycotting all local businesses—or, at least, those that refuse to support the strike—so that business owners have reason to pressure an administration to settle. That will also increase the amount of publicity a strike can generate. In a large city, it will be necessary to define a zone of impact, since one cannot expect to bring New York or Washington to a halt, but denial of patronage can still be part of a successful strategy, especially if it is honored by all campus workers and their friends.

Solidarity is obviously a critical component of effective economic actions of this sort. Students, faculty, and staff who join such efforts in large numbers can

254 / Cary Nelson

bring considerable power to bear on an administration. In a small town where
the college or university is the major employer, a coordinated economic boycott
can be decisive. Withhold rent, mortgage, and utility payments. Organize cara-
vans to shop in another city—or, still better, in another state if you are near a
border. Many businesses do not have sizeble ready-cash reserves. They cannot
long endure a sharply curtailed cash flow. Even large utilities are vulnerable to
cash-flow interruptions.

The absence of sufficient solidarity can be disastrous. That was one of the
key lessons of the Yale grade strike, where sufficient effort did not go into educating undergraduates about any of the issues at stake. They did not understand
that their instruction was being delivered by exploited workers or that crossing
a picket line is a significant ethical and political decision. I still wince at the
memory of the anti–GESO editorials and cartoons in the Yale student newspaper.
At one level, the Yale organizers had great publicity; their posters were clever and
striking. But they had not done enough of the hard work of undergraduate
instruction to build real commitment in the student body. At NYU, graduate-
employee support for the UAW-affiliated union was strong across the whole
range of disciplines, and there was a core of dedicated faculty support, but far
too many other faculty were indifferent or antagonistic. More time to educate
faculty would have helped, though timing was partly out of the union's control,
since the strike was prompted by the president's action.

Strike timing is nonetheless both complex and critical. Some of those involved
in the NYU planning held that delaying a strike would undermine its credibility
and chances for success. Others—among them NYU graduate activists and Yale
graduate employees playing key leadership roles in the NYU events—counseled
caution. A standard union warning is that it is easier to go out on strike than to
come back to work victorious. There really was no effective winning strategy in
place at NYU. Since, for example, a strike usually brings at least a temporary halt
to negotiations, plans must be in place to make it too costly for management
simply to wait out the strikers. Those who preferred waiting longer before striking
at NYU—waiting until support was assured—were almost certainly correct.

One obvious reason why relying on the local influence of the national UAW
would have been unwise is that the UAW simply does not have the political power
in New York that it has in Michigan. It cannot even rely on the same level of
cooperation from UAW locals in New York. Dealing with a private university,
rather than the public institutions it dealt with in California, put the UAW at a
still further remove from political influence. Corporate anxiety about the UAW's
potential political power was an effective component of a strike's threat, but the
added demands accruing to an actual strike presented a greater challenge. It is
also necessary to be realistic about prospects for cooperation in a fragmented
and sometimes competitive labor movement. The obvious place to turn for help
would be other unions representing college faculty, but if those unions not only
see themselves as competing to represent the same groups but also are inclined

to make tactical decisions based exclusively on a narrow view of their self-interest, then they are unlikely supporters.

Solidarity is the key. The United States will presumably eventually have a democratic president ready to appoint sympathetic NLRB members, but the NLRB has lost much of its credibility. It is now so fundamentally and irredeemably a political agency that any sense that it can apply labor law fairly is lost. The lesson for both graduate students and faculty at private universities seems increasingly clear: Ignore the NLRB. An employee group with campuswide solidarity can get whatever recognition and negotiating power it needs. Stand firm with secretaries and maintenance workers in their organizing drives and job actions. Then ask for their support when your turn comes. No administration can stand against a campus when a strong majority of all its labor groups support a job action. Many existing faculty unions were recognized by consent in the 1970s, not by the use of state or national labor law. In today's anti-union atmosphere, consent will now be forthcoming only with the application of force, but the principle is the same. Even in states that bar collective bargaining for public employees, faculty and students can force informal but effective negotiating. An AAUP chapter can discuss salary and working conditions with Mississippi or Alabama administrators if it chooses to do so, and it can place many sorts of potential job actions and non-cooperation on the table as points of negotiation. The challenge is to take possession of the power inherent in numbers and agency. The prevailing identities of recent generations have worked against that recognition, but growing graduate-employee and part-time–faculty activism is beginning to change the pattern.

This kind of organizing also requires a mix of wit and courage. Nonviolent civil disobedience may be a critical component, but only if economic pressures are in place. And sufficient solidarity must be present so arrests are engineered day after day. For me this is one of the unforgettable lessons of Vietnam protests: You have to make daily life unmanageable. The California Faculty Association has learned to give key administrators no peace. Place chanting pickets outside their homes. Disrupt every meeting they attend with sardonic or inspiring public theater. Arrange building occupations and street demonstrations every week. The goal is protest without end. Plan actions for members with different levels of commitment. You will certainly have some people willing to do almost anything nonviolent. Use them. Divert others to less confrontational support.

No employee group, it must be clear, acts simply out of self-interest in such struggles. Every union defeat empowers administrators elsewhere. Every union victory sets a precedent that other campuses and other industries will find increasingly difficult to resist. The issue is the worldwide exploitation of workers in all industries. The call is to rise up and take possession of economic justice. A university president who earns $1 million while denying classroom teachers a living wage is a criminal. He or she stands in opposition to all the values to which higher education has traditionally been dedicated. A campus that exploits its labor force educates all of its students in the logic of exploitation and sends them forth to practice it with untroubled consciences.

At the November 2006 invitational conference "Terrorism and the University," held at John Jay College of Criminal Justice in Manhattan, the president of NYU gave a keynote speech touting his unflinching dedication to high principle. Despite political and cultural pressures to compromise, he assured the audience, the satellite campus NYU was considering establishing in the Gulf region would not eliminate course components that were offensive to local tastes. Art classes would show slides of classic female nudes, despite objections. As he rose to speak, Eric Lott of the University of Virginia and I stood and prominently turned our backs on him, silently protesting what I regard as his administrative terrorism in denying his graduate employees the right to negotiate their working conditions. The next day, I told conference attendees I did not expect John Sexton to honor such rights in the Gulf, either. I anticipate that his satellite campuses—like so many others—will staff their courses with underpaid and unrepresented part-time faculty. The combination of high culture and wage slavery is the hallmark of the contemporary university. The city on the hill is built atop a mountain of hypocrisy.

Two weeks after I talked in New York, the news came through that the University of Toronto was planning to deny its part-time, or sessional, faculty access to research grants, a deplorable but typical act of de-professionalization and dehumanization. This proposal was defeated by union solidarity and a worldwide petition and letter-writing campaign. In the State of Washington, faculty unions, too, often exclude their part-timers from negotiated wage increases. Part-timer activists such as Keith Hoeller are writing editorials to draw attention to this tradition. Once again, we face not only local but also international pressures to adopt exploitive employment practices. For the globalized economy has made all such practices interdependent and co-present. The familiar adage "Act Locally, Think Globally" has been supplanted by forces that relentlessly internationalize local forms of exploitation. How higher education does or does not perform its commitment to human decency, how it does or does not enact community responsibility, now has the power to shape worldwide standards in all industries. Collective action is the one and only way we can guarantee that the academy's impact will be salutary rather than malicious. Graduate-employee activism can be an inspiration for other campus groups to join in group advocacy and organizing.

As the logic of corporatization is globalized and new opportunities for exploitation arise, the need for activism increases. American universities have been led to establish satellite campuses in other countries in part by the burdens placed on international students by the Patriot Act and the Department of Homeland Security. If Arab students cannot come to us, we will go to them. Homeland exploitation thus encourages us to secure profits by exploiting our academic labor force elsewhere. If local faculty resistance is a problem, circumvent it.

My university, the University of Illinois, Urbana-Champaign, is seeking to establish a global online campus. Touted as a cash cow, the enterprise may well prove a net financial loss, but the structure announced in 2006 also presented additional long-term dangers. In a particularly worrisome maneuver, the university announced a plan to establish a separate corporation to run its global online university. Local faculty would thus in one step have been excluded from influence or oversight over a major new curricular initiative. And there would have been no question of intellectual-property rights for faculty. The corporation would own all of the courses designed for the program. Since my administration is not known for original thinking, I assume it got the idea to form a corporation to deliver instruction without faculty oversight elsewhere and that administrators at other campuses have similar plans in the works.

With faculty solidarity unusual at any of the three Illinois campuses—Urbana-Champaign, Chicago, and Springfield—the AAUP locals and faculty senates united in opposition to the proposal and in 2007 forced the administration to withdraw the plan to establish a limited liability corporation to house the online university. Academic departments will now control the curriculum, a major victory for the faculty and—though some of the responsible administrators cannot understand this—a structure far more likely to produce viable degree programs. The experience once again proved that major campus constituencies, including both faculty and graduate employees, have the power they need to effect change if they are willing to exercise it.

Unfortunately, although this issue was the most pressing one, it was not the only one at stake in the plan. I have no doubt that the projected profitability for the online program was based on substandard wages for its part-time teachers. Having blocked a major breach of shared governance, it remains to be seen whether my Illinois colleagues will prevent the courses from being taught at slave wages. For a certain price was paid to obtain administrative cooperation. Long merely a rubber stamp for administration policy, the Faculty Senate (under new leadership) in this case slavishly endorsed the notion of an online university if only the governance problem could be settled. It is thus not well positioned to take a firm stand on other program components.

Will faculty at other schools let administrators get away with such initiatives? The experience at Illinois merits a general warning. Its potential for mischief is limitless, for it sets a precedent both for other ways to sever faculty from their traditional areas of responsibility and to increase reliance on exploited labor. We must resist. And while we can write and speak as individuals, most effective action must be collective. Perhaps fifteen years of graduate-employee activism will wake up my faculty colleagues to a broader oversight role. Responsible, community focused, internationally engaged unionization and AAUP membership are among its components.

The university is now being subjected to sustained political, cultural, and economic assault. To deny that is to cede the future to corporatization and a form of higher education with little purchase on cultural critique. To theorize the contemporary corporate university is to recognize there was nothing inevitable about its formation. It did not have to be, and it can still be dismantled. Set a $200,000 limit to faculty salaries and a $300,000 limit to upper-administrative salaries. Limit athletic coaches to $300,000, as well. At my institution, the executives working for the president earn $300,000. I would cut their salaries in half. Redirect the money saved to hiring assistant professors; to raising part-timers' salaries to parity and graduate-student employees' wages to the cost of living; and to eliminating all tuition payments for poor and lower-middle-class students. Deny administrators the right to fund gratuitous pet projects at the expense of a principled campus salary schedule. If administrators refuse to comply, sit in their offices, sit in front of their cars, block campus streets, block access to buildings, picket their houses. Use nonviolent civil disobedience to force change. Or if that seems too confrontational, form a union and negotiate these matters at the bargaining table. Increasingly, graduate employees and contingent faculty are doing just that. The key decisions about the job system are made on your own campus when budget priorities are set. Take the money in your own hands. You have nothing to lose but your colleagues' chains.

Contributors

Stanley Aronowitz is Distinguished Professor of Sociology at the Graduate Center of the City University of New York and Director of the Center for the Study of Culture, Technology and Work. He is the author or editor of twenty-three books, including *Just around the Corner: The Paradox of the Jobless Recovery, How Class Works, Food, Shelter and the American Dream, The Knowledge Factory, The Jobless Future: Sci-Tech and the Dogma of Work* (with William DiFazio), *Education under Siege* (with Henry Giroux), *Science as Power, False Promises: The Shaping of American Working Class Consciousness,* and *The Last Good Job in America.*

Barbara Bowen is Associate Professor of English at the CUNY Graduate Center and at Queens College and has published extensively on seventeenth-century English literature, Shakespeare, and African American literature. She is currently serving her third term as president of the Professional Staff Congress/CUNY, the union representing twenty thousand faculty and academic staff at CUNY.

Miabi Chatterji is a doctoral candidate in American Studies at New York University. Her areas of interest include race, gender, labor, and neoliberal globalization. Her dissertation work focuses on South Asian and Latino low-wage service workers and the ways that racial, gender, and ethnic difference is used by capital in the new service-based economy to manage and control workers.

Maggie Clinton is a doctoral candidate in the New York University History Department. She is writing her dissertation on culture and politics in 1930s China. She worked as a GSOC-UAW staff organizer in 2006 and 2007.

Andrew Cornell is a Ph.D. student in the American Studies program at New York University. An active member of United Students Against Sweatshops at the University of Michigan as an undergraduate, he served as a liaison between GSOC and undergraduate student activists during the 2005–2006 strike. He is a contributor to *Letters from Young Activists* and his writings have appeared in *Politics and Culture, Z Magazine, Left Turn, Utne Reader,* and *Clamor.*

Ashley Dawson is Associate Professor of English at the CUNY Graduate Center and at the College of Staten Island. He is the author of *Mongrel Nation: Diasporic Culture and the Making of Postcolonial Britain* and co-editor of *Exceptional State: Contemporary U.S. Culture and the New Imperialism.*

Stephen Duncombe is Associate Professor at the Gallatin School of New York University, where he teaches the history and politics of media and culture. He is the author, most recently, of *Dream: Re-Imagining Progressive Politics in an Age of Fantasy.*

Steve Fletcher is a documentary filmmaker and a Ph.D. candidate in American Studies at New York University. His dissertation research focuses on corporations' use of television and multimedia video to train and persuade internal employee audiences. His film about the GSOC strike, *I'm on Strike Because . . .* was featured at the Reel Work festival in Santa Cruz, California. He served as the broadcast press coordinator and an organizer for GSOC during the strike.

Jeff Goodwin is Professor of Sociology at New York University. His research and writings focus on social movements, revolutions, and terrorism. He is the author of *No Other Way Out: States and Revolutionary Movements, 1945–1991* and the coeditor of *Passionate Politics: Emotions and Social Movements; The Social Movements Reader: Cases and Concepts; Rethinking Social Movements: Structure, Culture, and Emotion;* and *The Contexts Reader.* He has been active in the American Association of University Professors (AAUP) and in the group Faculty Democracy.

Greg Grandin is Professor of History at New York University. He is the author of *The Blood of Guatemala; The Last Colonial Massacre: Latin America in the Cold War;* and *Empire's Workshop: Latin America, the United States, and the Rise of the New Imperialism.* He is co-editor of *Human Rights and Revolutions.* He has served on the United Nations Truth Commission for Guatemala and has published in the *Hispanic American Historical Review,* the *American Historical Review, Harper's, The Nation,* the *Boston Review,* and the *New York Times.*

Adam Green is Associate Professor of History at the University of Chicago and was until 2007 Associate Professor in the Departments of Social and Cultural Analysis and History at New York University. He is the author of *Selling the Race: Culture, Community and Black Chicago 1940–1955* and co-editor with Charles Payne of *Time Longer than Rope: A Century of African American Activism, 1850–1950.*

Monika Krause is a Ph.D. candidate in Sociology at New York University with research interests in critical theory and the sociology of culture. She is writing a dissertation on management practices in humanitarian relief organizations.

Kitty Krupat is Director of CUNY'S Joseph S. Murphy Center for Worker Education. A union activist and labor educator for more than thirty years, she was a founding member of GSOC at NYU. With Patrick McCreery, she is co-editor of *Out at Work: Building a Gay–Labor Alliance.* Her essays have appeared in *Radical History Review, Social Text, International Labor and Working-Class History,* and *New Labor Forum.*

Gordon Lafer is Associate Professor at the University of Oregon's Labor Education and Research Center and the author of *The Job Training Charade.* He became active in the labor movement as an organizer with the GESO at Yale. He has written widely on issues of economic and labor policy and has conducted strategic research for a wide range of labor unions.

Penny Lewis is a Ph.D. candidate in Sociology at the CUNY Graduate Center, where she is finishing her dissertation, "Rich Man's War, Poor Man's Fight? The Class Dynamics of the Vietnam Antiwar Movement." She is a member of the Professional Staff Congress's Delegate Assembly and co-chair of its Solidarity Committee and currently works as an instructor in the Social Science department at Borough of Manhattan Community College.

Natasha Lightfoot is Assistant Professor of History at Columbia University. She specializes in emancipation, race, and labor studies within the fields of Caribbean, Atlantic World, and African Diaspora history. She received a Ph.D. from New York University. While a graduate student at NYU, she was a GSOC-UAW organizer and served on the union's Organizing Committee.

Micki McGee is the author of *Self-Help, Inc: Makeover Culture in American Life* and has recently joined the Department of Sociology and Anthropology at Fordham University, the last university in New York City where tenure-track appointments still outnumber contingent faculty appointments. She held adjunct faculty appointments at New York University from 1989 to 1999 and an Assistant Professor/Faculty Fellow appointment from 2002 to 2005.

Sarah Nash is a Ph.D. candidate in Victorian literature at New York University and has worked as a UAW staff researcher since the strike started. Her dissertation is titled, "From Political to Purified: The Changing 'Function of Criticism' in Nineteenth-Century British Periodicals."

Cary Nelson is Jubilee Professor of Liberal Arts and Sciences at the University of Illinois, Urbana-Champaign, and national president of the American Association of University Professors. He is the author of several books and essays on modern American poetry, including *Revolutionary Memory: Recovering the Memory of the American Left,* and on academic labor, including *Office Hours: Activism and Change in the Academy.*

Christopher Newfield is Professor of American Studies in the English Department at the University of California, Santa Barbara. He is the author of *The Emerson Effect: Individualism and Submission in America* and *Ivy and Industry: Business and the Making of the American University, 1880–1980.* His recent articles have appeared in *Social Text, Critical Inquiry,* and *South Atlantic Quarterly.* He is active in faculty governance in the University of California, where he chairs the systemwide Committee for Planning and Budget, and is co-founder of UCSB's NSF Center for Nanotechnology in Society His new book, *Unmaking the Public University: The Forty Year Assault on the Middle Class,* will be published in 2008.

Mary Nolan is Professor of History at New York University. She is the author of *Social Democracy and Society* and *Visions of Modernity: American Business and the Modernization of Germany.* She is co-editor of *Crimes of War: Guilt and Denial in the Twentieth Century.*

Matthew Osypowski is an MFA candidate in the Creative Writing Program at New York University and holds an MA in English from the University of Texas, Austin. He was teaching in the Expository Writing Program at NYU until he was fired for participating in the 2005–2006 teaching assistants' strike. He is currently working on a novel.

Ed Ott is Executive Director of the New York City Central Labor Council/AFL-CIO, representing more than 1.5 million workers from four hundred affiliated labor organizations throughout New York City. Ott joined the labor movement in 1970 as a bottle washer at Columbia-Presbyterian Hospital, where he became active in an organizing campaign with Local 1199 of the Service Employees International Union. He later held leadership positions in the Public Employees Federation and the Oil, Chemical and Atomic Workers Union and served as political director of the Communications Workers of America Local 1180.

Michael Palm is finishing his Ph.D. in American Studies at New York University. His dissertation is titled "Phoning It In: Self-Service, Telecommunications and New Consumer Labor." He served as chairperson for GSOC/UAW Local 2110 from 2004 to 2007, and he has guest edited a special issue of *Workplace: A Journal of Academic Labor,* which featured analyses of the NYU strike written by GSOC members.

Andrew Ross is Professor of American Studies and chair of the Department of Social and Cultural Analysis at New York University. He is the author of several books, including Fast *Boat to China: Corporate Flight and the Consequences of Free Trade*; *Low Pay, High Profile: The Global Push for Fair Labor*; *No-Collar: The Humane Workplace and Its Hidden Costs*; and *The Celebration Chronicles: Life, Liberty and the Pursuit of Property Value in Disney's New Town.* He has also edited several books, including *No Sweat: Fashion, Free Trade, and the Rights of Garment Workers,* and, most recently, *Anti-Americanism.*

Naomi Schiller is a Ph.D. candidate in Anthropology at New York University. She is currently writing her dissertation on the production of community media and the state in Venezuela.

Ellen Schrecker is Professor of History at Yeshiva University and has written extensively on McCarthyism and academic freedom. Her books include *Many Are the Crimes: McCarthyism in America* and *No Ivory Tower: McCarthyism and the Universities.* The former editor of *Academe,* the magazine of the American Association of University Professors, she is currently working on a book about the contemporary academy.

Sherene Seikaly is Qatar Postdoctoral Fellow at the Center for Contemporary Arab Studies at Georgetown University and co-editor of the *Arab Studies Journal.* She received a Ph.D.

from the joint program in the Departments of History and Middle Eastern and Islamic Studies at New York University. She works on consumption and capitalism in early twentieth-century Palestine. At NYU, she was a GSOC-UAW organizer.

Susan Valentine is a Ph.D. candidate in History at New York University. The focus of her research is the religious culture of medieval Europe, with special regard to sex and gender. Her dissertation is titled, "'Because She Hath Loved Much': Mary Magdalene and Religious Reform, 1000–1215." She was an organizer and served as GSOC press spokesperson during the strike.

Index

Page numbers in *italics* indicate illustrations or tables.